JOHN RAWLS

JOHN RAWLS

His Life and Theory of Justice

THOMAS POGGE

Translated by
Michelle Kosch

OXFORD
UNIVERSITY PRESS

OXFORD
UNIVERSITY PRESS

Oxford University Press, Inc., publishes works that further
Oxford University's objective of excellence
in research, scholarship, and education.

Oxford   New York
Auckland   Cape Town   Dar es Salaam   Hong Kong   Karachi
Kuala Lumpur   Madrid   Melbourne   Mexico City   Nairobi
New Delhi   Shanghai   Taipei   Toronto

With offices in
Argentina   Austria   Brazil   Chile   Czech Republic   France   Greece
Guatemala   Hungary   Italy   Japan   Poland   Portugal   Singapore
South Korea   Switzerland   Thailand   Turkey   Ukraine   Vietnam

This book was originally published in German as *John Rawls* by Thomas W. Pogge.
Copyright © C. H. Beck'sche Verlagsbuchhandlung, Müchen, 1994

English translation copyright © 2007 by Oxford University Press, Inc.

198 Madison Avenue, New York, New York, 10016
Published by arrangement with C. H. Beck'sche Verlagsbuchhandlung

www.oup.com

Oxford is a registered trademark of Oxford University Press.

Library of Congress Cataloging-in-Publication Data
Pogge, Thomas Winfried Menko.
John Rawls: his life and theory of justice / Thomas Pogge; translated by Michelle Kosch.
p. cm.
Includes bibliographical references and index.
ISBN-13 978-0-19-513636-4; 978-0-19-513637-1 (pbk.)

1. Rawls, John, 1921– 2. Justice. I. Kosch, Michelle. II. Title.
JC578.R383P638 2006
320.01'1—dc22   2006043775

3   5   7   9   8   6   4

Printed in the United States of America
on acid-free paper

For
Sidney Morgenbesser,
Mensch

PREFACE

TRYING to introduce an important philosopher within a small volume, one must keep to the essentials. The adventures in Rawls's life largely concerned the developments in his thinking. And these I focus on—especially his theory of social justice, which occupied him for fifty years. Uniquely ambitious and illuminating, this theory is a brilliant achievement in political philosophy, the best there is. No one concerned for social justice in the real world can afford not to study it closely.

My hope is that this book will lead to a better understanding of Rawls's theory among nonspecialists. This theory is certainly worthy of a strict and detailed critique, to which I have tried to contribute elsewhere. But here the primary task is to achieve a clear understanding of it—to help the reader see it as a whole and appreciate its attractiveness, ingenuity, elegance, and systematic unity. Only with such an appreciation of the theory can a critique be fruitful.

Most of Rawls's important ideas are presented in his 1971 book, *A Theory of Justice*. "TJ" we used to call this bestseller, composed in twenty years of labor, and sometimes "green monster," alluding to its size and the color of its first edition. Surely no page turner; but once one has worked one's way through a few chapters of this difficult text, one stands before an elegant and amazingly unified intellectual structure that harmoniously reconstructs the complexity of political values and principles from a single basic idea: We citizens of a modern democratic society should design its basic rules in accordance with a public criterion of justice that purely prudential representatives of prospective citizens would agree upon behind a veil of ignorance.

A Theory of Justice was a formative event for twentieth-century philosophy. It showed how philosophy can do more than play with its own self-invented questions (Are moral assertions capable of being true or false? Is it possible to know that the external world exists?)—that it can work thoroughly and creatively on important questions that every adult citizen is or should be taking seriously. Many thought, after reading this book, that it was worthwhile again to read, study, teach, and write philosophy. It became a paradigm, within academic philosophy, of clear, constructive, useful work, a book that made the profession proud, especially also because its author was such a thoroughly good and likable person.

In appreciating Rawls and his achievements, I have the fortunate advantage of having been his student for five years and his teaching fellow for two of his courses. Like many of his other students, I have learned greatly from his teaching and example. His class lectures were structured with exceptional clarity, yet also so rich and dense that it was difficult, even with full concentration, to take everything in. Rawls carefully read new significant work appearing in his major areas of teaching and research: in ethics, political philosophy, philosophy of law, history of ideas, constitutional history (including seminal judicial verdicts), and the history of the United States with its eminent personalities. He took clearly structured notes on what he read and memorized these summaries.

Unlike other great philosophers in history, Rawls regarded his work neither as a revolutionary new beginning nor as the definitive treatment of a topic area. Rather, he studied his predecessors—Hobbes, Locke, Rousseau, Kant, Hegel, Mill, Sidgwick, and Marx—very carefully and tried to develop their best ideas in his own work. And similarly with his contemporaries—with Habermas, for example, whose writings Rawls knew well and with whom he has an extensive published debate.

I did not have the impression that this thoroughness came naturally for him or gave him much joy. Rawls had no photographic memory and was not an enthusiastic bibliophile. And he often found it painful, I think, to read secondary literature about his own work. The extraordinary range of his knowledge and the outstanding quality of his own work were mostly due then, I believe, to an iron discipline and to an intellectual focus that drew its strength from being directed at topics that were for him, personally and morally, of the greatest importance.

Rawls was unusual among the self-confident divinities of the Harvard Philosophy Department. His caring interactions with students and visitors, his modesty, his insecurity and conciliatory attitude in discussions—one could have taken him for a visiting professor from the countryside, next to his famous and overwhelmingly brilliant colleagues Quine, Goodman, Putnam, Nozick, Dreben, and Cavell. Rawls's astonishing modesty was not due to ignorance. He knew very well that he had written a classic that would be read for decades to come, while most other academic authors fall far short of such achievement. But the comparison he found relevant was not to others, but to the task of political philosophy. And this comparison must always be in some degree humbling.

I have sketched the picture of a serious person, and this is essentially true of Rawls. All through his life, he was uncomfortable in large groups, especially with strangers, and even more so when he himself (on the occasion of a public lecture perhaps) was the center of attention. On such occasions, he could seem shy or ill at ease and was sometimes still bothered by his stammer. In a Harvard lecture room, however, these problems were barely noticeable, especially after the first one or two weeks of term. By then, the audience had become familiar, and Rawls would even make an occasional joke—invariably with deadpan delivery, so the students took some time to catch on. In informal settings, such as a shared lunch with a familiar companion (or a few), Rawls could be at ease and might talk with sensitivity and warmth about the other's life and problems or about any of a wide range of topics, such as politics, meteorology, academic life, healthy food, or a recent movie about the U.S. war in Vietnam. On such occasions, he could be animated, even playful, and really enjoy himself. Perhaps only a few among us younger ones got to know this side of his personality. I got to know it only after completing my dissertation, especially through the conversations we had in preparation of this book.

What impressed me most in Rawls was the exceptional intellectual and moral honesty and thoroughness with which he pursued the development of his theory of justice. Moral language is all around us—praising and condemning as good or evil, right or wrong, just or unjust, heroism or terrorism. In all too many cases, however, such language is used only to advance personal or group interests, without any attempt at justification. Justification is avoided because it forces the speaker to assume more general moral commitments that may be vulnerable to critical objections and impose normative burdens on the speaker. Rawls sought out exactly what so many avoid. Publicly, in lectures and

in print, he tried to connect his moral commitments with one another and with various empirical and methodological commitments.
He thereby subjected his moral convictions, assumptions, and reasoning to the toughest test, finally endorsing only moral judgments that
had survived public critique and could be integrated into a complete
theory of justice. More admirable even than the resulting moral theory
is this relentless commitment to moral reflection. Rawls revised, re-
fined, and extended his theory to the very end. In grasping his theory
of social justice, we can understand what it means to make genuine
and credible moral judgments backed by a moral conception one has
fully thought through. And by appreciating Rawls's dedication to this
project, we can understand the fundamental element of being a just
person.

Rawls's theory, with its vast scope and intricacies, cannot be
simplified without distortion. I try to make it as accessible as it can be,
through clarity of exposition and a sharp focus on the core elements of
his theory of social justice (*justice as fairness*). This means that I must
leave aside much interesting work: Rawls's writings on the history of
moral and political philosophy, for example, and his views on civil
disobedience and conscientious refusal. I touch only lightly on his
writings on moral theory and on his political constructivism, and only
briefly on how his theory might address the claims of the disabled and
historical wrongs (against women and people of color, especially). I
do not discuss Rawls's late extension of his theory to international
relations, because I could not construct a sufficiently convincing account of it. I follow Rawls in setting aside our moral obligations relating to animals and the rest of nature. Finally, like Rawls, I say little
about transition problems: about how the ideal society can be reached
from where we are now, and what demands justice imposes on the
transition.

Though I have tried to keep the exposition of Rawls's views focused and clear, this book is not an easy read for those unfamiliar
with political philosophy. Students of Rawls's work need to absorb his
framework slowly, memorize key ideas, and rebuild the complexity of
justice as fairness in their own minds so as to understand how everything
hangs together. Here it helps greatly to play around with the parts. This
is similar to studying great games of chess: To appreciate the moves,
one needs to think through a lot of possible moves that never occurred.
Similarly here: To understand the moves Rawls makes in his complex
argument, one must also understand the moves he does not make, the

objections he is trying to preempt, and so on. I try to stimulate such play by raising questions, challenges, and objections throughout. The reader might wish to think about what could be said in reply and also, of course, wish to devise further challenges and counterarguments. The aim is always to treat the theory as Rawls treated it: not as a magnificent machine displayed behind velvet ropes in a museum, but as a work in progress to be used and developed, as well as improved and adjusted in the light of new arguments and objections, new knowledge and technologies, and new political developments.

Readers who engage with Rawls's work in this way will not be tempted to give up on the theory, even when they find Rawls committed to a moral judgment they cannot accept. A better response is to explore how deeply rooted the judgment in question is in his theory and how the theory might be revised to avoid that judgment. Following Rawls's example does not require accepting his theory hook, line, and sinker. At its best, it means pursuing one's own moral view with the intellectual seriousness and moral integrity that Rawls brought to his life's work. In doing so, one may find, more often than not, that he had deep and significant reasons for reaching the conclusions he left to us to study.

This book was originally published in German as *John Rawls* (Munich: Beck Verlag, 1994). It was written while I was a visiting scholar at Princeton University's Center for Human Values, which provided much wonderful support and intellectual stimulation during my stay (1993–94). Tom Nagel read the German book and was kind enough to recommend it to Oxford University Press. I am deeply grateful to Michelle Kosch, who has produced an outstanding translation. Taking advantage of a stay in the hospitable academic environment of the Centre for Applied Philosophy and Public Ethics at the Australian National University, I have worked through this translation carefully and, with much help from Rekha Nath, Ling Tong, Leif Wenar, and Andrew Williams, updated and revised a great deal. Any discrepancies with the German text, for better or for worse, are my own responsibility.

Let me also express a heartfelt appreciation to John Rawls. He spent many hours conversing with me about his life, searching old treasure boxes for photographs, and answering ever further questions about his biography and the details of his thought. The biographical account of chapter 1 is based mainly on taped interviews with him conducted in the summer of 1993. He read and commented on this chapter himself.

And so did his wife, Mardy Rawls, who has helped me greatly, frequently, and cheerfully in revising and updating this account for the present volume and also in finding and selecting some of the photographs here included. I thank her most warmly for that and for her hospitality over all these many years.

This book is dedicated to the memory of my dear friend and colleague Sidney Morgenbesser, who shared my admiration for Rawls and my fascination with his theory. We discussed Rawls's work for hundreds of hours over twenty-two years. Half a year younger than Rawls, Morgenbesser died in August 2004.

CONTENTS

1.   Biography   3

1.1 Family and Schooling   4
1.2 College and War   9
1.3 Academic Career   16
1.4 The Turbulent Decade 1962–1971   18
1.5 After *A Theory of Justice*   22
1.6 The Meaning of Rawls's Project   26

2.   The Focus on the Basic Structure   28

2.1 The Origin of the Theory   29
2.2 The Complexity of Modern Societies   31
2.3 The Idea of an Overlapping Consensus   34
2.4 The Scope of the Theory   38

3.   A Top-Tier Criterion of Justice   42

3.1 Purely Recipient-Oriented Criteria of Justice   43
3.2 The Anonymity Condition   48
3.3 Fundamental Interests versus Happiness   54

4.   The Basic Idea: *Justice as Fairness*   60

4.1 The Original Position   60
4.2 Maximin versus Average   67

4.3 Primary Goods   73
4.4 The Lexical Priority of the Basic Liberties   77

5.   The First Principle of Justice   82

5.1 The Structure of a Basic Right   83
5.2 Formulating the Required Scheme of Basic
     Rights and Liberties   85
5.3 The Fair Value of the Basic Political Liberties   91
5.4 Permissible Reductions of Basic Liberties   96
5.5 Impermissible Reductions of Basic Liberties   101

6.   The Second Principle of Justice   106

6.1 The Difference Principle in First Approximation   106
6.2 The Difference Principle in Detail   110
6.3 Advocating the Difference Principle in the Original Position   115
6.4 The Opportunity Principle   120
6.5 Advocating the Opportunity Principle in the
     Original Position   126
6.6 A Property-Owning Democracy   133

7.   A Rawlsian Society   135

7.1 A Well-Ordered Society   137
7.2 A Political Conception of Justice   139
7.3 Political versus Comprehensive Liberalisms   144
7.4 An Egalitarian Liberal Conception of Justice   148
7.5 A Society Well-Ordered by Rawls's Conception   153
7.6 A More Realistic Vision   156

8.   On Justification   161

8.1 Reflective Equilibrium   162
8.2 Fundamental Ideas   170
8.3 Truth and Reasonableness   174

9.   The Reception of *Justice as Fairness*   178

9.1 Rawls and Libertarianism   178
9.2 Rawls and Communitarianism   185
9.3 Rawls and Kant   188

Conclusion   196

Appendix   197

A.1 Timeline   197
A.2 Literature   198
A.2.1 Works by Rawls   198
A.2.2 Selected Secondary Works   199
A.2.2.1 Collections   199
A.2.2.2 Monographs   200
A.2.2.3 Essays   204

Index   215

JOHN RAWLS

One

BIOGRAPHY

Rawls's *A Theory of Justice* began a dramatic revival in political philosophy. The book has sold some four hundred thousand copies in English alone and—translated into twenty-eight languages—has become a staple in North American and European universities and an inspiration to many in Latin America, China, and Japan. It stimulated distinguished philosophers, economists, jurists, and political scientists to contribute to political theory and has drawn many young people into these fields to join the debates it began. *A Theory of Justice* is a true classic, likely to be read and taught for many decades to come.

We begin with a sketch of the life and personality of the man John Rawls, whose work has had such a profound and worldwide impact. Immediately striking about Rawls was his extraordinary intellectual and moral integrity. Over many years, he developed a thorough understanding of moral and political philosophy by studying its primary sources and its massive secondary literatures. An attentive and critical reader, he retained clearly structured synopses of the texts he studied and of their various strengths and weaknesses. Rawls's works show that he was equally strict and careful as a writer. He paid great attention to his choice of terms and phrases, as well as to the clear exposition of his thoughts, often taking months or even years to produce thoroughly reworked drafts of a text before allowing a final version to be published. The same care was apparent in his lectures, which were always rich and superbly crafted.

Rawls's extraordinary achievements as a scholar, author, and teacher can be traced to a variety of factors. He had great intellectual powers and virtues: an immense capacity for systematic thought, a good memory, a natural curiosity, and a critical attitude toward his own work, which generated productive dissatisfactions and further innovations. He was deeply committed to the intellectual life of his students, colleagues, university, and society. At least as important, Rawls focused his powers on two questions that were of the greatest significance to him: How it is possible for an institutional order to be just, and for a human life to be worthwhile? He pursued these questions within ethics and political philosophy and also beyond the traditional confines of these fields into economic theory, the political and constitutional history of the United States, and even into international relations. Rawls's profound aspiration to answer these questions, so apparent in his writings, sustained him during a lifetime of hard work.

1.1 Family and Schooling

John (Jack) Bordley Rawls was born on February 21, 1921, in Baltimore, the second of five sons of William Lee (1883–1946) and Anna Abell Rawls (née Stump, 1892–1954). His maternal grandparents came from affluent families residing in an exclusive suburb of Baltimore (Greenspring Valley, immortalized in the movie *Diner*). Both had inherited some wealth, consisting mainly of coal and oil holdings in Pennsylvania. The grandfather, Alexander Hamilton Stump, lost most of these inheritances, however, and the grandparents were eventually divorced. Their marriage produced four daughters, Lucy, Anna (Rawls's mother), May, and Marnie.

The Rawls family hailed from the South, where the name Rawls is still rather common. Rawls's paternal grandfather, William Stowe Rawls, was a banker in a small town near Greenville, North Carolina. Suffering from tuberculosis, he moved with his wife and three children to Baltimore in 1895 so as to be near the Johns Hopkins University Hospital. Rawls's father, William Lee, contracted tuberculosis some years after the move, and his health continued to be poor throughout his adult life. Money was scarce during William Lee's early years, and he never finished high school. Instead, he started working at the age of fourteen as a "runner" for a law firm. This gave the young man the opportunity to use the firm's law books in the evenings, and he educated himself well enough for the bar exam without any formal studies. William Lee went on to become a successful and respected corporate lawyer in the Marbury Law Firm—one of the best in Baltimore, its fame inaugurated in 1803 by the pivotal constitutional case of *Marbury v. Madison*. In the years after his bar exam, William Lee also occasionally taught at the Baltimore Law School, and in 1919 he was elected president of the Baltimore Bar Association, probably making him the youngest man to hold the office to that time.

Jack's parents both took a strong interest in politics. His father supported Woodrow Wilson and the League of Nations and was a close friend and unofficial advisor of Albert Ritchie, the Democratic governor of Maryland (1924–36). Ritchie asked William Lee to run for the U.S. Senate and offered him a judgeship on the Court of Appeals—both proposals he declined for health reasons. William Lee was a firm supporter of Franklin D. Roosevelt's New Deal. Yet his respect for Roosevelt ended abruptly with the Court-packing crisis of 1937, when Roosevelt attempted to break the Supreme Court's resistance to his legislation by appointing six new judges to the Court. Jack's mother—a highly intelligent woman, who excelled both in bridge and portrait painting—was for some time the Baltimore chapter president of the newly founded League of Women Voters. In 1940, she worked for the campaign of Wendell Willkie, who had quit the Democratic Party to run against Roosevelt as a Republican. Jack was rather distant from his father, whom he remembers as somewhat cold and aloof from the family. Yet he was very close to his mother and traces his lifelong interest in the equality of women to her influence (as well as to that of his wife and daughters).

William Lee and Anna Rawls had five sons: William Stowe (Bill, 1915–2004), John Bordley (Jack, 1921–2002), Robert Lee (Bobby, 1923–28), Thomas Hamilton (Tommy, 1927–29), and Richard Howland (Dick, 1933–67).

The most important events in Jack's childhood were the loss of two younger brothers, who died of diseases contracted from Jack. The first of these incidents occurred in 1928, when Jack fell gravely ill. Although Bobby, twenty-one months younger, had been sternly told not to enter Jack's room, he did so anyway a few times to keep Jack company. Soon both children were lying in bed with high fever. Because the family physician initially misdiagnosed the disease, much time passed until it was finally discovered that both were suffering from diphtheria. The correct diagnosis and antitoxin came too late to save Bobby. His death was a severe shock to Jack and may have (as their mother thought) triggered his stammer, which was a serious (though gradually receding) handicap for him for the rest of his life.

Jack recovered from the diphtheria, but the very next winter, while recovering from a tonsillectomy, caught a severe pneumonia, which

Figure 1.1. Jack and Bobby Rawls

soon infected his brother Tommy. The tragedy of the previous year repeated itself. While Jack was recovering slowly, his little brother died in February of 1929.

During his childhood, Jack's sense of justice was engaged through his mother's work for the rights of women. He also began his own reflections on matters of race and class. Even then, Baltimore had a large black population (approximately 40 percent), and Jack noticed early on that blacks were living in very different circumstances and that black children were attending separate schools. He also remembers vividly how his mother was not pleased when he made friends with a black boy, Ernest, even visiting him at his home in one of the small back-alley houses that were then typical abodes for Baltimore's black families.

By the time Jack was born, his father was a successful and respected lawyer, and that year, to escape the hot and humid Baltimore summers, bought a summer cottage south of Blue Hill (affording a beautiful view of Mt. Desert and the bay) and a small outboard motorboat to visit the outlying islands. Here Jack spent all his summers as he was growing up, and here he acquired his lifelong love of sailing. In the small village of Brooklin, he was also confronted with poor whites who lived there year-round, mostly fishermen and caretakers of the larger summer residences. While he did make friends among the "native" boys, he noticed that their educational opportunities and life prospects in their tiny impoverished village were much inferior to his own. These childhood experiences made a lasting impression on Jack by awakening his sense of injustice. They also deepened his lifelong feeling of having been terribly lucky. He had, after all, survived the diseases that killed two of his brothers and had enjoyed great undeserved privileges of affluence and education. Later, he would make it through the war with barely a scratch and also be fortunate throughout his chosen career.

Jack started his education in the private Calvert School, where he completed a year of kindergarten and his elementary schooling (1927–33). The school was coeducational, but boys and girls were taught separately in the last three grades. There was an emphasis on public speaking and acting, and Jack learned with some joy that he could overcome his stammer when speaking in rhyme. (In one performance of Schiller's *William Tell*, he mixed up his lines and announced to the delighted audience that the apple had split the arrow in two.) Jack's outstanding record at Calvert led to his selection as valedictorian of his class. His performance and early IQ score also impressed his teacher, John Webster, who provided special support and much encouragement to the boy, even giving him private tutorials well after he had left Calvert to attend Roland Park Junior High School. Jack was sent to this public school for two years (1933–35) because his father was then the (unpaid) president of Baltimore's school board and wanted to express support for the public school system. At the end of his father's term, Jack—as was not unusual among Baltimore's well-to-do—was sent to a private boarding school, where he completed the last four years of his schooling.

The boarding school Jack attended from 1935 to 1939 was the Kent School in western Connecticut, a strictly religious boys' school in the High Church Episcopal tradition headed by a monk of the Poughkeepsie-based Order of the Holy Cross. This principal was a severe and dogmatic man, who left little freedom to his teachers and students. Except for vacations, the students were not allowed to leave the school grounds to visit the shops in the nearby village or to see a movie. All students had to do house chores and attend religious services six days a week, and there were two mandatory church services on Sundays. Jack was certainly a success at Kent: high marks, senior prefect, a place on the football and wrestling teams, and advertising manager on the yearbook board. He also played hockey, baseball, tennis, and chess, as well as the trumpet for the school's jazz orchestra. Nonetheless, Jack did not much enjoy his years at Kent. The school offered him little intellectual stimulation, so it is not surprising that he remembers his time there as unhappy and unproductive.

Figure 1.2. Rawls with parents and brothers in Maine

Jack's older brother, Bill, was nearly six years his senior, and Jack followed Bill through Calvert and Kent schools to Princeton University. Bill was considerably bigger and stronger than Jack and very successful in football, wrestling, and tennis. Jack sought to follow Bill's example in sports but also developed independent interests in the biographies of famous scientists and in chemistry. The latter interest had been encouraged by a godfather who was a chemist. As a child, Jack owned an experimental chemistry set and, with the help of additional chemicals supplied by his godfather, produced all kinds of smells and explosions, preferably after Sunday school.

1.2 College and War

After completing boarding school, Rawls—like his brother Bill before him and his youngest brother, Dick, after him—was admitted to Princeton University. He entered in 1939, a member of the "class of 1943" containing some 630 young men. In those days, applicants were rarely rejected, so getting in was easy for those whose parents, like his, could afford the tuition. For the less affluent, it was a different story: Scholarships were scarce and awarded mostly to the athletes needed for intercollegiate sports.

The beginning of Rawls's first semester at Princeton coincided with the German attack on Poland, and Rawls recalls that most students in his class assumed that they would have to fight in a war. A large fraction of the class immediately signed up for the Reserve Officers' Training Corps (ROTC), securing the opportunity for a place in the officers' ranks after graduation. Rawls did not sign up but was moved by the imminent war to study World War I in the university library. Although no one was eager for war, those around Rawls (both at home and at Princeton) all agreed that the United States should support Great Britain. There was isolationist opposition ("America First") in some circles, but not among Rawls's family, friends, or acquaintances.

In his first year at Princeton, Rawls tried to imitate the brilliant athletic example of his brother Bill, who had been varsity in three sports (football, wrestling, tennis) and the captain of the tennis team. Rawls was indeed accepted onto the freshmen football team. But wrestling turned out to be a tougher challenge. Rawls was not good enough to secure a place in the 165-pound weight class and so tried to compete in the next class down (155 pounds). This meant that he had to lose a good bit of weight before each contest, which weakened him in the competition itself. Not particularly successful and increasingly averse to sports with one-on-one confrontation, Rawls quit the wrestling team even before the end of the season. He also gave up football after the first year. But he continued to enjoy baseball—though only as a casual pursuit.

Fraternities were banned at Princeton, and social life revolved around the eating clubs, consisting of juniors and seniors. Students could apply for membership at the end of their sophomore year (through a process called "bicker") and, if admitted, could eat all their meals at their club and spend their evenings there, talking or playing pool. The clubs also organized parties, especially on house party weekends, which were celebrated by all eating clubs simultaneously and attracted many young women from near and far. Propriety was, however, strictly enforced. Women were not allowed to spend the night at the eating clubs and had to break off visits to the dormitories at 7 P.M. All sexual contact was strictly prohibited, and students found guilty of such (or, indeed, found out to be married) were summarily expelled from the college. Once more in the footsteps of his brother, Rawls was admitted into the prestigious Ivy Club, which traditionally favored students from Baltimore.

At first, Rawls was not sure what major to choose. He tried chemistry, mathematics, music (he was a music critic for *The Daily Princetonian* for two years, covering local and New York musical events), and even art history. Finding himself insufficiently interested or talented in these subjects, he finally ended up in philosophy. In this choice, he did not follow his brother Bill, who went on to Harvard Law School and later became an attorney in Philadelphia.

Rawls's first teachers in philosophy were Walter T. Stace, David Bowers, and Norman Malcolm. In his sophomore year, Rawls took a course in moral philosophy with Stace, a utilitarian, in which Kant's *Groundwork*, John Stuart Mill's "Utilitarianism," and Stace's own work *The Concept of Morals* (1937) were discussed. Bowers (who died tragically during the war in an attempt to jump onto a departing train) was teaching Kant. The most important influence was, however, exercised by Malcolm, who was only some 10 years older than Rawls.

After a period of study in Cambridge (England), where he worked with Wittgenstein, Malcolm had returned to Harvard to complete his dissertation under C. I. Lewis. On the basis of a strong recommendation from Lewis, Malcolm was then offered a position at Princeton. Lewis soon came to regret this recommendation. The reason had to do with Malcolm's attitude toward phenomenalism, which, championed by Lewis, was then the dominant epistemological position in the United States. Under Wittgenstein's influence, Malcolm had come to dismiss phenomenalism—a fact that became painfully obvious during Malcolm's public defense of his thesis. Furious after the defense, Lewis fired off a retraction of his recommendation. But the Princeton philosophy department felt obligated to Malcolm and maintained its offer. Malcolm taught at Princeton until April 1942, when he joined the U.S. Navy.

The first meeting between Rawls and Malcolm was unpleasant, at least for Rawls. In the fall of 1941, Rawls gave Malcolm a philosophical essay that he himself thought rather good. Malcolm, however, subjected this essay to very severe criticism and asked Rawls to "take it back" and to "think about what you are doing!" Though temporarily disheartening, this sharp criticism contributed to a gradual deepening of Rawls's interest in philosophy, and he credits Malcolm's personal example with exerting a large influence on the development of his own way of doing philosophy.

During the spring term of 1942, Rawls took another course with Malcolm about the (as Rawls said) quasi-religious topic of human evil, with readings from Plato, Augustine, Bishop Butler, Reinhold Niebuhr, and Philip Leon. This topic was not among Malcolm's ordinary philosophical concerns, and his interest in it may have been inspired by the war. When Rawls mentioned the course to Malcolm much later (during Malcolm's term as president of the American Philosophical Association), he could not remember ever having taught it at all. Malcolm's lack of recall may also be due to the fact that Malcolm joined the navy midway through the course and so was swept up into larger events.

Rawls, by contrast, was deeply impressed by this class. It rekindled in him a latent interest in religion, leading him to write his senior thesis in this area and to seriously consider going to the Virginia Theological Seminary to study for the priesthood. Yet with most of his class going off to war, he decided instead to accelerate his studies.

Rawls received his AB in January 1943, after completing the special summer term in 1942 that had been added on account of the war. He graduated summa cum laude in philosophy, an accomplishment he (not untypically) credits to his good memory, enhanced through his habit of taking accurate and detailed notes. In February, Rawls entered the army as an enlisted man and, after basic infantry training, completed a course in the Signal Corps. He was then sent to the Pacific theater for two years, where he served in New Guinea, in

the Philippines, and finally for four months among the forces occu-
pying Japan (where his troop train went through the recently dev-
astated city of Hiroshima). During his time overseas, Rawls belonged
to the 128th Infantry Regiment of the 32nd Infantry ("Red Arrow")
Division. He served both in the regimental headquarters company and
in an intelligence and reconnaissance (I&R) unit that, in squads of
seven or eight men, reconnoitered enemy positions. He claims not to
have seen much combat, but his division was in heavy fighting in Leyte,
and he was awarded the Bronze Star for his radio work behind enemy
lines along the treacherous Villa Verde Trail in Luzon toward the end
of the war. His only wound came about when he removed his helmet
to drink from a stream and was grazed by a sniper's bullet. He had
gradually worked his way up to sergeant during his time in the Pacific
but was busted back to private in Japan for refusing to punish a soldier
as ordered by a first lieutenant whom this soldier had insulted. Having
declined the opportunity to become an officer at the end of the war
because he did not want to stay longer than necessary in what he
considered a "dismal institution," Rawls left the army in January
1946. He was still an enlisted man, and once more a private. As he
wrote in a little autobiographical sketch (composed for a Kent School
reunion fifty years after his graduation), he viewed his army career as
"singularly undistinguished." And so it may have appeared to him in
comparison to that of his brother Bill, who had volunteered for the air
force even before Pearl Harbor and had piloted four-engine Liberator

Figure 1.3. Rawls leaves the Army

bombers, flying many sorties from Italy over southern Germany, Austria, and Poland.

As noted earlier, before entering the army in 1943, Rawls had considered studying for the priesthood. By June of 1945, however, his experiences in the Pacific war had taken away his belief in orthodox Christianity, caused him to reject as evil the idea of the supremacy of a divine will, and taken away any desire to go into the ministry. In a brief unpublished essay—"On My Religion," composed during the 1990s—Rawls described this shift in these words:

I have often wondered why my religious beliefs changed, particularly during the war. I started as a believing orthodox Episcopalian Christian, and abandoned it entirely by June of 1945. I don't profess to understand at all why my beliefs changed, or believe it is possible fully to comprehend such changes. We can record what happened, tell stories and make guesses, but they must be taken as such. There may be something in them but probably not.

Three incidents stand out in my memory: Kilei Ridge, Deacon's death, hearing and thinking about the Holocaust. The first occurred about the middle of December, 1944. The struggle of F Company of the 128th Infantry Regiment of the 32nd Division to take the ridge overlooking the town of Limon on Leyte was over, and the company simply held its ground. One day a Lutheran Pastor came up and during his service gave a brief sermon in which he said that God aimed our bullets at the Japanese while God protected us from theirs. I don't know why this made me so angry, but it certainly did. I upbraided the Pastor (who was a First Lieutenant) for saying what I assumed he knew perfectly well—Lutheran that he was—were simply falsehoods about divine providence. What reason could he possibly have had but his trying to comfort the troops. Christian doctrine ought not to be used for that, though I knew perfectly well it was.

The second incident—Deacon's death—occurred in May, 1945, high up on the Villa Verde trail on Luzon. Deacon was a splendid man; we became friends and shared a tent at Regiment. One day the First Sergeant came to us looking for two volunteers, one to go with the Colonel to where he could look at the Japanese positions, the other to give blood badly needed for a wounded soldier in the small field hospital nearby. We both agreed and the outcome depended on who had the right blood type. Since I did and Deacon didn't, he went with the Colonel. They must have been spotted by the Japanese, because soon 150 mortar shells were falling in their direction. They jumped into a foxhole and were immediately killed when a mortar shell also landed in it. I was quite disconsolate and couldn't get the incident out of my mind. I don't know why this incident so affected me, other than my fondness for Deacon, as death was a common occurrence. But I think it did, in ways I mention in a moment.

The third incident is really more than an incident as it lasted over a long period of time. It started, as I recall, at Asingan in April, where the Regiment was taking a rest from the line and getting replacements. We went to the Army movies shown in the evening and they also had news reports of the Army information service. It was, I believe, here that I first heard about the Holocaust, as the very first reports of American troops coming upon the concentration camps were made known. Of course much had been known long before that, but it had not been open knowledge to soldiers in the field.

These incidents, and especially the third as it became widely known, affected me in the same way. This took the form of questioning whether prayer was possible. How could I pray and ask God to help me, or my family, or my country, or any other cherished thing I cared about, when God would not save millions of Jews from Hitler? When Lincoln interprets the Civil War as God's punishment for the sin of slavery, deserved equally by North and South, God is seen as acting justly. But the Holocaust can't be interpreted in that way, and all attempts to do so that I have read of are hideous and evil. To interpret history as expressing God's will, God's will must accord with the most basic ideas of justice as we know them. For what else can the most basic justice be? Thus, I soon came to reject the idea of the supremacy of the divine will as also hideous and evil.

The following months and years led to an increasing rejection of many of the main doctrines of Christianity, and it became more and more alien to me....

Having thus rejected the idea of theological studies, Rawls began graduate work in philosophy at Princeton in early 1946 (on the GI Bill). After three semesters at Princeton, he spent one year (1947–48) on a fellowship at Cornell University, where Malcolm and Max Black were working on Wittgenstein. The following year (1948–49), he was back in Princeton, writing his dissertation under the supervision of Walter Stace. [After completing his philosophical education in Dublin, Stace had become mayor of Colombo, the capital of Ceylon (today Sri Lanka), and, despite his official duties, had continued his philosophical studies, especially of Berkeley and Hegel, and even written a book, *The Theory of Knowledge and Existence*.] Rawls's thesis focused on character assessment and developed an antifoundationalist procedure—somewhat similar to his later idea of reflective equilibrium—for correcting one's initial considered moral judgments about particular cases by trying to explicate them all through checking them against a set of moral principles. (His first publication, "Outline of a Decision Procedure for Ethics," summarizes parts of this work.) While completing his thesis in late 1948, Rawls met his wife-to-be, Margaret (Mardy) Warfield Fox (born 1927), who was then a senior at Pembroke College, Brown University. They were married in June 1949 and spent the summer in Princeton, producing the index to Walter Kaufmann's book *Nietzsche: Philosopher, Psychologist and Anti-Christ* in exchange for the then princely sum of $500.

Drawn mainly to art and art history (in which Rawls, too, has had a lifelong interest), Mardy also took an increasingly active role in her husband's work. She helped him with proofreading, made stylistic suggestions, and edited his books and papers. She also brought home to him the importance of equality of opportunity for women. When they were married—they had known each other only six months—she told him that her parents had agreed they could afford to finance a college education only for her two brothers, not for herself, and that the boys' education was more important. Mardy had then successfully applied for a full-tuition scholarship to Brown and had managed, with additional income from various jobs, to pay for her own bachelor's degree. The young couple agreed that they would provide the same opportunities to their daughters as to their sons. And so they did: All four children studied with their parents' support—two at the University of Massachusetts at Amherst, the other two at Reed College and Boston University.

Rawls had won a fellowship for the 1949–50 academic year, and it made sense to spend it as a student at Princeton, even though his thesis was essentially done. During this year, he worked mainly outside the philosophy department. In the fall term, he participated in an economics seminar with Jacob Viner, and in the spring he took a seminar with Alpheus Mason on the history of U.S. political thought and constitutional law, in which the main text was an anthology edited by Mason, *Free Government in the Making: Readings in American Political Thought*. In this seminar, Rawls studied the most important views on political justice that had been articulated in the course of U.S. history and experimented in developing each of them into a systematic conception of justice.

1.3 Academic Career

Rawls taught the following two years (1950–52) as an instructor in the Princeton philosophy department. This was the time of the McCarthy accusations and hearings, from which Princeton was, however, largely insulated. Despite his teaching obligations, Rawls continued his studies outside philosophy. In the fall of 1950, he attended a seminar of the economist William Baumol, which focused mainly on J. R. Hicks's *Value and Capital* and Paul Samuelson's *Foundations of Economic Analysis*. These discussions were continued in the following spring in an unofficial study group. Rawls also studied Leon Walras's *Elements of Pure Economics* and John von Neumann and Oskar Morgenstern's *Theory of Games and Economic Behavior*. At the same time, he made friends with J. O. Urmson, an Oxford philosopher who was a visiting professor at Princeton in 1950–51. From Urmson, he first learned about all the interesting developments in British and particularly Oxford philosophy, which—with J. L. Austin, Gilbert Ryle, H. L. A. Hart, Isaiah Berlin, Stuart Hampshire, Peter Strawson, H. Paul Grice, and R. M. Hare—was then in an especially creative phase. On Urmson's advice, Rawls applied for a Fulbright fellowship and spent the 1952–53 year in Oxford as a member of the high table of Urmson's college, Christ Church.

The year in Oxford was the philosophically most important for Rawls since 1941–42 (his first year as a philosophy student, under the influence of Malcolm). Through Urmson, he got to know Oxford's most important philosophers. He attended a lecture course by H. L. A. Hart, who, freshly promoted to a professorship, was expounding some of the ideas he would later publish in *The Concept of Law*. Rawls was especially impressed with a seminar taught by Berlin and Hampshire, with Hart's active participation, in the winter of 1953. This covered Condorcet, Rousseau's *Social Contract*, John Stuart Mill's "On Liberty," Alexander Herzen, G. E. Moore, and two essays by John Maynard Keynes. Rawls continued to think of this seminar as an exemplar of excellent teaching that he should seek to emulate.

During this period, Rawls began developing the idea of justifying substantive moral principles by reference to an appropriately formulated deliberative procedure. He said that the inspiration for this idea may have come from an essay by Frank Knight, which mentions the organization of a reasonable communicative situation ("Economic Theory and Nationalism" in *The Ethics of Competition and Other Essays*, London, 1935, pp. 345–59, esp. the footnote on pp. 345–47). Rawls's initial idea was that the participants should deliberate independently of one another and forward their proposals for moral principles to an umpire. This process was to continue until agreement would be achieved. As with later versions of the original position, Rawls was hoping that he could derive substantive results from an exact and elaborately justified specification of a hypothetical situation—that is, without having to implement a procedure with actual participants.

After his return from Oxford (1953), Rawls accepted an assistant professorship at Cornell University, where he was promoted to associate professor with tenure in 1956. In the 1950s, Cornell had a rather attractive philosophy department whose character was shaped by Malcolm and Black. Among his other colleagues were Rogers Albritton and David Sachs, who had been Rawls's fellow students at Princeton. The department published (as it still does today) a highly acclaimed journal, the *Philosophical Review*, and Rawls became one of its editors.

Though professionally content at Cornell, Rawls considered the university's location a major disadvantage. Ithaca is a small town in upstate New York, hundreds of miles away from the nearest cultural centers of New York City, Princeton, Philadelphia, Baltimore, and Boston. While the region is beautiful, it has severe winters, which tend to intensify the feeling of isolation. This disadvantage seemed all the weightier as the Rawls family quickly gained four new members: Anne Warfield (born November 1950), today professor of sociology at Bentley College in Waltham with two sons; Robert Lee (born March 1954), now independent product designer and mechanical engineer near Seattle with one son and one daughter; Alexander (Alec) Emory (born December 1955), carpenter, builder, and writer in Palo Alto; and Elizabeth (Liz) Fox (born June 1957), a financial manager, sometime writer, fashion designer, and competitive ballroom dancer in Cambridge, Massachusetts.

The opportunity to leave Ithaca at least temporarily arose in 1959, when Rawls, who had meanwhile published several important essays, was invited to a one-year visiting professorship at Harvard (where his former colleague Albritton had taken up a permanent position). Rawls impressed many local philosophers during this year (1959–60), and MIT subsequently offered him a professorship with tenure. MIT was then heavily concentrated in the sciences and economics but also beginning to build a presence in philosophy, with one associate professor, Irving Singer, and two assistant professors, Hubert Dreyfus and Samuel Todes. There was no separate department, however, and the philosophers were part of a much larger humanities faculty. Rawls

Figure 1.4. Rawls with wife Mardy and their children, Ithaca, N.Y., 1959

decided to accept the offer to become the only tenured philosopher at MIT. This enabled him to develop his friendships at Harvard (especially with Burton Dreben) and to continue his old friendships with Albritton and with Sachs (who was now teaching at Brandeis).

The MIT administration understandably wanted to concentrate its philosophy presence on the history and philosophy of science. With the help of Noam Chomsky and others, Rawls was to build up a humanities subdivision in this field, and he hired James Thomson and then Hilary Putnam. Having spent considerable time and energy on mostly administrative service to a field in which he himself had little interest, Rawls was glad to receive an offer from Harvard in the spring of 1961. He nevertheless decided to postpone the move by a year in order to bring the changes at MIT to a successful conclusion. Rawls taught in the Harvard philosophy department from 1962 until his mandatory retirement in 1991. With special permission from Harvard's president, he continued to teach, for nominal pay, until his first strokes in 1995 made teaching impossible.

1.4 The Turbulent Decade 1962–1971

The following years were devoted mainly to the completion of *A Theory of Justice* (*TJ*). Rawls sought to combine the work on this book with his teaching duties as much as possible. Some of his courses were based, in part, on drafts of the book, which were sometimes distributed to the students. Rawls also used his courses for the study of the great historical figures of political philosophy, beginning in his first year at Harvard with a course on Kant and Hegel for which he composed an extensive lecture script on Hegel's philosophy.

Politically, the late 1960s were dominated by the Vietnam War. From the very beginning, Rawls believed this war to be unjust and repeatedly defended his assessment in public. Together with his colleague Roderick Firth, he took part in a Washington antiwar conference in May 1967. In the spring term of 1969, he taught a course "Problems of War," in which he discussed various views about whether the United States was justified in going to war in Vietnam (*ius ad bellum*) and in conducting this war the way it did (*ius in bello*). The last quarter of this course was canceled because of a general strike of the Harvard student body.

Rawls was deeply concerned to understand what flaws in his society might account for its prosecuting a plainly unjust war with such ferocity, and what citizens might do to oppose this war. In regard to the first question, he located the flaws mainly in the ways that wealth is very unevenly distributed and easily converted into political influence. The U.S. political process is structured so as to allow wealthy individuals and corporations (notably including those in the defense industry) to dominate the political competition through their contributions to political parties and organizations. Written during that time, *TJ* shows traces of these thoughts: "Those similarly endowed and motivated should have roughly the same chance of attaining positions of political authority irrespective of their economic and social class. . . . Historically one of the main defects of constitutional government has been the failure to ensure the fair value of political liberty. . . . Disparities in property and wealth that far exceed what is compatible with political equality have generally been tolerated by the legal system" (*TJ* 197–99). This critique is much expanded in a later essay, "The Basic Liberties and Their Priority" (1983, *PL* 289–371), which also severely reproaches the Supreme Court for blocking campaign reform legislation in *Buckley v. Valeo*.

In regard to the second question, Rawls deems it important to foster a public culture where civil disobedience and conscientious refusal are understood and respected as minority appeals to the conscience of the majority (*TJ* §§56–59). In the context of this discussion, Rawls offered a very brief account of international ethics (*TJ* 331–33), which is much elaborated in his later book *The Law of Peoples* (1999).

It was the second question that confronted Rawls most immediately. Many young people were unwilling to perform their military service, which was compulsory for men up to the age of twenty-six. The Department of Defense had decided not to conscript students in good standing, thereby giving professors an unusual power and responsibility: One failing grade could cause a student to be called up. Rawls thought that these "2-S deferments" for students were unjust (cf. *JFR* 47), quite apart from the injustice of the war itself. Why should students be treated better than others—especially when rich parents have a significant advantage in securing a place for their sons at some educational establishment or another? If young men are to be forced to participate in the war at all, then at least the sons of the rich and the well-connected should share this fate equally with the rest. If not all fit young men are needed for the war, then the requisite number

Figure 1.5. Rawls's passport photograph ca. 1963

should be selected by lot. With seven colleagues from the philosophy department—Albritton, Dreben, Firth, Putnam (who had joined Harvard after Rawls), Stanley Cavell, G. E. L. Owen, and Morton White (*not* W. V. O. Quine or Nelson Goodman)—and another eight from political science—including Judith (Dita) Shklar, Michael Walzer, Stanley Hoffmann, Harvey Mansfield, and Edward Banfield—Rawls defended this position and proposed its adoption at two faculty meetings in late 1966 and early 1967. The proposal was opposed by some of his colleagues and also by the university administration (headed by the conservative President Nathan Pusey) as an inappropriate interference with affairs outside the university. In response to this charge, the proponents were able to point out that the attorney general himself, Burke Marshall, had asked the universities for their views on the matter. A vote was finally taken, and the proposal went down in defeat. Intense disagreement relating to the Vietnam War continued at Harvard for many years.

Rawls spent the academic year 1969–70 at the Center for Advanced Study at Stanford University, where he finally completed *TJ*. He arrived there with a typescript of about two hundred single-spaced pages, which he was continuously revising through additions and substitutions. The revised parts were retyped by a secretary, Anna Tower, and the typescript grew (with alphabetized insert pages) in a way that eventually made it hard to survey. Can we still imagine, a mere thirty-six years later, how people wrote books without computers? It is easier for us electronic folk to imagine the sudden loss of a book in progress. This is what almost happened to Rawls toward the end of his Stanford year. In early April, the center's director called him around 6 A.M. with the terrible news that a few incendiary bombs had been exploded in the center overnight, concluding: "You have been wiped out." Rawls had left the latest version of the typescript on his desk in his office, and the only other extant version was the initial one of the summer of 1969. Eight months of intensive labor seemed irretrievably lost. But Rawls was lucky once again. His office had largely been spared by the flames and had merely sustained severe water damage. Though the precious typescript was wet through and through, it was still readable. Rawls laid it out to dry and then used it as the basis for further modifications.

In September of 1970, Rawls returned to Harvard and became chairman of the philosophy department. This tough and time-consuming job was made even harder by the political circumstances. The members of the department had diverse views on the war and on the issues it raised within the university. Putnam, for instance, was a member of the Maoist Progressive Labor Party, while Quine and Good-man held conservative views. These intradepartmental differences—though dealt with in a polite and civilized manner—required extra time and energy from Rawls. Because he also had to take care of his courses, he had to use evenings and weekends for the final polishing of the typescript.

Rawls remembers this academic year as the hardest of his career. But at its end, he had a text he was satisfied with. Because the typescript was full of insertions, he had no idea of its true length and was amazed when Harvard University Press sent him 587 pages of proof for corrections and indexing. Rawls prepared the index himself, and the long and widely anticipated book appeared in the United States in late 1971.

1.5 After *A Theory of Justice*

The following decades passed rather more calmly. Since 1960, the Rawls family has lived in Lexington, some eight miles from Cambridge. This town is governed by five elected, unpaid selectmen, who serve as a policy-making board; and by a representative town meeting of 189 elected delegates, who serve as the local legislature. Mardy Rawls was a town meeting member for about thirty years. In this capacity, she focused her efforts on matters of land use planning and environmental protection, and she has on occasion also engaged in environmental protection work professionally for the Commonwealth of Massachusetts. Recently, she has been pursuing her artistic career, originally begun at Brown University. Her watercolors have been on display in various places (including Harvard University), and one of them, a portrait of Lincoln, adorned Rawls's Harvard office. One of her portraits of her husband appears on the cover of *The Cambridge Companion to Rawls*.

Rawls himself continued to devote most of his time to his intellectual work, which he did mostly at home. He also continued to take an interest in the artistic work of his wife and enjoyed various sailing trips along the Maine coast. He tried to keep himself in good health by maintaining a strict dietary regimen and regular exercise. In 1983, he had to discontinue his hour-long jogs, however, because he had damaged a tendon while jumping rope. He switched to bicycling, which, thanks to a stationary exercise bike, he could keep up year-round.

In 1979, Rawls was promoted to the highest academic rank at Harvard, that of a university professor. Members of this exclusive group receive not merely an especially high salary but also complete freedom in regard to their teaching: They may offer courses in other departments, if they like, or skip a term to pursue research (though Rawls did not avail himself of these opportunities). Harvard had eight university professorships at the time, and Rawls was given the James Bryant Conant University Professorship (named for a former Harvard president), in which his predecessor had been the Nobel-laureate economist Kenneth Arrow.

Rawls taught at Harvard until 1995. His closest colleagues there were Albritton (who soon left for Los Angeles) and Dreben, as well as Firth, Cavell, Dita Shklar, Charles Fried, and in later years, the newcomers Thomas M. (Tim) Scanlon, Amartya K. Sen, and Christine Korsgaard. He left Massachusetts only for the year at Stanford (1969–70), a sabbatical year at the University of Michigan (1974–75), a term at the Princeton Institute for Advanced Study (fall 1977), and a term at Oxford (spring 1986). In Michigan, he made friends with William K. Frankena and Richard B. Brandt; in Oxford, he spent time, once again, with many of his old friends from 1952–53 (in particular, Hart, Hampshire, and Berlin), as well as with Philippa Foot, who had held a visiting professorship at MIT in the early 1960s.

As before, Rawls invested much effort into his courses (normally three per year, divided over two semesters), which have always been well attended and respected. The two mostly historical courses he offered regularly, though with somewhat variable readings, were moral philosophy (Butler, Hume, Kant, Sidgwick) and social and political philosophy (Hobbes, Locke, Rousseau, Mill, Marx, sometimes also *TJ*). These courses were open to graduate students and advanced undergraduates and generally had an enrollment of thirty to fifty students. They consisted of two excellent lectures per week (which Rawls often summarized for the students on a single handwritten Xeroxed page), plus a one-hour discussion session, which for the graduate students was conducted by Rawls himself and for the undergraduates by an advanced graduate student. Even when it had been given many times before, he would prepare each class lecture afresh, looking once more through the primary texts and familiarizing himself with any new and important secondary sources. It is not surprising, then, that many graduate students attended the same lecture course year after year to deepen their understanding of the field and to partake in the development of Rawls's thinking.

Rawls also regularly taught graduate seminars and tutorials (seminar-like courses for four to six advanced undergraduate philosophy majors) in which he discussed important new works in ethics and political philosophy, as well as other related topics such as the freedom and strength of the will (Kant and Donald Davidson).

Rawls also supervised dissertations and has trained an impressive group of philosophers over the years, including: David Lyons (Boston University), Tom Nagel (New York University), Tim Scanlon (Harvard), Onora O'Neill (Cambridge), Allan Gibbard (University of Michigan), and Sissela Bok (Brandeis) in the 1960s; Norman Daniels (Harvard School of Public Health), Michael Stocker (Syracuse University), Tom Hill (University of North Carolina), Barbara Herman (UCLA), Steven Strasnick (Agilent Technologies), Josh Cohen (MIT), Marcia Homiak (Occidental), and Christine Korsgaard (Harvard) in the 1970s; and since then Jean Hampton (deceased, last at the University of Arizona), Adrian Piper (Wellesley College), Arnold Davidson (University of Chicago), Andrews Reath (University of California at Riverside), Nancy Sherman (Georgetown), Thomas Pogge (Columbia), Daniel Brudney (University of Chicago), Sam Freeman (University of Pennsylvania), Susan Neiman (Einstein Forum, Potsdam), Sibyl Schwarzenbach (City University of New York), Elizabeth Anderson (University of Michigan), Hannah Ginsborg (University of California at Berkeley), Henry Richardson (Georgetown), Paul Weithman (Notre Dame), Sharon Lloyd (University of Southern California), Michele Moody-Adams (Cornell), Peter de Marneffe (Arizona State), Hilary Bok (Johns Hopkins), Erin Kelly (Tufts), and Anthony Laden (University of Illinois at Chicago).

This list shows that Rawls has done much to make a professional career in philosophy possible and attractive for women. It also shows that most good philosophy departments in the United States now have at least one prominent Rawls student. It is remarkable how many of these students have produced not only creative and original texts in moral and political philosophy but also excellent works of historical scholarship. Although Rawls himself has published only some of his many historical writings late in his life (*Lectures on the History of Moral Philosophy*, 2000), he has done much to broaden and improve the study of the history of moral and political philosophy in the United States. This achievement of his teaching is celebrated in a volume of essays by his students, *Reclaiming the History of Ethics: Essays for John Rawls*, which his students presented to him for his seventy-fifth birthday.

Figure 1.6. Rawls in retirement

Through his quality as a teacher and the interdisciplinary focus and presentation of his work, Rawls has also had a lasting impact on many other students who took his classes as undergraduates or as graduate students in political science, law, or economics. They have carried the influence of his teaching and writing into these neighboring disciplines and helped to make its reception there more sympathetic and accurate.

Sadly, Rawls was granted only four full years of life after his retirement. At a conference about his work in California in 1995, he suffered the first of a series of strokes, which caused a substantial mental and physical decline. Rawls nonetheless, with remarkable discipline and the untiring help of his wife and some former students, brought his life's work to completion through a volley of long-planned publications that explicate, defend, extend, and also revise his theory of justice.

His book *Political Liberalism* (*PL* 1993) includes many of these additions and improvements, but it has a different focus than *TJ*. *PL* elaborates on the role a conception of justice should play in a democratic society and in the lives of its citizens. In doing so, it prominently addresses the relation between religion and democracy and the conditions for their being compatible. Rawls's views on this question are most clearly expressed in his later essay "The Idea of Public Reason Revisited" included in his *Collected Papers* (*CP* 1999), which contain nearly all his published essays back to 1951. *Justice as Fairness: A Restatement* (*JFR* 2001) summarizes a modified conception of justice, going beyond the changes included in the revised edition of *TJ* (1999), which includes only revisions made before 1975. *The Law of Peoples* (*LP* 1999) adds a conception of international relations, greatly expanding and improving an identically titled lecture Rawls had given for Amnesty International six years earlier. A second volume of Rawls's historical lectures, this one covering political philosophy, is being edited by Samuel Freeman with the help of Rawls's wife, Mardy, and will appear as his last book in the near future.

1.6 The Meaning of Rawls's Project

All his life, Rawls was interested in the question whether and to what extent human life is redeemable—whether it is possible for human beings, individually and collectively, to live so that their lives are worth living (or, in Kant's words, so that there is value in human beings' living on the earth). This question is closely related to that of evil in human character, with which Rawls, still much influenced by religion, had been so fascinated during his student years. But even the life of someone whose conduct and character are above reproach may seem to lack worth. So much human time and energy are wasted on professional and personal projects that are ultimately pointless and do not really promote human excellence and flourishing. In light of such thoughts, Rawls has tried to lead a worthwhile life in part by trying to show what might make human life worthwhile.

He has focused these contributions to the political realm: Is it possible to envision a social world in which the collective life of human beings would be worthwhile? One can imagine all sorts of wonderful things, of course. But the question is to be understood in a realistic sense, asking us to envision the best social world within the context of the empirical conditions of this planet and of our human nature. The question is then whether we can envision a *realistic* utopia, an ideal social world that is reachable from the present on a plausible path of transition and, once reached, could sustain itself in its real context. By constructing such a realistic utopia, Rawls has sought to show that the world is good at least in this respect of making a worthwhile collective life of human beings possible.

Now one might think that our estimation of the goodness of the universe should not be affected by a merely theoretical demonstration of an ideal and stable social world, even one that can be shown to be reachable from where we are. What matters is the moral quality of our actual collective life. But Rawls held a different view. Without denying that the actual political achievement of the ideal is important, he believed that a well-grounded belief in its achievability can reconcile us to the world. So long as we are justifiably confident that a self-sustaining and just collective life among human beings is realistically possible, we may hope that we or others will someday, somewhere, achieve it—and can then also work toward this achievement. By modeling a realistic utopia as a final moral goal for our collective life, political philosophy can provide an inspiration that can banish the dangers of resignation and cynicism and can enhance the value of our lives even today.

John Rawls died at his home in Lexington, his wife, Mardy, by his side, on November 24, 2002, after a rapid but painless decline in his health. On Tuesday, December 3, 2002, the day of his memorial service in the First Parish Church beside the Lexington Green, the town of Lexington, in an unusual show of respect for a philosopher, flew the flag over the historic Battle Green at half-mast "in honor and memory of John Bordley Rawls whose wisdom and honor have inspired so many of us."

Two

THE FOCUS ON THE BASIC STRUCTURE

J USTICE is the first virtue of social institutions." Thus Rawls begins the first section of his most important work, *A Theory of Justice*. Many other things can also be called just or unjust—wars, contracts, accusations, laws, demands, verdicts, honors, fate, or even the world. Rawls, though, uses the word in a narrower sense: for the moral assessment of social institutions. This narrower sense is commonly marked by the expression "social justice," but, like Rawls, I generally suppress the adjective when the context makes clear that the narrower meaning is intended.

The word "institution" is often used for organized collective agents such as Harvard University or the World Bank. But this is not the sense in which Rawls uses the term "social institutions." He means to refer to the practices and rules that structure relationships and interactions among agents. This sense is exemplified by a social institution of promising. Its rules lay down what interactions between two agents count as creating a promise, what promisee conduct (if any) counts as releasing the promisor from the promise, what circumstances (if any) can be invoked as a justification or excuse for nonperformance, and so on. In all cultures, there are also more complex social institutions structuring kinship relations, economic cooperation, criminal punishment, and political decision making, for example. The moral assessment of such practices and rules is the domain of social justice. The moral assessment of individual and collective agents and of their conduct within some existing institutional scheme is the domain of ethics.

These two domains are not mutually independent. The social institutions of a society have a substantial influence on the options available to its members and even on the formation of their characters. And social institutions, in turn, are created, maintained, and changed through the conduct of individuals. It may thus appear impossible to treat one of these topics apart from the other. Because alternative social institutions generate different patterns of conduct and different characters, it seems that their moral assessment presupposes conduct and character assessments. On the other hand, it also seems that conduct in the context of particular social institutions cannot be assessed without a moral assessment of these institutions.

Rawls nonetheless concentrates on the domain of social justice—and, more narrowly still, on how to assess a society's major social institutions, its *basic structure*. Providing "the framework for a self-sufficient scheme of cooperation for all the essential purposes of human life," the basic structure "comprises the main social institutions—the constitution, the economic regime, the legal order and its specification of property," the family in some form, and how these institutions cohere into one unified system of social cooperation (*PL* 301, cf. *JFR* 10). The following sections discuss the emergence, meaning, and justification of this restriction of topic.

2.1 The Origin of the Theory

Rawls had initially been interested in ethics and especially in the basis of character assessments. In the course of his investigations, he developed a specific method for answering moral questions. First, one is to become familiar with all the different answers that may be given to a question—in particular, those that have already been set forth by distinguished thinkers. Next, one is to try, again with the help of historical materials, to criticize each of these positions as effectively as possible, both internally and from the outside. Third, one is to take up each of these positions and to defend it as well as possible. Here one may modify the position to make it more defensible, provided its essential elements are preserved. Only after one has rendered each of the competing positions as plausible as one can should one then, fourth, ask oneself which of them accounts best for one's moral convictions, which will probably have evolved further through the exercise. The judgment one is inclined to make after such a process is what Rawls calls *wide reflective equilibrium.*

An important moral position, which Rawls did not accept but nonetheless wanted to think through and formulate in its most plausible form, is utilitarianism. He made this attempt in his 1955 paper, "Two Concepts of Rules." The central idea of utilitarianism is that utility or happiness (understood as pleasure minus pain, desire satisfaction, or whatever) is the source of all moral value and that morality should therefore be concerned solely with raising the general happiness as high as possible. Applying this basic idea to conduct, however, leads to implausible prescriptions: We should lie and break promises, and judges should convict defendants they know to be innocent, whenever such actions produce more happiness than their alternatives. Such prescriptions run counter to commonsense morality, and perhaps even to happiness maximization itself: Lives lived among people seeking to maximize happiness would probably be less happy than ones lived among people generally observant of the constraints of commonsense morality.

Rawls tried to render utilitarianism more plausible by applying its central idea not to conduct but to *practices*. A practice is a set of rules through which human interactions are structured, as competitive team sports are structured by rules of the game. A practice defines various roles or positions (e.g., spouse, employee, jury member) and determines how occupants of these roles are required and/or permitted to act. Rawls claimed that the most plausible version of utilitarianism is *two-tiered*. Rather than enjoin agents to act so as to maximize happiness directly (single-tiered or act utilitarianism), two-tiered utilitarianism enjoins them to comply strictly with social rules and practices that in turn are to be designed so as to maximize happiness. According to this two-tiered utilitarianism, once optimal social rules and practices are in place, agents in their various roles must strictly observe them—even when more happiness could be produced by breaking these rules.

This institutional utilitarianism, which still has some supporters, got Rawls interested in the topic of practices or (as he later says) social institutions. But it did not ultimately convince him. He could not, in the end, bring himself to accept happiness as the source of all moral value. And he found himself unable to explain how someone who takes happiness to be the sole ultimate moral value can have a moral reason to comply with the rules of an optimal practice even when doing so leads to suboptimal results: If the authority of the rules is based solely on happiness, then it makes no sense to sacrifice some happiness for the sake of honoring the rules. (This criticism is clearly and convincingly presented by Rawls's student David Lyons in "Utility and Rights.")

Rawls's mature position nonetheless preserves the fundamental distinction between the justification of conduct and the justification of social institutions. To overcome the defects of institutional utilitarianism, he tried to formulate a criterion for assessing social institutions that would be more plausible than happiness maximization and would also be impossible to apply directly to the assessment of conduct. He succeeds in this attempt with his two principles of justice. They are a criterion of justice narrowly focused on the design of the basic structure, thereby ensuring that, if this criterion is satisfied by our society's institutional rules, we cannot promote the justice of our society by violating these rules.

2.2 The Complexity of Modern Societies

We have seen how Rawls came to shift his inquiry from the moral assessment of conduct and character (ethics) to that of social institutions. His concentration on social justice was due to the insight that ethics is increasingly unable to cope with morally significant aspects of modern societies. Such societies give rise to large-scale social problems that can be much better addressed through institutional rather than interactional moral analysis. Interactional moral analysis seeks to explain the deprivations some people suffer in terms of morally faulty (wrongful) conduct by other agents. Institutional moral analysis seeks to explain the statistical incidence of deprivations in terms of morally faulty (unjust) social institutions.

The advantages of institutional moral analysis are best illustrated in the economic sphere, where one encounters social problems like poverty and unemployment. Ethics might address such deprivations by enjoining agents to make special efforts outside their ordinary activities, to give to charities, for instance. But especially in the Anglophone countries, such positive duties to protect and assist are regarded as feeble or nonexistent. Here ethics is centered on negative duties, that is, duties not to harm.

Some social problems can be addressed through negative duties: Garbage on roads and trails and contamination of air and water can be controlled by enjoining agents to minimize their littering and pollution and can be explained as effects of wrongful conduct. But this model does not work for large-scale poverty or unemployment (as during the Great Depression), which cannot be prevented by assigning negative duties to agents and cannot be traced back to wrongful conduct by the poor themselves or to wrongful purchasing or hiring decisions by individual consumers and corporations.

The reason is that an individual market participant simply cannot anticipate the remote effects of her or his economic decisions. This inability is due not merely to ignorance of economics but mainly to the way in which the effects of such individual decisions intermingle with one another. Whether a particular purchasing or investment decision has a positive or negative impact on unemployment, for instance, depends upon countless other economic decisions, whose effects in turn depend upon yet others. In the contemporary world, it is thus beyond the capacity of typical individuals to shape their ordinary economic conduct so that it does not exacerbate poverty or unemployment. Any ethical command to this effect would produce only anxiety and guilt feelings, while bringing no relief for the poor and unemployed.

Conjoining this insight, that poverty and unemployment cannot be avoided by asking agents to refrain from specific harmful acts, with the common belief that there are no strong positive duties to relieve poverty, many have concluded that we must learn to accept poverty and unemployment as we must accept earthquakes and hurricanes. Without denying the two premises of this reasoning, Rawls challenges the inference and hence the conclusion. He does so by tracing disadvantages like poverty and unemployment back to social institutions. Any given society can be structured and regulated in many different ways, featuring diverse ways of organizing economic cooperation and control of resources and of the means of production. There are many different options for devising its governmental agencies and for formulating its laws governing property, taxation, labor, inheritance, and so on. Some of these institutional designs would tend to generate more poverty than others. Moral attention should be focused here: on the design and reform of society's institutional order—not on the particular acts and omissions of its participants.

This thought leads beyond the negative and any positive moral duties that apply to agents in their ordinary conduct (as buyers or sellers, employers or investors, etc.). It suggests an additional responsibility we have as citizens, through our participation in the imposition of our society's institutional order. This is a special political responsibility, typically borne by adult citizens (not foreigners). These citizens are then collectively responsible for excess unemployment and poverty that could be avoided through a better design of their institutional order. At the individual level, this collective responsibility might be associated with a strong negative duty not to cooperate in the imposition of an unjust institutional order without making adequate efforts to promote its reform.

Achieving institutional reform through collaborative efforts is difficult. It requires political cooperation. And it requires research into how the distribution of morally significant goods (income, employment, education, etc.) depends on the design of the institutional order and what these distributions would tend to be like under practicable alternative designs. Still, such efforts are far more promising than efforts to shape one's ordinary conduct so that it does not worsen the prevailing distribution.

Even social problems that can be analyzed interactionally may benefit greatly from an institutional moral analysis that considers alternative institutional design options. Without retracting the judgment that it is wrong to litter, we may then find that social rules are also at fault—perhaps because most of the garbage problem is avoidable by mandating biodegradable food containers and deposits on cans and bottles.

Analyzing how social problems are affected by institutional design brings out what ethical approaches generally obscure: In the modern world, an intricate framework of interrelated social institutions conditions the conduct of agents by shaping their options and by influencing profoundly the interests, desires, and abilities agents develop. Through these institutions, human lives have become increasingly interdependent so that decisions in one part of the world may have a strong impact on lives half a world away. (Food consumption among the children of Bangladeshi textile workers may well depend on summer beachwear fashions in the United States.) Interactional moral analysis cannot cope with these complexities. It can scrutinize the character of agents and their conduct in the different roles they play. But it must largely take as given the social conditions that mold the character of agents and the whole system of differentiated roles.

Some of the same limitations persist when social institutions are analyzed one by one. Such analysis cannot cope with the way social institutions are interdependent in their effects (so that the effects of any social institution depend on how the others are designed). Such analysis can get us to the point where every social institution, holding fixed the design of the rest, is well designed. But it may still be possible to do much better. To see this, consider the analogous case of optimizing some process of production as in a car factory. Even if each stage of the process is designed in the best feasible way given the way the other stages are designed, it may still be possible greatly to improve the entire process: by redesigning all its stages together or by altering its very structure (including the way it is divided into stages). Analogously, a society's institutional order may be much improved by reflecting on it as a whole. This enables mutual adjustment of the domains and functions of social institutions toward an optimal total arrangement.

Institutional moral analysis thus has important advantages in dealing with complex social systems. It enables a plausible assignment of responsibility for social problems such as poverty and unemployment. It indicates how such problems can be effectively solved. In addition, institutional moral analysis holds out the prospect of citizens upholding a just institutional order that relieves them from having to worry about these social problems in their ordinary conduct.

In Europe, these ideas were familiar when Rawls wrote. In the United States, however, they were new—all the more so as Rawls did not import them from Europe and its socialist heritage but developed them independently through his study of game theory and economics.

2.3 The Idea of an Overlapping Consensus

Rawls formulated an important further reason for his concentration on social institutions only after the publication of *TJ*.

The organization of a social system is necessarily settled one way or another—an institutional order can be designed in only *one* way at any given time. And it would then be good, of course, if all of its members could accept the prevailing design as just. With regard to ethics, aesthetics, and religion, by contrast, a limited pluralism is possible and, according to Rawls, even desirable. We can live together in harmony despite conflicting ideals of the good human being, of worthwhile living, of love and friendship, of ethical conduct, and the like, so long as we know that we share a moral commitment to our society's basic structure. For Rawls, this is one of the most important lessons of modernity: that it is possible to live together under common rules that have a moral basis, even without sharing a comprehensive moral or religious worldview or conception of the good.

The importance of this historical possibility is heightened by the *fact of reasonable pluralism* (PL 36–38): that there is in the modern world a plurality of deeply irreconcilable yet reasonable ethical, aesthetic, religious, and philosophical views and values—a plurality that can be eliminated, if at all, only through morally unacceptable levels of repression. Free democratic societies must live with such pluralism. With these points in mind, Rawls wants to concentrate on helping to achieve agreement where it is really needed. He seeks to develop, specifically for the basic structure, a conception of justice that the adherents of competing worldviews can morally endorse. And he wants then to describe a just basic structure that satisfies this conception.

The aim of extending moral consensus from this limited conception of social justice to a broader conception of how to live—into ethics, aesthetics, religion, or philosophy—is not merely less important, according to Rawls. Rather, it is positively counterproductive. We cannot hope to reach an unforced moral consensus on such a broader conception, and forced agreement is inconsistent with a free, democratic society. The same is true of a conception of social justice whose content is dependent on some broader moral, religious, or philosophical worldview (comprehensive doctrine or conception of the good). Only a conception of social justice that is derivable from, or at least compatible with, a wide range of such worldviews can sustain a social order that is *stable*, that is, supported by the unforced moral allegiance of all or most citizens. Rawls calls such a conception of justice—one that is not dependent on a more comprehensive worldview, but acceptable to adherents of diverse worldviews—a *political* conception of justice. And he calls a moral consensus whose content is confined to such a political conception of justice an *overlapping* consensus. His hope is for a free society in which the widely held moral, religious, and philosophical worldviews overlap in regard to a political conception of justice that justifies this society's basic structure.

The ideal of an overlapping consensus can be rejected in behalf of a more comprehensive consensus, which would include additional moral, religious, or philosophical contents. But one can also attack this ideal from the other side, asserting that an institutional order can be sustained, without *any* moral consensus, as a mere modus vivendi. It suffices that most participants see supporting this order as a prudent way of advancing their diverse interests and values.

This modus vivendi model can guarantee orderly coexistence only so long as most participating groups indeed believe it to be in their interest to support the existing institutional order. To satisfy this condition, the going rules must be especially accommodating to those who would do well even if the institutional order broke down. Such accommodation comes at the expense of those who would do poorly. But they have reason to accept such accommodation, nonetheless, because of their vital interest in avoiding such a breakdown. On the modus vivendi model, the institutional order that emerges is then a compromise between different groups, reflecting a bargaining equilibrium that accommodates the values and interests of each group according to its relative strength or threat advantage.

Now the interests, values, and especially also the relative strength of the various groups may change. Such changes require that the institutional order be continually renegotiated so that the equilibrium condition remains satisfied. A modus vivendi therefore involves serious danger: A group whose power declines in relative terms will have to accept revisions of the institutional order that will weaken it further. There is no limit to such a downward spiral because any institutionalized protections are always subject to renegotiation.

Understanding the danger, any participant in a modus vivendi will tend to give precedence to protecting and augmenting its power over honoring its moral values and principles. This model is then an example of might-makes-right, as the power of the various participants and their interest in power shape the terms of the institutional order they negotiate.

Terms negotiated in this way are unlikely to track justice on *any* participant's conception of it. This is a sharp contrast to the ideal of an overlapping consensus, which seeks an institutional order that *all* participants can morally endorse on the basis of their diverse moral, religious, or philosophical worldviews.

The familiar system of international relations—a web of conventions and treaties that clearly reflects the distribution of power among states—exemplifies the modus vivendi model. It also exemplifies its stated disadvantage: A state in such a system cannot through any number of treaties gain lasting security against the danger of having to retreat from territory it possesses, nor even against the danger of complete annihilation. Because states are aware of this danger, they must treat one another with suspicion and must always concentrate on their own power position—preserving and, if possible, even strengthening it at the expense of others. With the long-term survival of their values and form of life always at stake, they do not have the luxury of restraining themselves by their moral values or principles. This intense concern of each state for its own survival and power, understood by all the others, engenders considerable short-term dangers, amply illustrated by the frequency of wars.

A modus vivendi among groups within one society generates analogous dangers and problems. A rule-governed power struggle that is always also a struggle over these rules themselves, such a modus vivendi can provide neither lasting security nor justice on any group's conception of it. All groups interested in their long-term security therefore have reason to prefer, over the modus vivendi model, Rawls's ideal of an overlapping consensus. This ideal envisions an institutional order that the various groups endorse as just and are willing to support, even through changes in their respective interests and relative power. Such an institutional order is not a fortuitous and transitory product of negotiation and compromise but an enduring structure based on substantive moral consensus among, and genuine moral allegiance by, its participants.

The preference for a stable social order over a modus vivendi is not merely a prudential but also a moral one. In the first place, individuals and groups have a moral interest in securing the long-term survival of their values and forms of life, to which end a stable social order is far more suitable than a modus vivendi. Second, individuals and groups have a moral interest in conducting themselves in accordance with their own moral values—something they can do, within a modus vivendi, only at the cost of endangering the long-term survival of themselves and their progeny. And third, we all have a moral interest in living in a peaceful and harmonious society. This presupposes social institutions that, supported by widespread moral allegiance, stand above everyday political rivalries—regulating the political competition without themselves being an object of this competition.

These arguments may seem to support a narrower moral consensus than the one Rawls himself suggests. Instead of striving for agreement upon a moral framework consisting of a shared conception of justice and the basic structure it justifies, we should, it seems, aim for a moral consensus on the basic structure alone—a consensus that is narrower and thus more easily achieved. Rawls believes, however, that the limited moral consensus he envisions must include a shared moral justification for the basic structure. The reason is that a narrower moral consensus—including only the content of the constitution, for instance—could not provide adequate grounds for deciding how constitutional provisions are to be applied to controversial cases and how they are to be adapted to changing conditions. A narrower consensus would be too fragile, liable to break down in the face of competing interpretations or unforeseen new conditions.

So the moral consensus Rawls aims to facilitate has a more complex, tripartite object. It centrally includes a *public criterion of justice*, that is, a criterion for assessing the alternative basic structure designs that are simultaneously practicable for some society in its given conditions. It also includes a shared *moral justification* of this criterion. This justification should be shallow enough to be compatible with a wide range of more comprehensive moral, religious, and philosophical worldviews. Yet it should also be substantial enough to help guide the public interpretation and application of the public criterion in controversial cases, as may be triggered by environmental, technological, or cultural changes (*PL* 165). The sought consensus, third, includes a *basic structure* whose design and adjustment over time are justified by the public criterion and its associated application guidelines. The moral framework Rawls envisions for society thus consists of a basic structure that evolves with changing conditions in an orderly way controlled by an enduring public criterion of justice as applied in light of a common moral justification. This complex moral framework is stable in that its endurance is secured by the typical citizen's mutually reinforcing moral commitments to its three parts.

Within a moral framework that has this tripartite structure envisioned by Rawls, we can call the public criterion of justice and its moral justification, together, a *conception of justice*. And we can call the public criterion of justice and the basic structures it justifies, together, a *social order*. By including a public criterion in the consensus he aims for, Rawls can envision a social order that persists through institutional changes. Modifications of the basic structure are not fundamental changes but adjustments governed and justified by an enduring public criterion of justice.

2.4 The Scope of the Theory

Rawls offers a conception (or theory) of justice—dubbed *justice as fairness*—intended to help achieve such a stable social order. What he offers is in one sense more ambitious than his title, *Theory of Justice*, may suggest and less ambitious in another. It is more ambitious in that Rawls is not seeking a conception of justice that merely unifies and rationalizes moral judgments of a detached observer. Rather, he aims to construct a conception that can organize a real society through a moral content that is widely shared among its citizens. For this reason, *justice as fairness* includes a *public* criterion intended to play a central role in the political life of an actual society. To justify such a public criterion, one must show not merely that it delivers plausible judgments of justice but also that it would perform well in its political role. One must examine how it would be understood, implemented, and followed by actual citizens, what institutional designs they would actually implement under its guidance, how they would live under such social institutions, and to what extent they would continue freely to endorse this public criterion and any basic structure designed on its basis.

Rawls's conception is also less ambitious than his title may suggest: It does not cover the whole of social justice: the moral assessment of social institutions. There are organized social systems of many different sizes and types: families, tribes, states, universities, churches, trade unions, and the international system of states, to name only a few. Moreover, such social systems exist in very diverse conditions: primitive or modern, rich or poor, isolated or as regional or functional parts of a larger social system, and so on. Whether *one* theory of social justice can be developed to cover all of these cases is doubtful. Rawls, in any event, limits his efforts to a central case that can be characterized by six restrictions.

First, his theory is to address only one kind of social system: a *society*, defined as a large group of people living together in an organized way, in a fixed geographical area, over generations. He has in mind, of course, the modern state, the most important type of social system today. The life chances and environments of human beings, even our education, character traits, and ambitions, are profoundly shaped by the state in which we live—both directly and also indirectly through subsystems that are themselves deeply shaped by the state in which they are embedded. As part of this first restriction, Rawls also stipulates that a society is isolated and self-contained. He thinks of this stipulation as a plausible simplifying assumption for purposes of developing a conception of justice applicable to national societies. His late book *The Law of Peoples* (1999) develops a separate moral conception of international relations.

Second, Rawls adopts further idealizations by provisionally bracketing various special issues. Thus, his theory envisages a society of persons without severe mental or physical disabilities: All members are capable of taking part in education, work, and politics over a complete life. Problems of noncompliance are often left aside, though Rawls provides some guidance for how his theory can address such matters (*TJ* §§33–39). And questions concerning our duties to future generations as well as to animals and the rest of nature are also put aside.

Third, the context of the relevant society is, in other respects, to be imagined realistically. Thus Rawls assumes conditions of relative scarcity: Available resources are sufficient so that social cooperation

enables the comfortable survival of all members of society but not so
abundant that each can have all his heart might desire. Further, the
participants make conflicting claims on the social product; they do not
agree from the outset on the proper distribution of scarce goods (among
which Rawls lists rights and liberties, educational and employment
opportunities, income and wealth). Finally, Rawls has added the stipulation that the general conditions of the society must be "reasonably
favorable," that is, must make it possible for citizens, should they have
the political will, to realize certain basic rights and liberties. This stipulation does not imply that the envisaged society exists in the cultural
and technological conditions of the modern era—a constitutional democracy does not presuppose affluence and would have been possible
even in ancient times.

Fourth, Rawls does not want his conception of justice to address all
the rules and practices of a self-contained society but only its *basic
structure*. By this, he means the social institutions that exert a *profound*
and *unavoidable* influence on the lives of *all* members. These include at
least the structure of its political system, the organization of its economy, its legal, education, and health care systems, and the practices
regulating kinship relations and child rearing. In modern times, these
most fundamental rules are typically set forth in constitutions or statutes. Yet, the assessment of a basic structure design is to be based not on
how its rules are officially stated but on how they are actually understood and applied. Aside from the social institutions that make up the
basic structure, there are many other rules that do not affect all members
of society (laws governing the securities industry) or are simply less
important (traffic rules). Rawls supposes that a just basic structure goes a
very long way toward ensuring that these further rules and practices will
be justly structured as well.

Fifth, when assessing alternative public criteria of justice, Rawls is
asking not how well each would guide and organize people as they are
now, shaped by existing social institutions. Rather, engaging in *ideal
theory*, he is asking how well each candidate criterion would guide and
organize human beings as they would come to be if they grew up in a
society governed by this criterion. The sought public criterion is
meant to be used for selecting the best practicable basic structure
designs for any society in reasonably favorable conditions and for
guiding its citizens in maintaining and adjusting such an ideal design.
This criterion is not meant to be used for guiding the reform of an
unjust basic structure design: for judging the relative urgency of various
institutional reforms by examining which reform would result in the

least unjust design. (At times, Rawls understands ideal theory in an even more ideal sense: as based on the stipulation that each candidate public criterion would generate a solid commitment to itself on the part of all citizens. I leave such super-ideal theorizing aside, as many of Rawls's arguments involve reflections on how much commitment such candidate criteria would actually generate.) The focus on ideal theory complicates the comparison among criteria, because it requires envisioning and assessing social worlds that are remote from our own. It also involves neglect of questions that seem important: Which of the social worlds envisioned through such candidate public criteria are reachable from where our society is now, and on what path? But ideal theory is also important, lest we misunderstand features of human life produced by existing social institutions as unchangeable elements of the human condition.

Sixth, Rawls is seeking a conception of justice that can achieve *stability*, that is, can endure by engendering a firm moral allegiance to itself and to the social order it sustains on the part of all (or nearly all) citizens. He believes that, in modern conditions, a conception of justice can achieve stability only if it can be the object of an overlapping consensus, that is, only if it can be morally endorsed by citizens who are also committed to diverse and partially conflicting moral, religious, and philosophical worldviews. On this assumption, whether a conception of justice can achieve stability in some society depends then on what worldviews are actually prevalent in this society. What matters, however, is not whether the conception can be morally accepted by the now actually existing adherents of these worldviews but whether it can be so accepted by such adherents as they would be if their worldviews had adjusted themselves to the conception of justice and basic structure under examination. The fact that the members of an influential religion find a particular conception of justice morally unacceptable does not disqualify this conception. So long as it does not go against essential elements of the religion, it may come to be accepted and morally endorsed by its members. This possibility is illustrated by Catholicism, a conservative religion, which nonetheless has adapted throughout the ages to many variations in prevalent moral outlooks and in political and economic regimes.

Three

A TOP-TIER CRITERION OF JUSTICE

WHILE Rawls, like Jeremy Bentham, had conceived institutional utilitarianism as two-tiered, he conceived his own theory of justice as having *three tiers* corresponding to the three main contents of the overlapping consensus he seeks to facilitate (section 2.3). Rawls envisions a society whose citizens follow its going institutional rules and practices, particularly those of its (more narrowly defined) *basic structure*; this is the bottom tier, the same as in institutional utilitarianism. In designing, maintaining, and adjusting this basic structure, citizens are guided by a *public criterion of justice*; Rawls proposes his two principles of justice (with two priority rules) on this middle tier. In formulating and interpreting their public criterion of justice, citizens rely on a contractualist thought experiment; Rawls offers the original position on this top tier. Because the point of this thought experiment is to identify the morally best public criterion of justice, we can think of the original position as a *meta-criterion* of social justice.

In the society Rawls envisions, citizens have mutually reinforcing moral commitments on these three levels. Strongly held and widely shared, these moral commitments sustain a stable social order.

3.1 Purely Recipient-Oriented Criteria of Justice

Citizens with their diverse values and interests have divergent ideas about how the social institutions of their society should be designed and reformed. Such differences can be settled by force or through some widely acceptable procedure such as religious authority or voting. It is more appealing, however, to settle such differences through moral deliberation and agreement. This kind of settlement is more appealing because those whose initial preferences do not prevail genuinely accept the settlement. They are not outgunned, overruled, or outvoted (perhaps resentfully working to overturn the settlement in a rematch) but genuinely convinced.

To convince his compatriots, Rawls must offer them a justification. Central to the justification he offers is his thought experiment of the original position. I do not lay out this complex thought experiment immediately, however, but introduce first a few simpler elements that can be understood as its ingredients. Like the original position itself, these ingredient elements are meant to be widely sharable in a modern pluralistic society with many diverse religious, moral, and philosophical worldviews.

In introducing the simpler elements, I use language that is neutral between two-tiered and three-tiered theorizing. I discuss proposed elements of a top-tier criterion of justice while leaving open whether it is intended to be applied to candidate basic structures directly or (as a meta-criterion) to candidate public criteria of justice that in turn are applied to candidate basic structures. I use the expressions "how a society is organized" and "social order" in this neutral sense. Thus, a candidate social order, or *candidate* for short, is either a candidate basic structure ranked by a top-tier criterion of justice proposed within a two-tier theory or a candidate public criterion of justice ranked by a top-tier meta-criterion of justice proposed within a three-tier theory. By keeping the discussion more general in this way, we can learn more about the larger space of possible conceptions of justice within which Rawls specifies his own: We can appreciate particular structural features and problems shared by theories of a certain kind. And we can better understand the theory Rawls constructs by viewing it against the backdrop of its structural alternatives.

The first element is *consequentialism*. A moral criterion is consequentialist when it judges candidates solely by their consequences or effects. In comparing two basic structure designs, a consequentialist criterion gives preference to the candidate design whose implementation would have better effects. In comparing two public criteria of justice, a consequentialist meta-criterion gives preference to the candidate public criterion whose adoption would (mainly through the basic structures citizens would design and implement on its basis) have better effects.

The consequentialist element leaves entirely open which effects are morally relevant and how such morally relevant effects are to be scored. The second element of *humanism* begins to fill these gaps. A humanist consequentialist criterion focuses exclusively on each candidate's effects on human beings and considers effects to be better when they are better for human beings. Though Rawls is committed to humanism, his commitment is provisional in that he has explicitly set aside our relations with animals and the rest of nature.

The third element is *normative individualism*, which adds that the focus should be on *individual* human beings understood as temporally extended over a complete life. When a humanist consequentialist criterion is also individualist, it focuses on each candidate's effects on individual human lives. There are human entities other than individuals— time-slices of individuals, as well as groups, associations, and cultural communities (defined by a shared ethnicity, religion, language, or lifestyle), for example, and religions, values, and traditions. Like human individuals, these entities may be said to have interests and a good (something can be in the interest of the Red Sox or good for Catholicism). Normative individualism holds that effects on such other human entities matter only derivatively, only because and only insofar as individual persons identify with them. The only interests that count, in the final analysis, are those of individual human beings.

A moral criterion that incorporates these three elements is *purely recipient-oriented*. The rankings produced by such a criterion are based solely on how each candidate affects its recipients—here: human individuals. If one candidate leads to a better fulfillment of the interests of human beings than another, then the former is to be given preference.

The idea of a purely recipient-oriented conception of justice is immediately appealing: The best way of organizing a society is the way that is best for its individual members—how could one possibly disagree with this proposal?

One could object that the interests of foreigners should not be disregarded completely. They, too, might be affected, after all, by the way citizens organize their society. Rawls does not dispute or even discuss this point but sets it aside with his simplifying assumption that societies are isolated and self-contained. It is only for purposes of a first approximation that he focuses solely on the interests of individual members, holding that society should be organized in whatever way is best for them. (When lifting this simplifying assumption in his later book *LP*, however, Rawls does seem to overlook the question whether a conception of social justice ought to take account of the interests of outsiders.)

Rawls is not alone in endorsing the idea of a purely recipient-oriented conception of justice. Institutional utilitarianism is also committed to it, and so are many other conceptions of more recent vintage. But the idea also has its detractors. Especially in the United States, many believe that avoidable deprivations, such as poverty, suffered by members of a society are not necessarily indicative of social injustice. There may be no injustice if the society's institutional order satisfies certain intrinsic moral desiderata (by assigning appropriate rights and duties to its participants) and if the deprivations came about through a morally acceptable historical process. In a free society, some will succeed, and others, perhaps many, will fail. This is their own responsibility, and avoidable deprivations may therefore not indicate a moral defect in how the society is organized.

According to these critics, the moral acceptability of some given distribution among individuals depends then on the historical evolution of this distribution—not on whether it could be better if the society were differently organized. And similarly, some of the critics contend, the justice of a social order depends on how this order evolved historically—not on how it, relative to feasible alternatives, affects the distribution among individuals. Judgments of social justice require a historical examination of the *genesis* of present holdings and of the present social order—not a forward-looking examination of whether an alternative social order might have superior distributive effects. Rawls's most prominent critic in this vein has been the libertarian Robert Nozick, who developed a historical-entitlement conception of justice as an alternative (cf. section 9.1).

The consequentialist element in purely recipient-oriented theorizing can be opposed in a less radical way as well. This critique concedes that candidates should be judged in a forward-looking way. But it denies that all that matters about effects is how good or bad they are: It also matters what kind of causal pathway leads from a candidate social order to some particular effect or outcome.

This more moderate critique can begin from Rawls's own misgivings about applying a consequentialist criterion to conduct.

Notoriously, act utilitarianism treats the consequences of omissions on a par with those of actions. It holds that those who knowingly fail to donate lifesaving resources are morally on a par with killers and that one ought to kill seven when this is necessary to save eight. Most ethicists reject such purely recipient-oriented conduct assessment. They reject it on the ground that what matters morally is not merely what causal impact conduct has but also how it has this impact. The moderate critique of Rawls extends this rejection from ethics to social justice: In the assessment of social institutions and public criteria of justice, what matters morally is not merely what causal impact each has but also how it has this impact.

This critique can be supported by appeal to our intuitive understanding of justice, as two examples may illustrate. Avoidable unemployment is a hardship on individuals that detracts from the justice of the social order of their society. Yet, the moral weight of such avoidable unemployment seems to depend not merely on how severe and widespread it is but also on how it is causally related to the social order. Unemployment due to a legal restriction seems more serious, morally, than unemployment engendered by poorly designed economic institutions—even if the hardships on individual recipients are exactly the same. Similarly, a given avoidable risk of physical abuse seems morally more serious when the danger originates from the government than when it is due to criminals insufficiently deterred. The former risk detracts more from the justice of the society's social order than the latter—even if there is no difference in the injuriousness or probability of the abuse faced by individual recipients.

Our intuitive understanding of justice seems then to give more weight to burdens when these are mandated or authorized by law and administered by state officials than when they are due to insufficiently protective laws and officials. Purely recipient-oriented criteria are insensitive to this distinction because they assess candidates solely by how well the interests of individuals would be fulfilled under each. Such criteria therefore fail to match our intuitive understanding of justice. To fit this intuitive understanding, a criterion of justice must not simply tally up in some way the effects each candidate would have on individuals. It must weight these effects differentially by the kind of causal link that connects the candidate to specific benefits and burdens for individual recipients. A plausible criterion of justice must be sensitive to whether burdens on individuals are, for instance, *mandated* or *authorized* or *engendered* or *insufficiently deterred* by social institutions.

This more moderate critique has much to be said for it (cf. section 5.4). But it is nonetheless true that the consequentialist element is widely accepted among those Rawls sought to convince. This may be in part because the distinction highlighted by the moderate critique is often overlooked. This happens easily, because commonly used phrases are systematically ambiguous. When it is said, for instance, that an institutional order should be judged "by its effects" or "by how it affects individuals," it remains unclear whether the information to be consulted includes the causal pathways linking the institutional order to its effects. (An added emphasis—"by *how* it affects individuals"— can disambiguate.) It is easy, then, to slide from the idea of forward-looking assessment (candidates are to be judged solely by what they cause and how they cause it) to the idea of consequentialist assessment (candidates are to be judged solely by what they cause, regardless of how they cause it).

Utilitarians exemplify purely recipient-oriented moral theorizing. Bentham's institutional utilitarianism is an example. It assesses alternative designs of an institutional order solely by their (probabilistic) effects on pains and pleasures experienced by individuals—regardless of how the institutional order is causally involved in producing such pains and pleasures. Purely recipient-oriented moral assessment is also strongly dominant in modern normative economics, where it manifests itself in the (strong) *Pareto condition* (named for the Italian economist Vilfredo Pareto, 1848–1923). This condition requires that, of two candidates, C_1 must be ranked above C_2 if some affected recipient would be better off and none worse off under C_1 than under C_2. Thus, once again, alternative practicable social orders are judged by what causal impact each would have, without regard to how it would have this impact.

If one accepts that a criterion of justice should incorporate the three elements of consequentialism, humanism, and normative individualism (and hence should be purely recipient-oriented), one is still very far from a workable criterion of justice. In particular, two gaps remain to be filled: One needs an account of the human interests in terms of which a candidate's effects on individuals can be measured: an account of individual well-being or quality of life. And one needs a way of aggregating well-being information across individuals, because it will rarely be the case that the Pareto condition suffices to rank one candidate above all the rest. The next section discusses a step toward closing this latter gap: a fourth element of a top-tier criterion of justice. Philosophers have called this element *impartiality* or *moral universalism* or *equal consideration*. But because these labels are used in various other senses as well, I prefer the economists' term *anonymity*.

3.2 The Anonymity Condition

A criterion of justice incorporates the anonymity condition when it takes account of effects on a person equally, irrespective of who the person is. This element may seem to be contained in normative individualism, but it is not. Normative individualism requires that candidates be judged solely by their effects on individuals. This requirement is met even when the effects on some individuals (identified by name or by attributes) are given more weight than the effects on others. The fourth element rules out such partiality by requiring that individual well-being information be aggregated in a way that treats the information about any one individual the same as that about any other. The well-being information is, as it were, detached from the identity of the person: anonymized. A criterion incorporating this fourth element is equally sensitive to a deprived childhood, say, regardless of whether it is suffered by Alice or Beth, by a man or a woman, by a white or a black, by a Mormon or a Jew.

Suppose we have a society with three individuals—Alice, Beth, and Carl—and use an ordered triplet of numbers to represent how well off they would be under any candidate social order. The anonymity condition requires that all permutations of the same three numbers must lead to the same assessment. Thus, a candidate that produces a $<5,3,9>$ distribution of well-being is as good for its participants as other candidates producing distributions $<3,9,5>$ or $<9,3,5>$ or $<3,5,9>$ or $<9,5,3>$ or $<5,9,3>$. The well-being scores that a candidate produces for its participants are considered anonymously, that is, without regard to whose well-being each of these numbers represents.

Incorporating the anonymity condition adds discriminatory power to the idea of purely recipient-oriented assessment in that it allows many more contests to be decided. Thus consider two candidates, C_1 and C_2, that would, in our three-member society, produce well-being triplets of $<5,3,9>$ and $<4,9,6>$, respectively. Relying on the Pareto condition alone, one cannot rank either candidate above the other because, while Beth would be better off under C_2, Alice and Carl would do better under C_1. Invoking the anonymity condition in addition, a ranking is possible: The Pareto condition shows $<5,3,9>$

to be inferior to $<6,4,9>$, which in turn is equivalent to $<4,9,6>$ by the anonymity condition. It follows by transitivity that $<5,3,9>$ is inferior to $<4,9,6>$, and so C_1 must be ranked below C_2.

(This same result can be achieved on another path: The Pareto condition shows that $<4,9,6>$ is superior to $<3,9,5>$. But, according to the anonymity condition, $<3,9,5>$ is equivalent to $<5,3,9>$. Hence, by transitivity, $<5,3,9>$ must also be considered inferior to $<4,9,6>$ and C_1 therefore be ranked below C_2.)

Stating the point in general terms: A top-level criterion of justice satisfying the anonymity and Pareto conditions will hold that one candidate social order is superior to another just in case there is some one-to-one mapping of individual well-being scores under the former into those under the latter such that, for all pairs, the first score is in at least one case higher and in no case lower than the second.

When there are many affected recipients, the easiest way of comparing two candidates is by reordering the individual well-being scores each would generate by magnitude. (The anonymity condition requires that such a reordering should not alter the assessment.) This reordering yields the *distributional profile* associated with each candidate. Thus, the distributional profiles of the two ways of organizing the microsociety just discussed are $<3,5,9>$ and $<4,6,9>$, respectively. Here is a more complex example involving the distributional profiles of three alternative public criteria:

C_4 $<1,1,1,2,2,2,3,3,3,3,3,4,4,4,4,4,4,5,5,6,6,6,7,7,7,7,7,7,7,7,7,8,8,8,8,9,9,9,9,9,9,9,\ 9,\ 9,\ 9>$
C_5 $<1,1,1,1,2,2,2,3,3,3,3,3,3,3,4,4,4,4,5,5,5,5,5,6,6,6,6,6,7,7,7,7,8,8,8,8,8,8,8,9,\ 9,\ 9,\ 9>$
C_6 $<2,2,2,2,3,3,3,3,3,3,3,3,4,4,5,5,5,5,5,5,6,6,6,6,6,6,6,7,7,7,7,8,8,8,8,8,8,8,9,\ 9,\ 9,\ 9,\ 9>$

Employing such distributional profiles, one can see at a glance that the distribution C_5 would produce is inferior to the two distributions C_4 and C_6 would produce, and also that the anonymity and Pareto conditions do not suffice to rank C_4 vis-à-vis C_6.

The preceding discussion simplifies by assuming that, irrespective of which social order is chosen, the same persons would exist. This assumption is false of real-world societies, where the choice of social order makes a difference to who is born. This might be no problem if at least a society's population size were unaffected. But this weaker assumption, too, is false in the real world: The way a society is organized affects its birth and death rates. And there may then not be a one-to-one mapping of individuals across alternative ways of organizing society.

In response to this difficulty, one can compare candidates by matching up the well-being scores of individuals who occupy the same percentile rank. Here is an example:

C_7: <1, 1, 1, 2, 2, 2, 3, 3, 3, 3, 3, 3, 4, 4, 4, 4, 5, 5, 5, 5, 6, 6, 6, 6, 7, 7, 7, 7, 8, 8, 8, 8, 9, 9, 9, 9, 9>

C_8: <1,1,1,1,2,2,2,2,3,3,3,3,3,3,3,3,4,4,4,4,4,4,5,5,5,5,6,6,6,6,6,7,7,7,7,7,8,8,8,8,8,9,9,9,9,9>

The distributional profile produced by C_7 counts as Pareto-superior to that produced by C_8 on the ground that some persons under C_7 would be better off, and none worse off, than their counterparts (here shown immediately below) at the corresponding percentile under C_8. In general terms, of two ways of organizing the same society, C_x is to be ranked above C_y just in case the distribution produced by C_x is better than that produced by C_y at some percentile and worse at none.

This method of comparison can also be represented graphically by means of curves, each of which represents the individual well-being scores, ordered by magnitude, a candidate is estimated to produce. These curves, which are steadily rising toward the right, are *standard-*

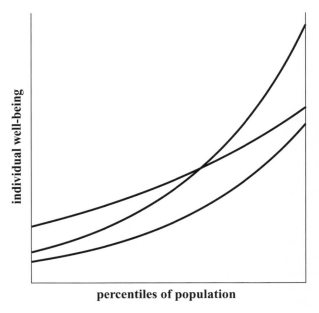

percentiles of population

Figure 3.1. Distributional Profiles Represented Graphically

ized so that their width is equal, irrespective of how many individuals would come to exist under each candidate social order. (Each hundredth of this width represents one percentile of the population.) In superimposing any two such curves upon each other, if one is above the other at some points and below at none, then the candidate associated with the former must be ranked above the candidate associated with the latter. Alternative social orders are compared via their standardized distributional profiles.

While this is the common way in which the Pareto and anonymity conditions are applied to different-number cases, it could be disputed. Consider again the preceding illustration. To compare C_8 with C_7, one might, in the first instance, consider only as many of the best-off persons under C_8 as are needed for a one-to-one mapping:

C_7: $<1,1,1,2,2,2,3,3,3,3,3,3,4,4,4,4,5,5,5,5,6,6,6,6,6,7,7,7,7,8,8,8,8,8,9,9,9,9,9>$
C_8: $<3,3,3,3,4,4,4,4,4,4,5,5,5,5,5,6,6,6,6,6,6,7,7,7,7,7,7,8,8,8,8,8,8,9,9,9,9,9,9>$

With this method of comparison, the distributional profile under C_8 is Pareto-superior to that under C_7. One might accept this ranking, provided only that the residual persons who would come to exist and would be the worst off under C_8 still have lives worth living. So C_8 is ranked higher, all things considered: In the pairs generated by the mapping, the persons who would exist under C_8 are in some cases better off and in no case worse off than their counterparts under C_7. And C_8 even offers a further bonus of additional lives that are worth living (with well-being scores 1,1,1,1,1,2,2,2,2,3,3,3,3,3).

Obviously, applying the Pareto and anonymity conditions in this alternative way would favor candidates under which more persons would come to exist. And so it is not surprising that, in an era when overpopulation has come to be a concern, most theorists (including Rawls and contemporary utilitarians) prefer to compare candidates via their standardized distributional profiles.

Though the anonymity condition so applied is widely endorsed as a plausible ingredient in a top-tier criterion of justice, it can be disputed in four distinct ways. Racists and other bigots who value the members of some race or religion more highly than those of another may resist the idea that the interests of all persons should be considered on a par. According to them, more weight should be given to the well-being of the members of their favorite group, presumably with the result that these persons are privileged in various ways and tend to fare better than others. This objection is morally offensive and not worth further discussion.

More appealing is the idea that the interests of morally deserving persons should count for more. But how morally deserving various persons will turn out to be depends in large part on the social order under which they live and thus cannot straightforwardly inform the choice of one such order over others. Still, one could say that, when comparing two candidates, it should count in favor of C_x that it better rewards those who would turn out to be morally deserving under C_x than C_y rewards those who would turn out to be morally deserving under C_y. Rawls rejects this idea on the ground that a just society should allow a wide diversity of judgments about what acts and lives are morally deserving. It must require compliance with its rules, of course, and punish some rule violations. But it need not and should not endorse any particular assessment of the lives individuals choose to lead within the freedom they have under the law.

A third objection to the anonymity condition, associated with David Gauthier, holds that the well-being of persons ought to reflect their differential bargaining power or threat advantage. Thus consider again the simple society consisting of Alice, Beth, and Carl. The anonymity condition holds that two candidates C_1 and C_3, producing well-being distributions of $<5,3,9>$ and $<3,9,5>$, respectively, should get equivalent assessments. But suppose that, were social cooperation to break down, the well-being scores of these three persons would be $<2,1,3>$. Alice and Carl can appeal to this fact, arguing that C_3 would involve an unfair distribution of the *gains* from cooperation, allowing Beth to gain 800 percent versus gains of only 50 percent and 67 percent for Alice and Carl. C_1, by contrast, involves a fairer distribution of gains: Alice gains 150 percent while Beth and Carl gain 200 percent each. Rawls can counter this objection by pointing out that any claims about how present citizens would fare if their society were dissolved are highly speculative, to put it mildly. He puts more stress, however, on the moral response that "to each according to his threat advantage" entails horrendous conclusions (*TJ* 116n10). This principle would celebrate as just a society in which those least able to fend for themselves would be severely disadvantaged in terms of rights and opportunities.

The fourth and most powerful objection to the anonymity condition maintains that, even if two distributions display the same distributional profile, one may still be morally inferior to the other if it displays a strong correlation between well-being scores on the one hand and skin color, gender, or religion on the other. Thus consider two identical distributional profiles with the scores of women (or people of color) highlighted in boldface:

<1,1,1,2,2,2,3,3,3,3,3,4,4,4,4,4,4,5,5,6,6,6,7,7,7,7,7,7,7,7,7,8,8,8,8,9,9,9,9,9,9, 9,9,9,9>
<1,1,1,2,2,2,3,3,3,3,3,4,4,4,4,4,4,5,5,6,6,6,7,7,7,7,7,7,7,7,7,8,8,8,8,9,9,9,9,9,9, 9,9,9,9>

Here the candidate public criterion producing the latter distributional profile would intuitively seem to be morally preferable because, unlike the former, it does not produce a distribution of well-being highly correlated with gender (or skin color). I return to this problem in section 6.4.

Purely recipient-oriented theorists who take individual human beings as recipients and accept the anonymity condition are two steps away from a workable top-tier criterion of justice: They must still specify a *metric of well-being* in terms of which one can estimate how well off or badly off the individuals living under any social order would be and in terms of which one can then sketch the distributional profile associated with each. And they must still specify an *interpersonal aggregation function* through which the data collected in each distributional profile can be synthesized into one *overall* assessment. The Pareto and anonymity conditions contribute to this latter task. But by themselves, they have too little discriminatory power, leaving many comparisons (such as that of C_4 and C_6) indeterminate, as their associated distributional profiles are Pareto-incomparable.

Contemporary utilitarians propose happiness or desire satisfaction for the first task, as the appropriate measure of well-being for individuals. For the second task, they propose *maximean* aggregation, which demands that the mean or average well-being should be as high as possible. Taking both elements together, (two-tier) institutional utilitarians propose then that, of two institutional designs workable in the same society, one should be ranked above the other if and only if the average happiness of individuals would be higher under the former than under the latter. Rawls rejects both elements of this utilitarian proposal. Let us discuss his two counterproposals in turn.

3.3 Fundamental Interests versus Happiness

Rawls has two main objections to using happiness as the appropriate measure of well-being for individuals. First, he holds that any happiness metric is insufficiently abstract to appeal to citizens with diverse worldviews. It is biased and controversial. In a free society, citizens have diverse views of the good life. Some do strive for happiness or desire satisfaction, to be sure. But even they differ deeply in how they understand happiness and make comparative judgments. Most citizens, in any case, pursue other aims, such as knowledge and culture, athletic success, love and friendship, artistic achievement, or some combination of these or yet further aims besides. Many deliberately sacrifice happiness in pursuit of such other aims. They could not accept the implication that, on account of such decisions, their lives are less worthwhile than they could be. Nor could they accept that their society ought to be organized to discourage such decisions—organized to shape its members into effective happiness producers and organized to prevent the emergence of any more challenging ambitions that would interfere with happiness production. Rawls wants his political conception of justice to avoid, as far as is reasonably possible, such implications about the value of different ways of life.

His second objection concerns the practical difficulties involved in applying a happiness metric. We cannot estimate, with anything resembling the needed precision, what distributions of happiness various alternative ways of organizing a society would produce. It could always be claimed, of course, that one basic structure design or one public criterion of justice would produce a better distribution of happiness than another. But such a claim is also easily denied, and there is no transparent public way of resolving such disputes. Even if it were possible to achieve agreement that society should be organized in a happiness-maximizing way and agreement also on the definition of happiness and its interpersonal aggregation, there would still be no way of determining, in a publicly accessible way, what organization of society would actually produce the best distribution of happiness so defined. A happiness-based criterion of justice would generate much disagreement about its application and may even fail to achieve stability (by facilitating widespread moral allegiance to the social order).

How can any purely recipient-oriented conception of justice avoid the first objection? Cannot any metric of well-being be rejected by some citizens as biased against their chosen way of life? Rawls sought to solve this problem by means of what he called a "thin theory of the good"—one that incorporates only widely acceptable ideas. In TJ, this thin theory featured the Aristotelian principle and the idea of a rational life plan. But Rawls replaced this account later, and I concentrate on the revised account. The revision is driven by the thought that a top-tier criterion of justice should be informed not by all the needs and interests of human beings but only by their needs and interests as citizens of a free democratic society. Such a criterion should be sensitive to the interests that, in our experience, citizens of such a society typically have and also must have, if a stable, free, and democratic social order is to be possible.

Rawls proposes three such interests (*PL* 74–75). The first two of these are interests in developing and exercising two moral powers, defined as the capacity for a sense of justice and the capacity for a conception of the good. The first interest is realized insofar as one has developed a sense of justice, that is, the ability and desire to govern one's conduct in accordance with a shared public conception of justice (Rawls's or another). The second interest is realized insofar as one has the ability to form, to revise, and rationally to pursue a conception of the good—a conception of a life worth living. The third is the interest in being successful in terms of the particular conception of the good one has chosen. In Rawls's three-tier theory, any candidate public criterion of justice is to be assessed by how well these three citizen interests would be fulfilled in societies whose citizens' institutional design decisions are guided by this criterion.

Rawls calls these *fundamental* or *higher-order* interests, suggesting both that they are interests in the content and fulfillment of other interests (like second-order desires are desires about desires) and also that they are deep, enduring, and normally decisive. Thus Rawls incorporates into his conception of justice the postulate that citizens have fundamental interests in cooperating with others on mutually and morally accepted terms, in being able critically to examine and rationally to pursue their (lower-order) interests within the framework of a larger conception of a worthwhile life, and in being successful in the pursuit of their chosen lower-order interests.

How can Rawls justify to his compatriots his reliance on these three fundamental interests at the expense of all other human interests? Is not his postulate no less biased than the utilitarian postulate of a fundamental interest in happiness? In fact, is it not even more biased? Happiness, after all, is pursued more widely than Rawls's fundamental interests, which play at best a subordinate role in many lives. Most people are not deeply interested in the justice of their society or in the formulation or critical examination of an overall conception of a worthwhile life. They live from one year to the next, care about their families, practice their religions, cultivate friendships, and cheer for their favorite baseball teams. Isn't it thus manifestly unfair for Rawls to base his conception of justice exclusively upon three "fundamental" interests that mean little to most people? Aren't his postulated interests congenial to intellectuals like himself and remote from most others whose lifestyles he nonetheless purports to respect as no worse than his own?

In response, Rawls can point out that more particular interests like those mentioned are not set aside but included within the third fundamental interest in being successful in terms of one's chosen ends. By avoiding any presumptions about the content of citizens' lower-order interests, Rawls renders his conception of justice more widely sharable than a utilitarian one would be. Thus, the stated objection is really applicable only to the first two fundamental interests: Why should they be given so much weight at the expense of the third fundamental interest, which includes ordinary lower-order interests?

Rawls might respond to the challenge as follows: The social order of a society should indeed be appropriate to the interests of its citizens. But these interests are profoundly shaped by the chosen social order (*TJ* 229–32, *PL* 68). Our attempt to envision an ideal social order thus cannot simply take existing interests as given (as if they were unaffected by how society is organized). We must, as it were, solve for two variables simultaneously. We must try to envision the best pairing: a society organized in a way that is congenial to the interests its citizens would have if it were so organized. This best pairing must do well in three respects: The envisioned social order must be morally appealing to us now, to those Rawls is seeking to convince. The envisioned social order must tend to develop in its participants interests that we find morally appealing. And the envisioned social order must be well suited to the fulfillment of these interests that it itself produces.

So Rawls need not claim that the first two fundamental interests are deeply felt now but only that we now, on reflection, find ourselves committed to their moral desirability and importance and therefore have moral reason to work toward a social order in which these two interests would be deeply felt. But why should this be so?

Rawls's answers to this question exemplify two different but compatible justificatory strategies. One of these emphasizes the moral appeal of his postulate. The first two fundamental interests involve our capacity to develop a sense of justice and a conception of the good. According to Rawls, these are the two *moral powers* of human beings—valuable capacities that ought to be developed and exercised, as he urges emphatically: "The role and exercise of these powers (in the appropriate instances) is a condition of good. That is, citizens are to act justly and rationally, as circumstances require. In particular, their just and honorable (and fully autonomous) conduct renders them, as

Kant would say, worthy of happiness; it makes their accomplishments wholly admirable and their pleasures completely good" (*PL* 334). This formulation is perhaps too emphatic, venturing beyond the terrain where overlap of reasonable worldviews can be hoped for. Remaining closer to ideas that are available in the public political culture of our society today (cf. section 8.2), Rawls might still say this: Even if not all of us today are interested in developing and exercising a sense of justice or in critical reflection about how to lead a worthwhile life, we nonetheless respect and value these moral powers. This is shown in our commitment to a public education system designed to enable everyone to develop these powers to a minimally sufficient extent. It is shown in widespread respect and admiration for people— be they reflective high school students, political leaders, or great philosophers—who strive to develop these powers in themselves. And it is also shown in our positive attitude toward a future state of our society in which interests to develop these powers would be more prevalent and reflections these powers enable thus more prominent in our culture.

Endorsing such valuations, Rawls's conception of justice cannot claim to be equidistant from all conceptions of the good. It has greater affinity to those who devote serious efforts to developing their two moral powers than to those who devote most of their spare time to cheering on their baseball teams. Still, there is no narrow bias because the first fundamental interest involves no determinate conception of justice and the second no determinate conception of the good. All three fundamental interests Rawls stipulates are therefore more abstract than a stipulated interest in happiness would be and, for this reason, better suited to form part of a political conception of justice for a pluralistic society. Individuals with entirely different interests and world-views can value these interests and can thus accept and employ them in evaluating alternative ways of organizing their society.

This thought can be extended to help defend Rawls against objections that propose adding further fundamental interests to his account. Many such proposals would be too partisan in the sense that they could not be accepted by the adherents of many reasonable moral, religious, or philosophical worldviews. An interest in redemption or the salvation of one's soul is an example. Overridingly important as this interest is for many believers, it is wholly unacceptable to others as part of the moral basis on which agreement about the social organization of our society is to rest.

This brings us to the second justificatory strategy, pursuant to which Rawls derives the first two fundamental interests from the (uncontroversial) third—by showing them to be constituent parts of it or means to its fulfillment. This strategy occurs in two variants. In one variant, Rawls tries to show that each citizen, whatever her other interests may be, also has an interest in herself having the first two fundamental interests. Along these lines one can, for instance, argue that the second moral power—to form, to revise, and rationally to pursue a conception of the good life—is itself a useful tool for fulfilling particular interests, whatever these might be (*PL* 312). A further argument along the same lines appeals to self-respect as a requirement for fulfilling whatever other interests we might have: "Without self-respect nothing may seem worth doing, and if some things have value for us, we lack the will to pursue them. . . . Self-respect is rooted in our self-confidence as a fully cooperating member of society capable of pursuing a worthwhile conception of the good over a complete life. Thus self-respect presupposes the development and exercise of both moral powers and therefore an effective sense of justice" (*PL* 318).

In the other variant of the second strategy, Rawls tries to show that each citizen, whatever her other interests may be, also has an interest in her *fellow-citizens'* having the first two fundamental interests, as this would greatly contribute to stability. Those who have a well-developed sense of justice can maintain their allegiance to a social order even when doing so runs counter to their own individual or group interests. Those with an interest in developing and exercising the ability to form, to revise, and rationally to pursue a conception of the good will help protect and maintain a pluralistic diversity of worldviews and forms of life. If both of these dispositions are widespread in a society, one has less reason to fear that some political victory will be misused to revise the basic structure or to persecute some particular group. Because such stability protects all citizens in the pursuit of their diverse interests, there is reason to favor a social order that tends to produce in citizens the first two fundamental interests—and then reason also to structure society in such a way that it is suitable to persons with these interests.

These reasons are strengthened by another, more positive consideration: When citizens do not feel threatened by, and are disposed to protect, other ways of life and conceptions of the good, then they can benefit from them even without fully participating in them. Borrowed from Wilhelm von Humboldt, the basic idea is that, within a harmonious society, persons can partake in the pursuit of many interests and ambitions vicariously and can thereby console themselves for the depressing fact that each of us can seriously pursue only a few interests

and ambitions oneself. Thus, a society in which the first two fundamental interests are prevalent can facilitate a harmonious synergy of
complementary interests (*PL* 320–23).

These considerations invoke the fact of reasonable pluralism: It is
empirically impossible in free modern societies to achieve stability or a
harmonization of complementary interests by means of a comprehensive consensus that covers all moral topics or most. A social order
supported by widespread moral allegiance and a harmony of complementary interests—both of which benefit citizens in the pursuit of their
own particular interests—is best secured through an overlapping consensus that is confined to a conception of justice and the basic structure
design it justifies. Such a consensus is possible only where citizens can
count on being able to pursue their various values and interests freely,
under the protection of a culture of liberal tolerance. The fundamental interests Rawls stipulates are meant to support such tolerance.

One may still question whether a society organized on the basis of
this stipulation would actually produce citizens that have the stipulated
interests. This question can be addressed only later (chapter 7), aided
by a clearer picture of a Rawlsian social order. Only an affirmative
answer would render Rawls's two justificatory strategies fully successful and, in particular, vindicate the last two arguments by showing
that a Rawlsian society is best able to achieve stability and a harmony
of complementary interests.

Four

THE BASIC IDEA: *JUSTICE AS FAIRNESS*

Purely recipient-oriented moral theorizing can be rationalized through the idea of a hypothetical contract. Such a contract is a fiction, a thought experiment, not an actual historical event. Its moral significance does not then depend upon the supposition that we or our ancestors made some promise or contract. What then is the moral significance of such a purely fictional agreement? The best answer to this question varies with the subject matter to which the contractualist thought experiment is applied. Rawls's subject matter is a society's social order, the way it is organized. (As a three-tier theorist, Rawls thinks of this subject matter as involving not merely the society's major social institutions, its "basic structure," but also a public criterion of justice that guides the design, maintenance, and adjustment of the basic structure in light of prevailing circumstances. We can continue to disregard this complication a little longer.) Let us examine the specific thought experiment Rawls proposes for this subject matter.

4.1 The Original Position

A society's social order has profound and pervasive effects on its members. It involves rules and social expectations, many of which are backed by sanctions that can be very severe. This raises the question whether it is morally justifiable to constrain and condition individual conduct so severely and, if so, how and under what conditions.

Compliance with society's rules is not merely commanded with threats of sanctions but also presented as a moral obligation. This raises the further question whether individuals really have moral reasons to comply with their society's rules and social expectations and, if so, why and under what conditions. Finally, individuals are born, through no choice of their own, into an ongoing society whose social order has a deep influence on their development, on who they will come to be. Not only the options and incentives individuals face but also their very identity—their character, temperament, personality, values, ambitions, goals, ideals, hopes, and dreams—are profoundly shaped by the way their society is organized. To be sure, it is all but unavoidable that individuals are deeply shaped by the social environment in which they grow up. Yet, some ways of molding the character of individuals are clearly wrong. And this raises the third question of what kinds of social shaping of individual development can be morally justified, and how.

In a democratic society, citizens are not merely shaped and bound by the social order but also collectively responsible for it. The three questions are then not discretionary questions that one may press against one's society if one wishes, but questions we must face in view of our participation in imposing a particular social order on our compatriots and, especially, on those who are (without choice) born into our society. How can we justify what we together do to each of us when we coercively impose rules and social expectations on our fellow citizens, regard them as morally bound by these rules and expectations, and shape their very identity through the social environment in which they grow up? One possible justification involves the attempt to base what we together do to each solely on plausible conjectures about what she herself would have rationally wanted or agreed to. Contractualist thought experiments are such attempts.

This rationale for contractualist thought experiments makes clear why it is appropriate to describe the contracting parties as motivated by a rational concern for their own interests alone. If we imagined these parties as altruistically motivated, the thought experiment would lose its justificatory force. One can describe a social contract in which women, altruistically motivated, agree to do all the housekeeping and child-rearing work without receiving any promise of reciprocal service from men. But such a description does not give actual women even the slightest moral reason to accept a rule or social expectation to this effect. To justify to others that they *ought* to accept certain rules or obligations, one needs to show them that it would have been in their own interest to agree to them. Thus one might justify a social rule that requires people to help one another whenever the cost to the helper is greatly outweighed by the benefit to the recipient in this way: by pointing out that this rule is antecedently in everyone's best interest and therefore would have been rationally agreed to by all.

Contractualism makes vivid the basic idea of purely recipient-oriented moral theorizing: Something is morally justified if and only if it is in the best interest of all affected, without regard to the kind of causal pathway through which it affects these recipients. Imagine a society's members having to agree beforehand on how their society is to be organized. Rational persons would rate each candidate social order on the basis of how well they could expect to do under it. They would not care whether specific benefits or burdens they might encounter are officially called for by laws and practices, engendered by agents' uncoordinated conduct under such rules, or due to poorly deterred breaches of the law. Each would care only about the impact of such benefits and burdens on her own well-being and about the probability of encountering any of them. A hypothetical-contract approach is by its very nature purely recipient-oriented. And conversely, one may conjecture that any purely recipient-oriented moral conception can be couched in terms of some hypothetical contract functioning as an "expository device" (*TJ* 19, 105).

The features of Rawls's theory already introduced go well beyond the bare idea of purely recipient-oriented moral theorizing in various respects: Rawls focuses on a specific moral topic, the social order of a society (which is my term for what in his theory ideally consists of a public criterion of justice and the basic structure designed, maintained, and adjusted by reference to this criterion). He thinks of the relevant recipients as individual human members of the society in question. He endorses the anonymity condition (equal consideration for all recipients). He rejects the moral relevance of threat advantage: of how well each citizen would fare if the society were to be dissolved. And he proposes the three fundamental interests as an appropriate account of human well-being at the top tier.

Rawls wants to present a hypothetical-contract account that serves as an expository device for a conception of justice that has these (and yet further) features. This requires corresponding specifications of the hypothetical contract idea, resulting in the detailed thought experiment of the original position. This thought experiment can be summarized in the following five points. It is immediately apparent from these points how the original position incorporates Rawls's focus on a specific topic, his commitment to humanism and normative individualism, and his stipulation of the three fundamental interests. The anonymity condition and the exclusion of threat advantage are discussed after the summary.

(1) The contracting parties in the original position have a specific *task description*: They are charged with agreeing on a public criterion of justice for the comparative assessment of practicable basic structure designs. Their choice is final; it is binding upon the society for its whole indefinite future. The society in question is self-contained, exists in reasonably favorable conditions of relative scarcity, and is characterized by the fact of reasonable pluralism. Its members are human beings who have no grave physical or mental handicaps and possess the two moral powers to some sufficient degree. The criterion to be chosen is to play a public role: It should be understandable to all adults and should facilitate a public, transparent, and definite assessment of the social institutions of the basic structure. This criterion should also be a suitable object for a lasting overlapping consensus and thus should invariably select a design of the basic structure under which citizens would tend to develop a sense of justice that inspires a moral commitment to the social order that generally outweighs their other motives.

(2) The contracting parties choose their public criterion of justice from a *list of historically influential candidates*. Rawls says that this list can be lengthened if desired. He is initially mainly concerned to demonstrate that the parties would prefer his criterion to various utilitarian candidates.

(3) Rawls imagines the *contracting parties* endowed with rationality but does not ascribe to them morality, moral powers, or any richer faculty of reason. Representing one prospective member of society over his or her complete lifetime, each party aims to do as well as possible in safeguarding this individual human client's interests. (Rawls sometimes wrote as if he imagined prospective citizens themselves to assemble in the original position. But he came to regard this image as expositionally inferior because it invites the false belief that Rawls envisions citizens themselves as rational maximizers akin to the lawyerly parties; cf. *TJ* 457, *JFR* 83–85.)

(4) The parties are made to assume that *citizens* have the three fundamental interests and therefore (this follows from the third interest) determinate conceptions of the good that they want to realize as fully as possible. In accordance with the second justificatory strategy discussed in section 3.3, one might alternatively make the parties assume only the third fundamental interest and then show that it entails

the other two as constituent parts or means to its fulfillment: The parties understand that citizens are generally better able to fulfill their particular interests if they have the two moral powers (especially the second) and live in a society whose other members also have them (especially the first). Thus they have an interest in their society being so organized that it motivates its members to develop these two moral powers, and they will then assess alternative social orders from the standpoint of these two additional interests (*PL* 312–23).

(5) The contracting parties make their agreement behind a *veil of ignorance*. They know nothing about the particular individual each represents, about that citizen's gender, skin color, natural endowments, temperament, interests, tastes, and preferences. Nor do they know anything about the specific conditions of the society whose social order is at stake—the size, quality, climate, and location of its national territory, for instance, its natural resources, its population and population density, its wealth, and its level of technological development. The parties have only general knowledge of the social sciences (including human psychology), as well as the information stated under points (1) through (4).

New for us in this summary is the last point, the veil of ignorance, which is meant to model the anonymity condition and the exclusion of threat advantage.

In conditions of scarcity, persons with similar interests and needs have competing interests in regard to the distribution of goods that many want. This competition is not merely about the goods available under existing social institutions but also about the design of such institutions themselves. Which such design is best for some participant varies with his or her family background, talents, gender, and other characteristics. How is it to be possible, nonetheless, to justify one social order to all participants? If a hypothetical contract is to provide such a justification to all, then it must somehow balance their competing interests against one another. This can be done in two ways.

One way of balancing—best elaborated by David Gauthier—involves hypothetical negotiations in which differently endowed participants (or their representatives) reach agreement through mutual concessions and compromises. Such concessions would be motivated by the fear that without them the result would be either an unregulated Hobbesian war of all against all in the absence of any social order or else a social order agreed upon by some who, together, are strong enough to impose it on the rest. A social contract of this kind reflects the differential bargaining power and threat potentials of the various participants and may result in an agreement that treats these participants very unequally.

As a crude illustration of the problems with this way of balancing, imagine negotiations in which men offer women a social order under which they have certain rights but are excluded from politics and government. The men declare that, should their offer be rejected, they will agree among themselves to a social order that would give women no rights at all. Given this threat and the greater physical strength of men, women might prudently accept the offer. But does this hypothetical negotiation and its hypothetical result give *us* any reason to establish such gender-based political inequality and even to pronounce it just?

Moreover, it is not rational for actual agents to honor concessions made on the basis of merely hypothetical threat potentials in a fictional contract situation. It would be foolish for women to renounce voting rights in their actual society, if the threat of depriving them of all rights exists and can be implemented only in some hypothetical scenario. It may well be rational to make concessions in response to actual threats, as we observed in discussing a modus vivendi. But this valid point is not illuminated, but only obscured, by introducing the idea of a hypothetical contract.

There is also no moral reason to make concessions on the basis of hypothetical threat potentials in a fictional contract situation. We are told that, if it would have been rational for women to succumb to the hypothetical blackmail as described, then actual women ought to be willing to renounce their voting rights. But this conclusion is so offensive to our intuitive understanding of justice that it provides a powerful reason for rejecting any hypothetical-contract view committed to the inference.

Rather than balance competing interests by appeal to the parties' differential bargaining power and threat advantage, a hypothetical contract view can balance them by depriving the contracting parties of knowledge. Here one imagines each party as representing the interests of a prospective participant without knowing anything about the individuating features of this client—about his or her gender, skin color, talents, temperament, tastes, specific interests, values, and worldview. Placed behind a veil of ignorance, such hypothetical contractors have only general information about the distribution of natural endowments among individuals (not about the distribution of other personal features, because this distribution depends on the social order yet to be chosen). Because each contractor must reckon with any possible combination of natural endowments, the balancing of interests is accomplished not through negotiations among the parties but through identical deliberations by each: Whatever agreement it is rational for any one contractor to want is also rational for all the others.

Only this latter kind of balancing of competing interests, exemplified by Rawls's original position, can explain why the agreement reached, albeit merely hypothetical, should nonetheless be morally binding on actual people: In the original position, the needs and interests of all prospective participants are represented and, thanks to the veil of ignorance, which eliminates threat advantage and implements the anonymity condition, represented *fairly*. This thought inspires the name Rawls has given to his conception: *justice as fairness*. A social order is to be accepted as *just* if and only if it could be the object of a *fair* agreement—of an agreement that takes equal account of the interests of all the individuals who are to live under this social order.

The veil of ignorance deprives the parties not just of all particular knowledge about the individuals they represent. It also deprives them of any—even probabilistic—knowledge about the particular enduring conditions of their society (over and above its existing in "reasonably favorable" conditions, defined as ones that make it possible for citizens, should they have the political will, to realize certain basic rights and liberties). This second deprivation is unnecessary for ensuring that the original position is fair. And it prevents the parties from formulating an optimal public criterion of justice—one tailored to the more enduring conditions of their particular society. Rawls is prepared gradually to lift the veil of ignorance, after his public criterion of justice has been chosen, to allow the parties to specify this criterion further so as to adapt it to the conditions of a particular society (*TJ* §31). He thinks it important, however, that the public criterion itself be chosen from behind a "thick" veil of ignorance. This is meant to highlight how closely the thought experiment of the original position models the fair placement of free and equal individuals and how the argument in which this thought experiment is embedded does not depend on the contingent conditions of some particular society (*CP* 335–36).

Rawls's employment of a thick veil is, however, problematic. For one thing, he does not explain why the contracting parties should not find it rational to circumvent their ignorance by agreeing on a complex disjunctive public criterion that specifies the demands of justice differently for different sets of enduring conditions. In fact, Rawls had initially argued that the parties would reach such a disjunctive solution, prescribing the *special conception* if society exists in reasonably favorable conditions and the *general conception* otherwise (*TJ* 54–55, *PL* 297; he later excluded unfavorable conditions from the scope of *justice as fairness* and jettisoned the general conception). Pushing this strategy further, the parties could distinguish various different sets of conditions their society might be in and could then adopt a different criterion for each set, thereby completely negating Rawls's thickening of the veil (which denies them all knowledge about the size, quality, climate, and location of the society's national territory, as well as about its natural resources, its population and population density, its wealth, and its level of technological development).

To be sure, Rawls might somehow prevent or forbid this disjunctive strategy. This would force the parties to adopt a public criterion that is suitable for a vast range of sets of reasonably favorable conditions, many of which would be very remote from the actual world. (It is most unlikely that the United States will ever be landlocked, have fewer than fifty thousand citizens, or lack the technology to generate electricity.) Such a broadly serviceable criterion may well be suboptimal for the particular conditions that actually obtain or could realistically come to obtain in the target society. Learning more about these actual conditions (as the veil is gradually lifted; *TJ* §31), the parties might then deeply regret their choice. (For example, given how little information they had, it may have been rational for them to adopt expensive precautions that turn out to be superfluous in the enduring conditions this society is actually facing.) It is unclear why we should feel morally obligated to structure our society according to a public criterion that it is rational to adopt only if nothing is known about the particular enduring conditions in which our society exists— when we could all be better off with an alternative public criterion better adapted to these enduring conditions.

4.2 Maximin versus Average

We have seen that Rawls's top-tier criterion of justice features the three fundamental interests as its well-being metric. Let us now examine the interpersonal aggregation function that is to synthesize the individual well-being data of any distributional profile into a single assessment for the candidate social order producing this profile.

One obvious way to aggregate these data—consistent with the purely recipient-oriented mode of assessment and the anonymity condition—is to average them. This *maximean* aggregation function, employed by most contemporary utilitarians, favors the candidate social order that would lead to the highest *average* level of fundamental interest fulfillment.

As an important alternative, Rawls proposes the *maximin* interpersonal aggregation function, which synthesizes the well-being data of any distributional profile by taking the *lowest* individual well-being as representative for the whole. According to this proposal, distributional profiles are compared by reference to their respective worst-off members. The just social order we should aim for is the one that would engender the highest floor or highest minimum (*maximum minimorum*, in Latin): the social order under which the worst-off participant is better off than the worst-off participant under any practicable alternative social order would be. Rawls's top-tier criterion of justice is then *maximin fundamental interest fulfillment*. We ought to opt for the social order that would result in the highest achievable floor of fundamental interest fulfillment.

Rawls seeks to support maximin aggregation in the first instance by claiming that it is generally rational for the parties in the original position to deliberate according to the maximin rule. This is a decision-theoretic rule for situations in which at least one of the possible options can lead to a number of different outcomes. Here the maximin rule enjoins that one choose the option with the best worst-case scenario. Suppose you have $10,000 that you won't need for the next two years. If you deposit it in a savings account, it will grow to $11,000 over this period. If you invest it in the stock market, it will be worth between $7,000 and $17,000 in two years. The maximin rule recommends the savings account in this case, because it offers a superior worst-case scenario: a gain of 10 percent versus a loss of 30 percent in the stock market.

Whether it is rational to choose according to the maximin rule depends on the decision situation. According to Fellner and Rawls (*TJ* 134–39, *JFR* 98), it depends in particular on the degree to which this situation exemplifies three features: The best worst-case scenario is acceptable (it is not very important to do better), and all other options involve intolerable worst-case scenarios (it is very important to avoid these), whose probability is unknown.

Thus, if having $11,000 in two years is acceptable to you, if you find having in two years only $7,000 to be wholly intolerable, and if you know nothing about the probability that the stock market would reduce your wealth so drastically, then it is rational for you to employ the maximin rule and thus to choose the savings account.

On the other hand, if you do care about future money increments in the $11,000 to $17,000 range, no less than about money decrements in the $7,000 to $11,000 range, and if you know the probabilities of the various stock market outcomes, then it is rational to choose the option with the higher probability-weighted expected payout. For the stock market option, this is calculated by multiplying each possible outcome by its probability and then adding these products. If the probabilities of the various possible outcomes of investing in the stock market display an arithmetically normal distribution, the probability-weighted expected outcome is midway between $7,000 and $17,000, that is, $12,000. The maximean rule then favors the stock market investment, which offers an expected return of 20 percent—twice that of the savings account (10 percent).

Decision situations often lie between these two extremes. Each of the three conditions can hold to a greater or lesser degree and can do so independently of the degree to which any of the others holds. For this reason, it may be difficult to decide between the two decision rules. In such intermediate cases, it makes sense to examine the choice in both ways, aiming for a decision that seems rational under both decision rules.

Rawls allows that it may be rational to examine the decision problem posed in the original position under the maximean rule. But he insists that the situation is one in which the maximin rule has a certain preeminence. That this is so is, to some extent, an artifact of the thick veil of ignorance Rawls chooses to impose on the parties, a choice we have already seen to be problematic. How a society's social order affects the well-being of its individual members depends not only on the details of this social order but also on the features of that society: on the size, quality, climate, and location of its national territory, its natural resources, its population and population density, its wealth, and its level of technological development. By depriving the parties of any—even probabilistic—knowledge about such features of their clients' society (*TJ* 134), Rawls ensures that they cannot develop credible probability estimates with regard to specific outcomes. It is therefore indeed rational for the parties to employ the maximin rule. Still, Rawls's reasoning here depends on his own stipulation of a thick veil, which is not well justified. We will see, however, that Rawls has further reasons for favoring a top-tier criterion of justice that focuses attention on the worst off.

The parties employ the maximin rule and know very little about the society whose social order they are supposed to agree upon. Therefore, they would want to agree on a candidate social order that would reliably protect the fundamental interests of all members of society over the whole range of sets of reasonably favorable conditions. An agreement they would find it rational to endorse must fulfill two desiderata that go in opposite directions. On the one hand, it should be flexible enough to fit all the many sets of reasonably favorable conditions that may turn out to obtain. The parties would not want to accept a meticulous agreement with detailed descriptions of the major social institutions because the described institutions might not work well in the particular conditions of the society in question. On the other hand, the agreement should be firm and specific enough reliably to protect the three fundamental interests of citizens. Both desiderata are well accommodated by the public criterion of justice Rawls proposes: his two principles with the two priority rules.

That the parties are supposed to agree on a public criterion of justice is simply part of their task description as stipulated by Rawls. Still, this stipulation is here, as it were, reaffirmed: Quite apart from the stipulation, the parties would find it rational to agree on a public criterion of justice, rather than on a basic structure design directly, in order to avoid the risk that the chosen basic structure design would be (or come to be) ill fitting to the society's actual conditions in a way that involves very bad outcomes for some of its members. As is often the case, the parties' reasoning mirrors our own—here Rawls's reasons for conceiving his theory of justice as three-tiered and aiming for an overlapping consensus on more than merely the constitution or design of the basic structure (section 2.3).

Employing the maximin rule, the parties examine the public criterion Rawls proposes for agreement as follows: They canvass all the diverse sets of reasonably favorable conditions in which their society may find itself. They contemplate the basic structure designs that actual citizens guided by Rawls's public criterion might implement in each such set of conditions. They anticipate the worst individual position (in terms of fundamental interest fulfillment) each of these basic structure designs would generate in the conditions in which citizens might implement it. They estimate how bad each of these worst individual positions would be (in terms of fundamental interest fulfillment). They compare all these worst positions across sets of conditions and basic structure designs in order to identify the worst of these worst-case scenarios. This is the *very-worst-case scenario* associated with Rawls's public criterion of justice, by reference to which the parties compare this criterion to other public criteria they might agree on instead.

This summary account makes clear how one could reject the thick veil of ignorance as biased. One might say that the very-worst-case scenarios the parties pay so much attention to are simply irrelevant when they arise in reasonably favorable conditions that our society does not confront and never will. We ought to restrict attention to the sets of conditions that our society may conceivably face in the future, and perhaps even (departing from the maximin rule) invoke probability estimates with regard to sets of such conditions. We should not base the assessment of any candidate criterion on a single very-worst-case scenario that involves conditions that our society certainly will not, or is extremely unlikely ever to, encounter. One important reason against doing this is that it might hurt the interests of those who are actually worst off in our society, who may be much worse off than anyone would need to be in existing conditions. How can we allow their fate on the ground that it is a necessary by-product of a public criterion of justice that wins the very-worst-case scenario contest— when the very-worst-case scenarios the winning criterion allows us to avoid arise in conditions that we know will never obtain in our society?

This rejection of the thick veil could be especially attractive to advocates of utilitarian criteria of justice, whom Rawls regards as his main competitors. It is easy to think up reasonably favorable conditions in which a utilitarian criterion might justify social institutions under which some would be very badly off. Utilitarians may want to dismiss such "counterexamples" when these describe conditions that do not and will not exist. To circumvent this response, it would be good if Rawls's proposed public criterion also won the worst-case-scenario contest for various realistic sets of conditions. Insofar as it does, we gain assurance that its adoption will not lower the worst position for the sake of avoiding some unrealistic very-worst-case scenario.

In Rawls's theory, the thought experiment of the original position functions as a meta-criterion of justice. It ranks candidate public criteria of justice by how high a minimum level of fundamental interest fulfillment each would secure. One might think that the public criterion so chosen would be identical in content to the meta-criterion. But this is not so. A public criterion of justice is assessed not by whether what it values matches closely what the meta-criterion values, but solely by its effects. What matters is what basic structure designs actual citizens, guided by some public criterion of justice, would maintain under diverse sets of reasonably favorable conditions and how well the worst off under these basic structure designs would fare. The parties in the original position seek not the public criterion of justice that, in any given conditions, *requires designing* the basic structure so that the worst lives, in terms of fundamental interest fulfillment, are no worse than is unavoidable. Rather, they seek the public criterion that, in any given conditions, *would reliably guide citizens to design* the basic structure so that the worst lives, in terms of fundamental interest fulfillment, are not (much) worse than is unavoidable.

Under realistic conditions, any public criterion of justice falls short of realizing what it itself requires. Any society guided by the end of maximizing average happiness will fall short of maximizing happiness, for example. Possible causes for such shortfalls are of two types. One is that officials and citizens make mistakes in applying the criterion, which results in losses through misapplications and disputes. The other type of cause is that officials and citizens do not even try to apply the criterion correctly because their moral commitment to it is weak or nonexistent. This results in losses from deliberate misjudgments, noncompliance, disputes, even civil war. Rawls clearly wants problems of the first type to be considered in the original position. Problems of the second type, at least insofar as they are serious enough to subvert stability, are to be examined at a second stage, where an entire conception of justice is checked for whether it can generate enduring moral allegiance (*PL* 64–65, 140–43), though Rawls also presents stability considerations within the original position (*TJ* 398, *JFR* 115–17). I suppose that one reason to think about serious instability separately is that the parties, insofar as they employ the maximin rule, would have no basis to compare public criteria that involve some risk of serious instability. The very-worst-case scenario of all such candidate criteria is the same: civil war.

If instructed to resolve questions of basic structure design by reference to a metric of fundamental interest fulfillment, citizens would be highly prone to error and interminable disagreement. Citizens would not be able to develop a clear and shared understanding of how fulfillment of each of the three fundamental interests should be measured and how such measurements should be aggregated into assessments of personal well-being and then be brought to bear on the design of the basic structure. Many citizens would reject public justifications of institutional design decisions as (perhaps deliberate) misapplications of the shared public criterion of justice. Such error and interminable disagreement would greatly reduce the degree to which citizens' fundamental interests would actually be fulfilled. This thought closely parallels Rawls's complaint that a principle of utility, deployed as a public criterion, would fail to achieve what by its own lights matters: the production of happiness. Let us see what Rawls proposes, within his public criterion of justice, as a substitute for fundamental interest fulfillment.

4.3 Primary Goods

Rawls aims to propose a public criterion of justice that citizens can understand and apply together in a transparent way to all questions concerning the design, maintenance, and adjustment of the basic structure of their society. Because this middle-tier public criterion is supposed to be justifiable by reference to Rawls's top-tier meta-criterion, it is not surprising that it also incorporates the elements of consequentialism, humanism, normative individualism, anonymity, and irrelevance of threat advantage. Rawls needs then a metric of individual well-being that better lends itself to transparent public application than the metric of fundamental interest fulfillment. He proposes a list of primary goods for this role (see *TJ* §15; *CP* 313–14, 454; *PL* 181, 308–9):

1. certain basic rights and liberties, themselves given by a list (*TJ* 53, *PL* 291);
2. freedom of movement and free choice of occupation;
3. powers and prerogatives of offices;
4. income and wealth;
5. residual social bases of self-respect ("residual," because Rawls views the first four primary goods as bases of self-respect as well).

Access to as much of these primary goods as possible is supposed to be advantageous to all citizens, important for the development and exercise of their two moral powers, as well as for the realization of whatever lower-order interests each may have.

It is notable that the proposed public criterion assesses individual well-being in terms of social goods alone, ignoring all the natural features of citizens. This would seem to make Rawls's proposal less acceptable for agreement in the original position. The parties are concerned with their clients' fundamental interests, whose fulfillment is certainly affected also by their natural constitution.

One might want to defend Rawls's decision by pointing out that the distribution of natural endowments is not under society's control and should be disregarded for this reason. But this is a bad argument. Even if the distribution of natural assets is fixed, this distribution can be taken into account in assessing a distribution of social primary goods. A public criterion of justice would then assess the well-being of a disabled person as being below that of an able-bodied person with the same social primary goods. It would do so because the disabled person is likely to be less successful in his or her pursuit of the three fundamental interests—both because of the additional expenses (wheelchair, hearing aid) this disability makes necessary and because of the handicap that remains even with such compensatory expenditures. Looking at each citizen's share of social primary goods alone, Rawls's public criterion may seem to miss important components of well-being as the parties understand it.

In response, Rawls can point out that he has explicitly bracketed the problem of chronic illnesses and disabilities. And he can adduce the further assumption that citizens, capable of taking part in education, work, and politics over a complete life, have access to adequate insurance against temporary illnesses and disabilities. There are, however, other natural goods that are unequally distributed from birth and affect the well-being of citizens: native intelligence, memory, perceptual acuity, energy and stamina, quick reflexes, various special talents (for music, mathematics, sports, and the like), personal appearance, and many others besides. Rawls appreciates this fact and explicitly recognizes such natural primary goods (*TJ* 54). But his proposed public criterion of justice assesses individual well-being in terms of social primary goods alone.

One could give a principled justification for this exclusion: Social institutions should not be designed with an eye to the resulting distribution of natural endowments but should allow this distribution to emerge from the free choices of consenting couples. Newly born citizens can then be regarded as bringing their natural endowments with them into society. They do not, of course, deserve their natural characteristics and are not in any way responsible for having them, but this does not mean that *society* must take responsibility for them and hence organize itself so as to compensate for natural inequalities. Society is responsible not for the justice of the universe but only for that of its own social institutions. It should therefore concern itself only with the goods whose distribution is regulated or intentionally affected by its social institutions.

Such a principled justification—which Rawls does not offer himself—occupies a plausible midpoint between two extremes. Some (luck egalitarians) want to compensate for natural inequalities: to assign more social goods to those who fare worse in terms of natural goods. Others (utilitarians and perfectionists) tend to aggravate natural inequalities, assigning more social goods to those whose natural endowments enable them to make the best use of them, to those already naturally favored: education to those most capable of learning, income to those who can enjoy it most, and so on. Rawls's criterion of justice stands between these extremes: the given distribution of natural abilities is not to be taken into account—either positively or negatively—in assessing the distributional effects of alternative designs of the basic structure.

Nonetheless, I see two difficulties. Granted, we do not think of a society as being, ceteris paribus, more just if it provides more primary goods to, say, its less good-looking or less gifted members. But we think differently about genuine disabilities. It *is* worse if those already struck with blindness must also occupy the lowest position in terms of social primary goods. Whether the principled justification can succeed must depend, then, on a solution to the problem of chronic illnesses and disabilities. Rawls brackets this problem by stipulating that all citizens have the capacities needed to be fully cooperating members of society over a complete life (*PL* 182–85).

Another difficulty for the principled justification is that of reconciling it with the thought experiment of the original position. Rawls himself has never even attempted to do this. Employing the maximin rule in the original position, the parties would reason as follows: We want to agree on a public criterion of justice that, in any given conditions, tends to select the basic structure under which the lowest level of fundamental interest fulfillment is higher than it would be under any other practicable basic structure design. Now the extent to which a person's fundamental interests (especially the third) are fulfilled depends not only on her or his access to social primary goods but also and substantially on her or his natural endowments. We should therefore agree on a public criterion of justice that, by employing an appropriate list of social *and natural* primary goods for assessing individual well-being, is sensitive also to natural endowments. Such a public criterion is better able to preclude very low levels of fundamental interest fulfillment than a public criterion that disregards information about individuals' natural endowments and is sensitive only to their social positions. The plausibility of this reasoning suggests that Rawls must either jettison his account of the three fundamental interests, or even the whole thought experiment of the original position, or else must give up his public criterion's exclusive concern with social primary goods.

But there is a third option. One could attempt a reconciliation through pragmatic arguments: Institutionalized compensation given to the less gifted is liable to undermine both the self-respect of the citizens so classified and the sense of equal citizenship across society. Institutionalized compensation required from the better endowed would undermine their freedom to choose low-paying jobs. A further problem is that there would be no agreement on the proper measurement of ugliness or bad memory, or on the proper exchange rate between such natural goods and ills and social benefits and burdens. Disagreements are all the more likely as members of a society governed by such a complex public criterion of justice would have an incentive to conceal their natural endowments—to pretend to have a bad memory, for example, or to let their looks deteriorate. Including natural factors in the list of primary goods, one would never arrive at a widely accepted public criterion of justice that can be publicly applied in a transparent and convincing way. Therefore, even if we should ideally take account of all factors relevant to fundamental interest fulfillment, it would nonetheless be better, for the sake of transparent applicability, to exclude from the public criterion most natural factors—with the possible exception of chronic illnesses and disabilities.

Such pragmatic arguments may carry some weight with the parties in the original position. As we saw, the parties are seeking not the criterion that requires designing but the criterion that would reliably guide citizens to design the basic structure so that the worst lives, in terms of fundamental interest fulfillment, are no worse than is unavoidable. When a society is governed by a public criterion that takes account of the distribution of all primary goods, natural and social, there is much reason to expect that its social institutions would not even approximately track this criterion. The parties may therefore find it rational, even if they have reason to care about their clients' endowment with primary goods overall, to choose a simpler public criterion that takes account only of social primary goods, perhaps with an exception to cover chronic illnesses and disabilities. Affording the prospect of superior tracking and transparent application, such a criterion is more likely actually to sustain a social order that avoids very bad outcomes—or so its pragmatic justification would assert.

Rawls's public criterion disregards not only natural differences but also differences in personal interests and values. Some people have expensive conceptions of the good—hang-gliding, trips around the world—while others prefer hiking and playing chess. Would a basic structure not be more just if those with expensive interests had greater access to the means for fulfilling them? Rawls thinks that a just society can and should hold its citizens responsible for adjusting their goals and interests to their material means. He might again offer a principled or a pragmatic justification for this view. How a pragmatic justification would look is clear enough. A principled justification would have to take account of the fact that interests are not entirely freely chosen but are based in part on values and preferences that are formed in childhood or even inborn. Inborn preferences and aversions could be handled in the same way as other aspects of the natural constitution. They have to do with the justice of the universe, not that of society—a plausible distinction that nonetheless, as we have seen, would be hard to maintain in the original position. The case of childhood preferences is new. Suppose, for example, that a young girl has begun, at her parents' expense, an excellent musical education and that this has awakened in her an enthusiastic interest in its continuation. The financial means for this, however, are not available—neither from her parents nor from another source. Is she, because of her frustrated interest, worse off than others with the same access to primary goods? There are certainly good pragmatic reasons for saying that a public criterion of justice, and social institutions, should not attempt to take account of such frustrated interests. I do not, however, see good principled reasons for this conclusion within Rawls's justificatory apparatus.

4.4 The Lexical Priority of the Basic Liberties

Suppose it can be shown that a public criterion of justice should take account of the distribution of social goods only and, indeed, should focus exclusively on the social primary goods on Rawls's list. Then the parties in the original position, deliberating according to the maximin rule, would be inclined to agree on a public criterion that ranks alternative designs of the basic structure by the worst share each such design would generate. In *TJ*, more prominently in the first edition, Rawls indeed formulates such a criterion, calling it the *general conception*: "All social primary goods . . . are to be distributed equally unless an unequal distribution of any or all of these goods is to the advantage of the least favored" (*TJ* [1971] 303, cf. *TJ* 54).

In the role of public criterion of justice, this general conception may not do much better than happiness or the three fundamental interests: It is difficult to specify a widely acceptable way of aggregating individual shares of these goods intrapersonally into a single metric of well-being, and difficult also to apply any such aggregation in practice.

In response to this problem and in recognition of the great importance of the listed basic rights and liberties, Rawls proposes a dramatic simplification: Information about the distribution of basic rights and liberties is to be *separated* from information about the distribution of the remaining social primary goods, and the assessment based on the first set of data is to be given *lexical priority* over the assessment based on the second set of data. This proposal simplifies the problem of aggregation by eliminating an entire class of trade-offs. In comparing alternative basic structure designs, one that produces a better distribution of basic liberties is always to be preferred, regardless of the distribution of the remaining social primary goods. Basic liberties are never to be traded off against anything else. Rawls recognizes that this simplified public criterion is not plausible in all conceivable societal conditions, and he confines its applicability to *reasonably favorable conditions*, defined as ones that, "provided the political will exists, permit the effective establishment and full exercise of these liberties" (*PL* 297, cf. *JFR* 47).

Rawls formulates his public criterion of justice in two principles, which are meant to apply to different parts of an institutional order. The first principle applies specifically to the political and legal order of a society—the sphere in which its members are considered as citizens in the narrow sense. This part of the basic structure is to be assessed by the distribution of basic rights and liberties it produces. The second principle applies specifically to the society's social and economic arrangements—its education and health care systems, for example, and the organization of its economy. It governs spheres where members of society are considered in light of the many roles they play in the physical and cultural reproduction of their society: as producers and consumers, employees and employers, students and teachers, patients and doctors. This part of the basic structure is to be assessed by the distribution of the remaining social primary goods it produces. Let me use the adjectives *political* and *socioeconomic* to mark the distinction between these two parts of an institutional order and between the corresponding social spheres. Of course, these two parts are not independent of each other. Socioeconomic institutions are shaped through political decision making, and political institutions are often influenced by socioeconomic factors. We will examine later whether the differing demands Rawls places on political and socioeconomic institutions take adequate account of their mutual interdependence.

The lexical priority of the first principle means that the various practicable basic structure designs are to be judged primarily by the distribution of basic rights and liberties each is expected to produce. The second principle comes into play only insofar as these distributions are estimated to be equivalent. The word "lexical" here is short for *lexicographical* (cf. *TJ* 37–38). Alternative practicable basic structure designs are to be ranked in analogy to how words are ordered in a dictionary. One is to estimate first, through Rawls's first principle of justice, the quality of the distribution of basic rights and liberties each basic structure design would produce. If one basic structure design does better than another on this score, it is ranked higher for this reason alone (like a word beginning in *d* is listed before one beginning in *f*, regardless of their subsequent letters). When two basic structure designs are estimated to produce equivalent distributions of basic rights and liberties, then the tie is broken through Rawls's second principle of justice: by assessing their respective distributions of the remaining social primary goods. Rawls initially defends this lexical priority by arguing that citizens animated by the three fundamental interests would value basic rights and liberties much more highly than the remaining social primary goods (*TJ* §82, §39).

Both components of Rawls's simplification are problematic. The lexical priority is problematic by assuming that even the smallest superiority in terms of the distribution of basic rights and liberties is more valuable than even the greatest superiority in the distribution of the remaining social primary goods. It would be better, for example, to institute a basic structure design B_1 that would produce two classes whose individual members would have scores of [81,*30*] and [81,*10*], respectively, than to institute B_2, which would produce equal scores of [80,*60*] for all citizens. (In these ordered pairs, the first number expresses a person's share of basic rights and liberties; the second, in italics, expresses the same person's share of the remaining social primary goods.) This ranking implausibly directs us to accept huge increases in poverty and inequality for the sake of only a slight gain in basic rights and liberties.

The informational separation is also problematic because, by assigning political and socioeconomic primary goods to two distinct assessment exercises, Rawls's proposed public criterion loses all information about correlations between them. The criterion becomes blind to whether social inequalities of the two kinds offset or aggravate each other. To illustrate the problem, consider a society for which two basic structure designs are practicable. Both would produce the same two equal-sized classes. Both would generate, for their two classes, the same first-principle scores of 90 and 70. B_3 would generate, for its two classes, second-principle scores of *50* and *19*, whereas B_4 would generate second-principle scores of *50* and *20*. Rawls's first principle would rank these two basic structure designs equivalent, and the second principle would break the tie in favor of B_4. Yet this result may be implausible once the informational separation is removed. We then find that members of the two classes under B_3 have scores of [90,*19*] and [70,*50*], respectively, whereas members of the two classes under B_4 have individual scores of [90,*50*] and [70,*20*]. Their maximin concern would incline the parties to agree on a criterion that favors B_3 over B_4 in such a case, but Rawls's public criterion favors B_4 over B_3.

The problem is even more obvious, perhaps, when we consider basic structure B_5, producing scores [90,*20*] and [70,*50*]. B_5 would be ranked equal with B_4 by Rawls's two principles and yet is clearly preferred over B_4 from the standpoint of the original position— because at [70,*20*] the members of the worse-off class under B_4 are plainly worse off than the members of either class under B_5. The problem arises from the fact that the two interclass inequalities produced by B_4 are positively correlated, mutually aggravating—whereas the opposite is true of B_3 and B_5, which produce negatively correlated or mutually offsetting social inequalities. By disregarding this information, Rawls's public criterion delivers what the parties would regard as the wrong result.

In response, Rawls can claim that these two objections are not realistic once one bears in mind that his criterion is primarily intended for ideal theory: for selecting the best practicable basic structure designs for any society in reasonably favorable conditions and for guiding its citizens in maintaining and adjusting such an ideal design. A choice like that between B_1 and B_2 can easily arise for those seeking to reform an unjust society that is currently featuring two classes with scores of [80,*30*] and [80,*10*], say. But Rawls does not endorse this use of the lexical priority: as an implementation priority. He is committed to this priority as a design priority only (cf. *TJ* 215–16, 267), used for identifying the final goal of basic-structure reform for a society in reasonably favorable conditions: the best basic structure design practicable for this society. And if B_1 and B_2 are both practicable, then there are bound to be other practicable designs similar to B_2 that achieve a small gain in basic liberties (from 80 to 81 or above) at a much smaller cost in socioeconomic goods. The objection to informational separation is similarly unrealistic: Basic structure designs in which political and socioeconomic inequalities are negatively correlated are costly and difficult to maintain. Thus, when B_3 or B_5 are practicable, then something substantially better than B_4 should likewise be practicable as well.

Rawls can add that the advantages his proposed public criterion offers in terms of clear and transparent public applicability outweigh the disadvantage that it may deliver (what from the parties' standpoint is) the wrong result in rare and special cases. We have yet to examine how well Rawls's public criterion does in enabling citizens to reach public judgments about actual basic structures in a transparent way.

Five

THE FIRST PRINCIPLE OF JUSTICE

T HE first principle applies specifically to the political order of a society and assesses it according to the extent to which it secures certain basic rights and liberties to its members. In the most recent formulation, it reads as follows: "Each person has an equal claim to a fully adequate scheme of equal basic rights and liberties, which scheme is compatible with the same scheme for all; and in this scheme the equal political liberties, and only those liberties, are to be guaranteed their fair value" (*PL* 5). Rawls never distinguishes precisely between basic rights and basic liberties, and for the sake of brevity, he often refers only to basic liberties or only to basic rights. I will follow him in this.

Rawls explicates the basic liberties, in the first instance, by a list (*TJ* 53, *PL* 334–40). This list is based on historical experience and hence rather conventional. It is also rather short, as Rawls seeks to include only the most important rights and liberties (*PL* 296) lest the special concern for these important ones be watered down or the priority (further discussed later) of the first principle over the second be rendered implausible to the parties in the original position.

Rawls's list is organized under four headings:

> The *political liberties*: freedom of thought and of political speech, freedom of the press, freedom of assembly, and the right to vote and to hold public office.
> *Liberty of conscience and freedom of association*, which between them cover freedom of religion.

Freedom and integrity of the person, which are incompatible with slavery and serfdom and which also include freedom from psychological oppression, physical injury, and abuse, as well as freedom of movement and the right to hold personal property (not including rights to inheritance, rights to hold personal property in means of production and natural resources, or rights to share collective control of means of production and natural resources; *JFR* 114).

The *rights covered by the rule of law*: protection from arbitrary arrest and seizure, habeas corpus, the right to a speedy trial, due process, and uniform procedures conducted according to publicized rules.

5.1 The Structure of a Basic Right

How are we to judge whether and in what degree a person living under some institutional order has the basic rights and liberties Rawls requires? Different answers to this question differ in what information they deem relevant. One might think of rights in a formal way and look narrowly only at the extent to which any basic right is explicitly assigned by the text of the constitution or the relevant laws. Alternatively, one might think of rights in a de facto way and look more broadly also at the security of any explicitly assigned basic right, at how effectively its exercise is actually protected against interference by officials and private citizens. Finally, one might think of rights in terms of their value or usefulness and then look even more broadly also at the availability of means (money, education, etc.) for enjoying or taking advantage of each basic right.

Rawls opts for the second answer. Judging whether and in what degree some institutional order affords a person a particular basic liberty requires two investigations: We must examine the relevant legal texts as officially interpreted to determine to what extent the rights they guarantee adequately cover the basic liberty in question. And we must examine how well the rights covering the basic liberty are in fact adequately protected and enforced. Yet, we are to disregard the distribution of resources needed to enjoy or take advantage of the guaranteed rights covering the basic liberty in question. Basic liberties may be worth much less to poor citizens than to wealthy ones, who may have much richer options for travel, for publicizing their opinions, or for filing lawsuits. But Rawls does not consider the scheme of basic liberties guaranteed to the poor to be any less fully adequate for this reason. By engendering poverty and inequality, an institutional order does not violate the first principle of justice—though it may of course violate the second. Emphasizing this division of labor between his two principles (*TJ* 179, *PL* 326), Rawls also recognizes two important exceptions (to be discussed in sections 5.3 and 5.5).

Rawls thus understands basic rights and liberties, and the adequacy of a scheme of such, two-dimensionally: in terms of their extent and security. *Extent* is determined by what the assigned legal rights guarantee according to standard judicial practice—which conduct is taken to be protected by a particular basic liberty, for example. In this dimension, an institutional order is assessed by the extent to which the legal rights it guarantees cover what they ought to cover. There is the additional requirement that these legal rights must be equal across citizens. Such equality of rights is strongly supported by historical experience and pragmatic considerations, but there are also plausible exceptions (e.g., group-differentiated rights in a multicultural society), which Rawls does not discuss. *Security* is determined by how well the object of a right is actually protected. There are plenty of countries where the right to the free exercise of religion is officially guaranteed but by no means secure—where adherents of an unpopular religion are persecuted by the police or tax authorities, for example, or beaten up by thugs with impunity. In such societies, Rawls holds, the basic right to the free exercise of religion, and with it the first principle of justice, is not realized.

In the case of many rights, total security is unattainable. There is no practicable institutional design under which every guaranteed exercise of religion or every guaranteed expression of an opinion would be certain to come off unimpeded. And no society can absolutely protect its citizens from injury or death from crimes or traffic offenses. Should we then strike such rights from the list of basic rights or content ourselves with their official legal recognition while paying no attention to how well protected they are? Or does the lexical priority of the first principle mean that a society must maximize the security of such rights to the exclusion of all else, even if security expenditures then preempt all spending on arts and travel, even food and clothing?

Both of these extremes are clearly absurd. Rawls must therefore be understood to mean that a scheme of basic rights and liberties can be fully adequate when the security of each guaranteed right reaches a determinate, comfortably attainable threshold level for all citizens. Each of the guaranteed rights must be well protected for all. To judge whether it is, one may need to consider different categories of citizens separately, because a society may systematically fail to protect a basic

right for a certain gender, for certain minorities, or in certain neighborhoods. Such a society does not fulfill the guaranteed rights of
members of the disadvantaged groups and therefore fails to satisfy the
first principle—even if all the guaranteed rights are secure enough on
average.

The idea of security thresholds makes it possible for the first principle to be fully satisfied, as Rawls clearly intended. But it raises
another problem for the lexical priority of the first principle. When
the security of a guaranteed basic right is (for some citizens) below the
threshold, then raising this security to the threshold counts as infinitely more important than any improvements in the distribution of
the other primary goods. But when the security of a guaranteed basic
right is (for all citizens) at or above the threshold, then achieving even
greater security is justice-irrelevant because the scheme of guaranteed
basic rights and liberties is already secure enough to satisfy the first
principle. This discontinuity in the treatment of marginal gains in the
security of guaranteed basic rights seems absurd. But without the stipulation of security thresholds, somewhat below absolute security, the
first principle could never be fully satisfied, which would render its
lexical priority indefensible.

5.2 Formulating the Required Scheme
of Basic Rights and Liberties

The list of basic liberties Rawls offers in the first instance is too vague
to guide the assessment or reform of an actual basic structure. To be
sure, neither Rawls nor the parties in the original position have reason
to seek the precision generally found in constitutional documents and
legal statutes. Such precision would impede the flexible adaptation of
the public criterion of justice to the specific conditions of actual societies (including here also their historical traditions, which may favor
a specific kind of political or legal regime). Rawls envisions such
adaptation when he formulates his first principle with the indefinite
article. There is to be *a* fully adequate scheme of equal basic rights and
liberties. This clearly suggests that there is not only one such scheme,
to be realized regardless of the society's territory, culture, and level of
technological development.

Despite the obvious reasons for flexibility, neither Rawls nor the
parties would want to count as a fully adequate scheme just any as-
sortment of equal basic rights and liberties that fits Rawls's preliminary

list. There are compelling reasons for wanting the first principle to be more demanding than this. In particular, one should consider inadequate any scheme featuring equal basic rights and liberties that would often come into conflict by being plausibly invoked on both sides of a political disagreement among citizen groups. Such conflicts may be difficult to settle genially, through a legislative vote or judicial verdict, as the losing side may feel that the settlement runs roughshod over fundamental rights of citizens. Such a scheme also courts the danger that procedural settlements will come out the wrong way—paradigmatically by allowing the majority to have its way at the expense of fundamental minority interests that the parties, insofar as they employ the maximin rule, are especially concerned to protect. Given these dangers, a fully adequate scheme must be one that defines its equal basic rights coherently and precisely enough to preclude in advance, as far as is reasonably possible, conflicts among plausible basic-right claims.

The first principle should thus be understood as requiring a *scheme* of the listed basic rights and liberties—carefully defined so as to be well adjusted to one another—but not some particular such scheme irrespective of each society's specific conditions. The first principle contains the recognition that there are many ways of formulating a fully adequate scheme through careful mutual adjustment of the basic rights and liberties on Rawls's list.

Still, not every scheme formulated in this way should count as fully adequate in extent. The first principle must also demand that the required mutual adjustment should, as far as reasonably possible, leave the listed rights and liberties intact in their essence. It must demand that mutual adjustment ought to shield the *more significant* aspects of the listed rights and liberties from conflict and disagreement by pruning *less significant* aspects. And it should demand that permissible regulations of guaranteed basic liberties—rules of order in political debate, traffic rules, building codes, zoning laws, rules protecting public order and nocturnal tranquility, and the like—leave the essence of the regulated liberty unrestricted. Without incorporating such a notion of significance, the first principle would leave too much leeway for schemes featuring equal rights and liberties that, though nicely adjusted to one another, insufficiently protect citizens' fundamental interests.

Discussing the needed notion of significance, Rawls proposes to understand it as the significance that defined rights and liberties have for the first two fundamental interests (*JFR* 112–14). Here the first fundamental interest is especially relevant for confirming and defining the basic political liberties: In order to develop and exercise a sense of justice, especially with regard to the design of the basic structure, one must be able to participate in the political life of one's society and to express one's opinions freely. The second fundamental interest is especially relevant for confirming and defining freedom of conscience and freedom of association: In order to develop and pursue a conception of the good, one must be free to choose and to change one's values and aims—and therefore also one's friends, occupation, religion, and lifestyle—and this presupposes freedom of conscience, free access to literature and art, and the freedom to interact with others in consensual ways. The freedom and integrity of the person and the rule of law are to be confirmed and defined as "supporting" liberties "necessary if the other basic liberties are to be properly guaranteed" (*JFR* 113). On Rawls's understanding, the first principle requires then that, in light of a society's specific traditions and conditions, the listed basic rights and liberties be defined and mutually adjusted into one scheme formulated to protect citizens' first two fundamental interests.

One may wonder why Rawls offers so narrow a notion of significance, so narrow a basis on which to specify the content of a fully adequate scheme of basic rights and liberties. Why does he leave aside the third fundamental interest in being successful in terms of one's chosen conception of the good? This interest could well make a difference in the assessment of the adequacy of candidate schemes. It would increase the weight of liberty of conscience, for example. This liberty is supported by the second fundamental interest, to be sure. But it is supported even more strongly by the consideration that citizens may be deeply devoted to some particular religion (or other conception of the good) whose legal prohibition would be devastating to them—a case Rawls vividly describes (*TJ* §32, *PL* 310–15, *JFR* 104–5). Understanding significance in light also of the third fundamental interest would similarly increase the weight of some of the "supporting" liberties: freedom from slavery and serfdom, freedom from physical injury and abuse (torture), freedom of movement, freedom from arbitrary arrest and seizure, and the right to a speedy trial. To illustrate: As the case of Immanuel Kant demonstrates, it is possible (and even easier with modern communications) to develop and exercise the two moral powers without ever leaving the vicinity of one's hometown. But travel beyond these confines tends to be highly valued by citizens of modern democratic societies as part of their conception of the good. Such citizens would regard it as a drastic restriction of their freedom if they were confined to one locale (e.g., by a system of local ration cards as existed in China during and after the Great Proletarian Cultural Revolution). It seems odd, then, that Rawls wants to understand significance in a way that excludes the third fundamental interest and thereby citizen-specific interests and values that, as discussed (section 3.3), typically are, and are likely to remain, the most deeply felt interests in the lives of most citizens.

Rawls does not explain why he uses the narrower notion of significance in this important role. But two obvious reasons are easily supplied. One is that the third fundamental interest is too indeterminate: Given their thick veil of ignorance, the parties know little about the particular society to which their public criterion is to apply and little in particular about what conceptions of the good the citizens of that society may have. And we, Rawls and his readers, are similarly ignorant, given that the proposed public criterion of justice is supposed to cover all human societies existing in reasonably favorable conditions. This problem of indeterminacy is compounded by the ideal-theory circularity: what interests citizens develop depends in part on the basic structure of their society, whose design in turn is to be guided by the public criterion yet to be chosen.

The other possible reason for Rawls's reluctance to broaden the notion of significance by invoking also the third fundamental interest is that, once citizen-specific interests and values are brought in, assessments of significance themselves become citizen-specific. Consider, for instance, the significance of the right to perform animal sacrifices as a possible component of citizens' liberty of conscience. By the test Rawls proposes, this significance is low: Animal sacrifices are not "essential for the adequate development and full and informed exercise of their two moral powers" (*JFR* 112). More important, this significance is the same for all citizens: A legal ban on animal sacrifices does not interfere with any citizens' fulfillment of their first two fundamental interests. Were the third fundamental interest to be held relevant to assessments of significance, such assessments would become much harder: The right to perform animal sacrifices would then turn out to be of very little significance to some citizens—and of great significance to others, adherents of Santeria, for instance. Such discrepancies make it very much harder to provide clear guidelines for how the listed rights and liberties should be mutually adjusted into a fully adequate scheme. This is so because one would now have to balance the standpoint of Santeria adherents—for whom the gain from including the right to perform animal sacrifices within liberty of conscience is much greater than the gain from including the collective right to ban animal sacrifices within the political liberties—with the standpoint of most other citizens, for whom the opposite holds true.

Such balancing may not be so hard in any given case (in the case before us, it would presumably support the inclusion of the right to perform animal sacrifices in liberty of conscience). But it would be prohibitively complicated to base judgments about whether a scheme of basic liberties is fully adequate in extent on considering an indefinite number of possible conceptions of the good. And doing this could also be socially divisive, as any such balancing would produce winners and losers among conceptions of the good.

Rawls's view on how the first principle is to guide the formulation of a fully adequate scheme of basic liberties changed over time. He gave up (*JFR* 112) his initial idea of "the most extensive total system of equal basic liberties compatible with a similar system of liberty for all" (*TJ* 266), as well as the appeal to "the rational interest of the representative equal citizen" (*PL* 333, 356; cf. *TJ* 187). But he remained deeply committed to the postulate that "equal citizenship defines a general point of view. The problems of adjudicating among the basic liberties are settled by reference to it" (*TJ* 82). This postulate greatly facilitates such adjudication. But there are yet further grounds for questioning its viability—grounds arising from citizens' diverse natural attributes and diverse socioeconomic positions.

A very important natural attribute is gender. It is possible that the interests of women and men with regard to the specific formulation of a scheme of basic liberties diverge—more so if the third fundamental interest is included, but even otherwise. Thus consider the question to what extent the liberty to have an abortion should be included within the freedom and integrity of the person (cf. *PL* 243n). This liberty is obviously much more significant for women's fundamental interest in developing and exercising their moral powers than for men's. Or consider the questions whether the marriage rights protected as part of the freedom of association should extend to polygamous marriages as well and should include provisions protecting the economically weaker spouse(s). Here again, the interests of men and women with regard to the formulation of a scheme of equal basic rights and liberties are liable to diverge—and this not only in existing societies, deeply scarred, as they are, by a long history of male domination, but also in any ideal society in which each birth is preceded by a *woman's* pregnancy.

Other natural differences may also give rise to discrepant significance assessments—differences in natural intelligence, for example.

But let us turn to differences in socioeconomic position (which would persist and could be large in Rawls's ideal society). To see the possible relevance of such differences, consider the option of propagating opinions through the mass media. The first principle is consistent with mass media being privately owned (in a property-owning democracy). But private ownership may lead to concentration of ownership or at least to a heavy dominance of opinions favored by the rich. The question is then whether the basic political liberties include any passive rights to have some public mass media (such as the PBS or BBC) or any active rights to address one's fellow citizens through existing media, irrespective of one's ability to pay the commercial rate. From the standpoint of the poor, the inclusion of these rights within the political liberties is likely to be much more significant than from the standpoint of the rich.

To satisfy the first principle, a society's basic structure must guarantee, equally to all citizens, legal rights that are defined and mutually adjusted into a coherent scheme that is fully adequate in security and extent. A scheme is fully adequate in extent just in case it covers the basic liberties Rawls lists, guaranteeing their more significant component liberties partly at the expense of less significant ones. Here "a liberty is more or less significant depending on whether it is more or less essentially involved in, or is a more or less necessary institutional means to protect, the full and informed exercise of the moral powers" (*JFR* 113). Such assessments of significance are to be made without regard to differences among citizens: differences in their needs, interests, values, natural characteristics, and socioeconomic position. We are not to run through various categories of citizens, examine how adequate a candidate scheme is from each standpoint, and then aggregate into an overall assessment of adequacy. Rather, we are to examine the matter from a single standpoint: that of the first two fundamental interests of the representative citizen.

Having outlined important advantages and disadvantages of this simplification, let me offer one last point on it, which Rawls suggests in his discussions of stability and strains of commitment. By agreeing on the first principle of justice, the parties hope to advance the fundamental interests of their clients: Each citizen benefits from being assured of a well-defined set of legally protected claims, options, and immunities. Yet each citizen also benefits in another way as well—from *other* citizens having like assurance. When one's fellow citizens can count on their most important needs, interests, and values being firmly protected, they are much more likely to respect the democratic rules of the game in case of political disagreements and are more inclined to be trustworthy partners generally. This is something citizens have reason to want in one another. But the simplification undermines the hope for such assurance. A scheme of equal basic liberties whose extent is fully adequate for general citizens concerned solely with advancing their first two fundamental interests may not be felt to be fully adequate by human beings with particular interests and talents, with a particular gender, socioeconomic position, and conception of the good.

We would be in a better position to assess this and the other disadvantages of Rawls's simplification had he had a chance to apply his late account of significance to more difficult cases of judging the adequacy of the extent of some scheme of basic liberties. We might then have been better able to judge the parties' reasons for and against adopting the first principle with Rawls's explication as part of their agreement in the original position. The parties do take account of the third fundamental interest and examine possible agreements from the many standpoints citizens might occupy—standpoints defined in terms of natural endowments, conception of the good, and socioeconomic position. Rawls was presumably hoping that the parties' more complex deliberations would reconfirm the simplified explication of "fully adequate in extent" he chose to incorporate into the first principle. But this hope is realistic only if the explication is definite enough to permit citizens to reach public judgments about actual basic structures in a transparent way. Citizens like ourselves, Rawls's readers, must be able, with the guidance he provides, to reach reasoned agreement on whether the rights and liberties guaranteed in this or that actual society today cover what they ought to cover and, if not, what is missing. Unless we can do this, at least for the most part, the first principle fails in its intended role of part of a public criterion that citizens can use together to design, maintain, and adjust the basic structure of their society.

5.3 The Fair Value of the Basic Political Liberties

We have seen that, to count as affording a person some particular listed right, the basic structure must legally guarantee this right in its essentials and also effectively protect the object of the right as guaranteed. The basic structure need not ensure that the person has the necessary means to enjoy or take advantage of the basic rights it guarantees. But there is an exception to this latter statement: In the case of the basic political liberties, and in their case alone, the first principle demands *fair value*. Here adequacy depends not merely on the extent and security of existing rights but also on their worth or usefulness, on whether citizens have the means needed to enjoy or take advantage of these rights.

The adequacy of a scheme of basic rights and liberties is then judged in three dimensions after all: by the *extent* to which guaranteed legal rights as officially interpreted cover the listed basic liberties, by the actual *security* of these rights attained through institutionalized protection of their enjoyment and exercise, and by the *value* of specifically those legal rights that cover the basic political liberties. To be fully adequate, a scheme of guaranteed basic rights and liberties must be fully adequate in all three dimensions. Here small variations across citizens, above the threshold of full adequacy, are permissible (and inevitable), but in the first dimension, strict equality is required.

Rawls defines the fair value of the basic political liberties as requiring that "citizens similarly gifted and motivated have roughly an equal chance of influencing the government's policy and of attaining positions of authority irrespective of their economic and social class" (*JFR* 46).

The reference to class need not be taken to suggest that the first principle is consistent with gross inequalities in political influence associated with other factors, such as gender, skin color, other physical characteristics, religious affiliation, marital status, and sexual preference. Rawls does not specifically mention such other factors because he is working within ideal theory and therefore focusing attention on factors that "tend to generate troubling inequalities even in a well-ordered society" as his theory envisions (cf. *JFR* 65). Under a fully just institutional order, he assumes, the other factors would not generate troubling inequalities in citizens' political influence. There is reason to believe that this assumption may be false regarding some such other factors: height and good looks, most obviously. In any case, those asked to adopt or apply Rawls's public criterion of justice need to know whether the first principle requires rough equality of political influence only across socioeconomic classes or more generally. I conjecture that Rawls would have understood the exception to rule out *all* systematic and gross inequalities in chances of influencing government policy and of attaining political positions. To be *systematic*, an inequality must be correlated with generic features of citizens;

THE FIRST PRINCIPLE OF JUSTICE 93

an inequality between any two citizens similarly gifted and motivated is not systematic, nor is the inequality between the fifty most influential and the fifty least influential citizens within some set of equally gifted and motivated persons. A *gross* inequality is one that exceeds in magnitude whatever Rawls means by roughly an equal chance. This parameter of the exception would, of course, need to be specified.

In support of the exception, Rawls argues that what the political liberties are meant to secure, political participation, is highly symbolic of the (equal) status of citizenship—more so than anything secured by other basic liberties. Moreover, the basic political liberties organize a competition that essentially has the character of a constant-sum game—a game in which gains for some entail losses for others. Someone too poor to travel as many others do can still feel equal as a citizen. But he or she cannot do so when those others dominate the political process through large campaign contributions and thereby effectively eliminate him or her from collective deliberations and decisions about justice and the common good.

One might ask why the exception should apply to the basic *political* liberties only. After all, a closely parallel argument could be made for other listed liberties as well. When only wealthy citizens can afford good lawyers, their chances of winning in court are greatly improved, and others' chances of defending their rights correspondingly diminished. Rivalry in the courts, in civil cases, has the same constant-sum character as political rivalry. And inequalities in the fair value of being secure in one's legal rights (rule of law) undermine any shared sense of equal citizenship because politicians, officials, and private citizens need not take the legal rights of the poor too seriously when they know that lack of means will prevent the poor from causing these rights to be effectively enforced. Rawls decides against this extension of the fair-value requirement without explaining why.

Rawls does explain why the first principle should not guarantee the fair value of *all* basic liberties. Such a requirement would implausibly rule out inequalities that improve all socioeconomic positions. The availability of exceptional options that only the rich can afford to take advantage of provides incentives that may make our economy more productive in a way that enhances the options of all. Insofar as they do, unequal options can be approved from the standpoint of all socioeconomic positions and therefore easily agreed to in the original position.

Rawls can then reason as follows: When there is no constraint on the distribution of chances to enjoy or take advantage of noncompetitive basic liberties, then these chances vary with citizens' (possibly very unequal) socioeconomic positions. The distribution of socioeconomic means, however, is constrained by the difference principle, which demands that social institutions should give rise to all and only those socioeconomic inequalities that raise the lowest socioeconomic position. It follows that, when the difference principle is satisfied, inequalities in chances to enjoy or take advantage of noncompetitive basic liberties can be endorsed from the standpoints of all socioeconomic positions and from that of the lowest such position in particular. The poorest chances to enjoy or take advantage of noncompetitive basic liberties would be poorer still, if the existing inequality were in any way diminished. Any further requirement to equalize such chances would therefore be rejected even from the standpoint of the lowest socioeconomic position which is salient to the parties insofar as they employ the maximin rule.

Rawls considers two ways of assuring the fair value of political liberties: limits on economic inequalities and limits on the impact of money on politics and legislation. In *TJ*, Rawls emphasized the first way: "Historically one of the main defects of constitutional government has been the failure to ensure the fair value of political liberty. . . . Disparities in the distribution of property and wealth that far exceed what is compatible with political equality have generally been tolerated by the legal system" (*TJ* 198–99). In later works, he has focused more on insulating the political sphere from financial interests (*PL* 356–63), for instance through public funding of, and limits on private and corporate contributions to, political campaigns. This shift in emphasis makes sense within his framework. Limiting socioeconomic inequality more tightly than the difference principle would favor (*TJ* 70) entails a reduction in all socioeconomic positions. It makes sense, then, to impose such limits only insofar as insulation proves insufficient. However, even insulation has its socioeconomic costs: The incentive effects of money which, when the difference principle is satisfied, benefit all socioeconomic positions are greater the more things money can buy. When money cannot buy political influence, it loses some of its motivating power.

Insulation can be achieved by tight limits on private and corporate funding in conjunction with broad and generous public funding of political deliberation and elections. Rawls offers a rich discussion of a court decision that struck down a congressional effort to limit political contributions. In *Buckley v. Valeo* (1976), the U.S. Supreme Court found such legislation unconstitutional on the ground that it would abridge the freedom of speech guaranteed by the First Amendment to the U.S. Constitution.

Rawls is highly critical of this decision. He criticizes that the Court gave far too central a place to a right Rawls sees as marginal within freedom of speech: the right to spend money on advertising political programs and candidates. Giving this right a central place amounts to viewing "democracy [as] a kind of regulated rivalry between economic classes and interest groups in which the outcome should properly depend on the ability and willingness of each to use its financial resources and skills, admittedly very unequal, to make its desires felt" (*PL* 361).

Rawls also criticizes that the Court gave no weight to securing the fair value of the basic political liberties and therefore failed to recognize that "the liberties protected by the First Amendment may have to be adjusted in the light of other constitutional requirements, in this case the requirement of the fair value of the political liberties" (*PL* 362). It may be more accurate to say that the Court took there to be no such constitutional requirement to which freedom of speech might need to be adjusted. Like much legal and political thinking in the United States, the Court invoked exactly the distinction Rawls himself emphasizes: It is of great importance, indeed a constitutional essential, that citizens should *have* certain guaranteed rights and liberties (which depend on extent and security alone), but it is of much less importance, and not to be constitutionally protected, that citizens should have the means to enjoy or take advantage of those guaranteed rights and liberties. The disagreement stems from the fact that Rawls wants to recognize an exception specifically for the fair value of the basic political liberties, whereas the Court and much U.S. opinion prefer not to break the straightforward analogy to other basic rights and liberties.

We have seen that Rawls justifies the exception by invoking the constant-sum character of political influence and the great symbolic value of political participation for equal citizenship. These points could easily be used to justify the exception by appeal to the standpoint of those in the lowest socioeconomic position. Continuing to eschew appeals to citizen-specific factors, Rawls bypasses this argument to appeal to the interest of citizens in general: "without the public recognition that background justice is maintained, citizens tend to become resentful, cynical, and apathetic" (*PL* 363). To be sure, the rich are not likely to become resentful and apathetic when they find themselves able to convert their riches into political influence. But, and this is Rawls's point, even their first fundamental interest is set

back when substantial portions of their society's electorate are resentful and apathetic.

5.4 Permissible Reductions of Basic Liberties

It might seem that the parties in the original position should prefer to
agree on a first principle that calls for unequal schemes of basic liberties when such inequalities work to the benefit of those with the
least adequate scheme. That this is not so is due to the combination of
two reasons: To vindicate the lexical priority and to render it truly
effective, the first principle covers only the more significant components of the most important rights and liberties. And Rawls's public
criterion, of which the first principle is a part, applies only to societies in reasonably favorable conditions, which make it possible for
citizens, should they have the political will, to satisfy the first principle. Unlike other social primary goods such as income, of which one
might always have more than one has, the basic liberties have an upper
limit. And this upper limit is necessarily (by definition of "reasonably
favorable") attainable for all citizens through a suitable basic structure
design.

Rawls's public criterion of justice is simply inapplicable to societies
in unfavorable conditions. And it instructs the citizens of the remaining societies to maintain a basic structure that satisfies the first
principle. They can do this, and they can do no better for any citizen's
basic liberties. Hence there is no reason for allowing any differentials
in the adequacy of schemes of basic liberties—ideally, anyway.

Reasonably favorable conditions notwithstanding, a society may
fail to satisfy the first principle. Rawls stated clearly that he took the
United States to be an example of this: Reasonably favorable conditions obtain (PL 297), but the first principle is not satisfied (PL 360–
62, JFR 101n23). Such a failure to realize the basic liberties may be
due to obstacles of three kinds: First, people holding high legislative,
judicial, or executive offices are blocking, perhaps supported or bribed
by citizen groups, needed reforms of the basic structure. As a result,
the basic structure is such that the basic liberties are not extensive
enough (fail to cover all they ought to cover) or not secure enough or
the fair value of the basic political liberties is not ensured. Second,
groups of citizens fail to comply with existing social institutions. Such
noncompliance does not affect the extent of basic liberties, but it can

affect their security (e.g., through bias attacks, domestic terrorist activities, religious or racial strife, even civil war) or the fair value of the
basic political liberties (e.g., through illegal political contributions).
Third, temporary external phenomena (e.g. wars, embargoes, political
or economic pressures or terrorist attacks from abroad, epidemics, natural catastrophes) undermine the security of basic liberties. In contrast
to obstacles of the other kinds, these obstacles involve no lack in
citizens' political will. One might think, therefore, that, when such
external phenomena make it impossible to satisfy the first principle,
reasonably favorable conditions cease to obtain. But Rawls thought
of the *conditions* in which a society exists as having some endurance
and robustness—as persisting through even a severe temporary threat
to citizens' health and survival. Thus he applied his public criterion to
state that military conscription, though "a drastic interference with the
basic liberties of equal citizenship," can be justified by a compelling
need to defend these equal liberties themselves (*JFR* 47).

Obstacles of the first two kinds call on Rawls's theory of justice as a
means of convincing citizens to help implement the missing requirements of the first principle. Obstacles of all three kinds raise the
question: Is it justifiable to adjust the basic structure in a way that reduces the basic liberties of some or all in order to overcome such
obstacles when circumstances make it impossible, with *any* design of
the basic structure, to ensure for all citizens a fully adequate scheme of
equal basic rights and liberties? Rawls provides guidance in regard to
such adjustments by proposing, as part of his public criterion of justice, a priority rule attached to his first principle of justice. Slightly
updated to take account of subsequent revisions, this *first priority rule*
says: The principles of justice are to be ranked in lexical order, and a
basic liberty may therefore be restricted only for the sake of basic
liberties (the same or others). There are two cases. The general restriction of a basic liberty must strengthen the total system of basic
liberties shared by all; and unequal basic liberties must be to the
benefit of those with the lesser basic liberties (*TJ* 266; cf. *PL* 356).

The language suggests that Rawls is mostly thinking of institutional
designs that restrict the *extent* of basic liberties of some or all citizens.
But his discussion can be extended to institutional designs that
compromise the *security* of basic liberties or the *fair value* of basic
political liberties. Any such *reduction* of the basic liberties of some or all
citizens infringes the first principle and thus requires special justification. The general question is: In what circumstances is it justified
deliberately to design the basic structure so that some or all citizens fall

short of a fully adequate scheme of basic rights and liberties as required by the first principle?

The first sentence of the priority rule—that basic liberties must never be reduced for the sake of anything other than basic liberties—is discussed in section 5.5. Here we examine the two cases of justified unequal and equal reductions of basic liberties.

As an example of an *unequal* restriction of a basic liberty, Rawls uses John Stuart Mill's proposal that educated citizens should have extra votes and hence more weight in political decisions. Rawls holds that such an inequality "may be perfectly just" (*TJ* 205) if, by improving the outcomes of political decision making, it renders more adequate the extent or security of other basic liberties. To see whether it is justified, Rawls writes, we must adopt "the perspective of those who have the lesser political liberty" (*TJ* 203), showing that, in terms of their basic liberties, they gain more than they lose from the dilution of their vote.

The priority rule illustrated here is, however, more permissive. It can permit extra votes for the educated to be justified on the ground that they are necessary to protect the basic liberties of the educated themselves. To see this, suppose equal franchise results in legislation that jeopardizes other basic rights of the educated, but not of the uneducated. In this case, we must compare the inadequate scheme had by the uneducated if their voting rights are diluted with the inadequate scheme had by the educated if voting rights are equal. If the latter scheme of basic liberties is more inadequate than the former, then the dilution of voting rights is justified by the first priority rule.

The first priority rule accords well on this point with what the parties, insofar as they employ the maximin rule, would want to agree on. Considering circumstances in which the first principle cannot be satisfied because of obstacles of the second or third kinds, the parties would favor a basic structure design under which the least adequate scheme of basic liberties is as adequate as possible. They would want the criterion they agree on to reflect this preference by ranking basic structure designs in terms of the least adequate scheme of basic liberties each is expected to generate in the particular society and period.

Rawls himself interprets his first priority rule in this more permissive way when he discusses the justification for restricting the freedom of an intolerant sect: "its freedom should be restricted only when the tolerant sincerely and with reason believe that their own security and that of the institutions of liberty are in danger" (*TJ* 193). There is no suggestion here that the unequal restriction of the freedom of the intolerant must be to their own benefit. According with the parties' preferred understanding, the centerpiece of Rawls's public criterion is then: In reasonably favorable conditions, the basic structure should be designed so that the least adequate scheme of basic liberties is as adequate as possible. This understanding also has the advantage of being perfectly general across all reasonably favorable conditions, justifying, for any prevailing circumstances, either *no* or *unequal* or *equal* reductions in basic liberties.

This more permissive understanding stands a better chance of justifying practices that are widely accepted, also by Rawls. Consider conscription into the U.S. or Canadian military to fight overseas in the Second World War, or a mandatory quarantine deemed necessary to contain a virulent epidemic. Such drastic restrictions of basic liberties are usually not to the benefit of the basic liberties of those selected. The prospects for being able to justify such selective restrictions improve when a deficit in basic liberties suffered by one group can also be justified by a greater deficit thereby avoided for another (measuring deficits, in both cases, relative to a fully adequate scheme). Here it would be important to clarify how the comparison is to be made. Is the size of the two groups relevant? And how does one identify the relevant comparison group and its loss? Is one to focus on the group of those not targeted for quarantine and on the increase in the risk of infection they would suffer (*ex ante*) in the absence of the quarantine? Or is one to focus on the smaller group of those who would actually (*ex post*) be infected as a consequence of there being no quarantine?

Rawls gives this example of an *equal* restriction of the extent of a basic liberty that could improve the whole scheme of basic liberties for all (*TJ* §38): Armed unrest is feared because of sharp tensions among religious communities. In order to safeguard citizens' freedom from bodily harm, the government wants to take weapons out of circulation. It therefore passes a criminal statute forbidding the possession of firearms, stipulating that sufficient evidence for conviction is that the weapons be found in the defendant's home or property, unless he or she can prove that someone else put them there. This statute restricts a basic liberty associated with the rule of law by exposing citizens to criminal conviction for something they did not intend and could not reasonably have known or prevented: Citizens cannot watch all of their property all the time. This restriction is nonetheless justified if the loss is outweighed by a gain in the security of other basic liberties—in this case, by a gain in physical safety: "Citizens may affirm the law as the lesser of two evils, resigning themselves to the fact that while they may be held guilty for things they have not done, the risks to their liberty on any other course would be worse" (*TJ* 213).

Rawls's reasoning ignores the possibility that the two dangers here compared will not be of equal magnitude for all members of society. Some would be exposed to an unusually large risk of injury if the statute is not enacted and armed unrest breaks out; this might be true, for instance, of members of a religious community who live in an area dominated by members of another. Likewise, some would be exposed to an unusually large risk of conviction under the criminal statute, perhaps because they own substantial real estate where weapons can easily be hidden without their knowledge. Rawls suggests that he considers all citizens' basic liberties to be affected equally by the decision, which can therefore be assessed from the standpoint of "the representative citizen." This might be a normative choice: The differences in question do not count as affecting the security of citizens' basic liberties (perhaps because citizens control where they live and how much real estate they own). It could be an empirical claim: The differences in question are slight or unpredictable. Or it could be a pragmatic choice: The attempt to take such differences into account would excessively complicate decisions and make them too vulnerable to self-deception and abuse by interested parties.

There are two further objections to Rawls's reasoning that justifies the government's reducing basic liberties whenever it takes this to be necessary to forestall an even larger reduction from another source. For one thing, such an authorization of government involves risks of its own. Abuse of authority, deception, and self-deception are not unknown among politicians, who are likely to restrict basic liberties too much and too often if empowered to do so. A party in power, appealing to Rawls, might well justify legislation reducing citizens' basic liberties with the false claim that such legislation best safeguards citizen's basic liberties overall. Such claims are made in defense of much antiterror legislation passed and proposed these days in all too many countries. Given such dangers, the parties in the original position, departing from Rawls's reasoning, would conduct the weighing in a different way: The government's authority to reduce basic liberties for the sake of better protecting such liberties should be formulated in such a way that the dangers forestalled by the government having this authority outweigh, by as large a margin as possible, the dangers this authority poses to citizens' basic liberties.

The deepest objection to Rawls's reasoning challenges the whole idea that an official reduction in basic liberties is morally justified when it "might be accepted by the representative citizen as a lesser loss of liberty" (*TJ* 213). The objection holds that these two kinds of losses are not on a par. Even if suspensions of habeas corpus, preventive detentions, torturous interrogations, sedition laws, or draconian punishments for communicating government secrets really do serve the representative citizen's basic liberties overall, they may still diminish the justice of the society imposing them. This objection challenges once more the purely recipient-oriented approach of Rawls's theory by maintaining that the justice of a society depends not merely on what effects the laws have on citizens as recipients but also on how citizens treat one another through the laws they enact (section 3.1).

When considering ourselves solely as recipients, it makes sense to authorize our government to institute brutal antiterror measures when our small risk of being brutalized by the security services is outweighed by a larger reduction in our risk of being brutalized by terrorists. But this argument for the authorization fails to take into account that we are much more implicated in brutalities we authorize state officials to commit than in ones that result from our failure to authorize such aggressive measures. As it is generally wrong to kill two innocent persons for the sake of saving three, so it seems unjust to structure a society so that it harms or kills some innocents for the sake of saving a somewhat larger number from a similar fate.

This objection is compatible with allowing social institutions to do harm, even harm to innocents, as unavoidably results from any realistically conceivable system of criminal law enforcement. The objection need claim merely that, in deliberations about institutional design, harms we authorize through social institutions should be weighted more heavily than otherwise equivalent harms our social institutions merely fail to prevent. A reduction in basic liberties imposed by the state serves justice only if it forestalls a considerably larger reduction in basic liberties from other sources.

5.5 Impermissible Reductions of Basic Liberties

Basic liberties may be reduced *only* for the sake of basic liberties, not for the sake of any other social primary goods. This lexical priority of the basic rights and liberties must seem strange at first. Their importance may indeed be indisputable, particularly from the perspective of the three fundamental interests. But their importance does not entail their absolute priority: that it is *always* unjust, in any and all reasonably favorable conditions, to reduce basic liberties for the sake of socio-economic goods. After all, these socioeconomic goods are by no means unimportant.

The listed basic liberties guarantee neither food nor clothing nor shelter. Members of society are supposed to satisfy such basic socio-economic needs out of their income, whose distribution is governed by the second principle. And so the question arises whether having the basic liberties is really infinitely more important than the satis-faction of these basic socioeconomic needs.

One reason for the parties to agree on Rawls's public criterion of justice is supposedly that it is "the maximin solution to the problem of social justice" (*TJ* 132): By choosing it, the parties ensure the best achievable very-worst-case scenario for their clients. Is the criterion Rawls advances, with the lexical priority of basic liberties, really a plausible candidate for maximin solution? Is it rational for the parties to assign more significance to minute reductions of basic liberties than to great losses in socioeconomic goods? Is a basic structure in which some starve, though they have a fully adequate scheme of basic lib-erties, really more just than one in which all are economically well-off, though some lack the full complement of basic rights—for in-stance, are not allowed to own a newspaper?

Rawls makes some headway against this obvious objection by limiting the task of his public criterion of justice so that it applies only in ideal theory and only to societies in reasonably favorable condi-tions (section 4.4). Still, these limitations do not fully cope with the objection. When it is in reasonably favorable conditions, a society is affluent enough to satisfy the first principle, that is, affluent enough not only to give (cheap) formal legal recognition to basic rights but also to ensure their security for all citizens, which requires parliaments, ad-ministrators, judges, police, and so forth. But reasonably favorable con-ditions as defined do not ensure that the society is affluent enough to satisfy the first principle *and* to ensure that all citizens' basic socio-economic needs are met. So there remains the danger that the lexical priority leads to implausible design choices that involve serious sacri-fices of citizens' basic needs for the sake of marginal enhancements of their basic liberties.

In response, one could plausibly conjecture that Rawls would have wanted to understand "reasonably favorable conditions" more am-bitiously as conditions in which both a fully adequate scheme of basic liberties and the fulfillment of basic socioeconomic needs can be assured to all society members. But even this conjecture does not quite overcome the objection.

Despite reasonably favorable conditions (ambitiously understood), the basic needs of some society members may be unmet in fact. This may be due to obstacles of three kinds (analogous to those discussed in section 5.4): First, people holding high legislative, judicial, or executive offices are blocking, perhaps with the support of citizen groups, needed reforms of the basic structure. Second, groups of citizens fail fully to comply with existing social institutions. Third, temporary external phenomena (e.g., wars, droughts, or other natural catastrophes) interfere with the production or distribution of basic necessities. Such obstacles raise the question: Is it justifiable to adjust the basic structure in a way that reduces the basic liberties of some or all in order to overcome such obstacles when circumstances make it impossible, with *any* design of the basic structure, to satisfy the first principle and to ensure that all citizens' basic needs are met? Rawls's answer, it seems, is an unequivocal *no*. Even a great gain for basic needs fulfillment does not justify any adjustment of the basic structure that would ever so slightly reduce the basic liberties of some or all—by outlawing a political party, perhaps, or by reducing public security expenditures (police) or by subverting the fair value of some group's political liberties. Would the parties agree on so rigid a public criterion of justice? Many of Rawls's readers, in any case, have found it implausible.

After much criticism of this sort, Rawls has suggested a remarkable addition (the second of the two exceptions announced in section 5.1) to his proposed public criterion of justice: "the first principle covering the equal basic rights and liberties may easily be preceded by a lexically prior principle requiring that citizens' basic socioeconomic needs be met, at least insofar as their being met is necessary for citizens to understand and to be able fruitfully to exercise those rights and liberties" (*PL* 7). Rawls adds that the level of well-being and education required depends on the level of development of the society in question. Someone's basic socioeconomic needs are met if she has the requisite means (including education) to take part in the social and political life of the society as a citizen (*PL* 166). This new top principle finally clarifies that Rawls does not in the end want to follow the U.S. constitutional tradition by prioritizing basic liberties over the fulfillment of basic socioeconomic needs. Indeed, he even advocates the opposite priority relation.

Given the rationale Rawls offers—that all must be enabled to take part in the social and political life of their society as citizens—it would seem reasonable to place basic liberties and basic socioeconomic needs on a par. This can be done by expanding the first principle so that it covers all means minimally necessary to take part as a citizen in the social and political life of one's society: the basic liberties, basic education, and some basic level of income. Rawls suggests this idea in two passages where he characterizes political questions that touch on either basic liberties or basic needs as concerned with *constitutional essentials* (PL 166, 228–30) and includes, by implication, basic needs fulfillment among the "equal basic rights and liberties of citizenship" (PL 227).

Treating basic liberties and basic needs on a par would have the further advantage of balancing Rawls's increased divergence from the U.S. constitutional tradition with increased conformity to the human rights documents of the United Nations. In any case, whether Rawls's public criterion places basic needs lexically above basic liberties or on a par, this criterion now allows reductions of basic liberties to be justified as necessary for avoiding deficits in basic necessities.

Rawls's criterion still categorically prohibits reductions of basic liberties for the sake of satisfying needs and interests beyond the basic needs level. Rawls believes that, with this prohibition, his criterion is more suitable for clear and transparent public application than competing candidate criteria that allow trade-offs across all goods. The parties in the original position are seeking the criterion that would reliably guide citizens to design the basic structure so that the worst lives, in terms of fundamental interest fulfillment, are no worse than is unavoidable. They assume that the criterion they agree on will be used by real human beings—neither geniuses nor angels—in an actual society. A criterion requiring all primary goods to be weighed against one another is more vulnerable to abuse and reasonable disagreement.

Rawls can admit that the lexical priority involves the risk of implausible rigidity: of a small inadequacy in some group's scheme of basic liberties being avoided at the expense of much greater poverty, for example. In response, he can say that this risk is reduced by his having incorporated only genuinely essential rights and liberties into the first principle. He can add that rejection of the lexical priority involves more serious dangers to the fulfillment of citizens' fundamental interests: A public criterion that instructs citizens to weigh all primary goods against one another would often be misapplied and also tend to generate much more disagreement about how the basic structure should be designed, maintained, and adjusted. Insofar as citizens cannot appreciate public applications of their shared criterion as correct or at least plausible, many may view such political judgments as arbitrary or even self-interested. This view weakens their moral allegiance to their social order and thereby diminishes its stability.

Rawls can further point out that the risk of implausible rigidity is easily overestimated. One can indeed describe scenarios where reductions of some group's basic political liberties or freedom of expression would make it possible to structure the economy in a more poverty-avoiding way. But what matters is not whether politicians' enhanced powers *could*, but whether they actually *would*, entail lower poverty. The historical record suggests that politicians are far better at invoking the interests of the poor than at serving them, and that the poor often end up losers when politicians successfully claim greater powers in their name. By placing clear and narrow limits on permissible reductions of basic liberties, Rawls's criterion at least firmly protects the political influence of the poor, who are generally the most reliable guardians of their interests.

Rawls also stresses the cost of unequal restrictions of basic rights in particular. It is desirable that members of society see themselves as equal citizens. Such a shared sense of equal citizenship cannot plausibly be sustained through socioeconomic equality, which is very difficult to maintain and would entail substantial economic losses for all. A shared sense of equal citizenship can be sustained, however, on the basis of equal basic rights and liberties, including the fair value of the equal basic political liberties. If all citizens see themselves and one another as equals in this important respect, then social and economic inequalities, moderated by the second principle, will not threaten the stability of the social order.

Six

THE SECOND PRINCIPLE OF JUSTICE

W E have seen that Rawls distinguished two parts of the basic structure: a society's political and legal order and its social and economic institutions. The latter are to be governed by Rawls's second principle of justice, which says, in its most recent formulation: "Social and economic inequalities are to satisfy two conditions: first, they are to be attached to positions and offices open to all under conditions of fair equality of opportunity; and second, they are to be to the greatest benefit of the least advantaged members of society" (*PL* 6, *JFR* 42–43). Known as the opportunity and difference principles, these two conditions are lexically ordered (*TJ* 77, 264–67): The demands of the difference principle on socioeconomic institutions are subject to the demand of fair equality of opportunity. My discussion nonetheless begins with the difference principle.

6.1 The Difference Principle in First Approximation

The difference principle makes the following demand on a society's basic structure: *Social and economic inequalities are to be to the greatest benefit of the least advantaged members of society* (*PL* 6, *JFR* 42–43). The reference here is not to particular persons—for example, those who are actually least advantaged in the existing institutional order. If this were the idea, then every basic structure would violate the difference principle because institutional reforms benefiting the presently least advantaged are always possible. The difference principle must be interpreted in light of the anonymity condition: A basic structure that creates socioeconomic inequalities must be to the greatest possible benefit of the lowest socioeconomic position. The basic structure must be such that no practicable alternative design of it would lead to a superior least advantaged socioeconomic position. This interpretation fits precisely with the use of the maximin rule in the original position: concerned with the worst case, the parties assess each design of socioeconomic institutions from the standpoint of the worst socioeconomic position it would generate. As a first approximation, then, one can say that the difference principle favors, for a given society and time period, those designs of socioeconomic institutions that would produce the best possible worst socioeconomic position.

Socioeconomic positions and inequalities are defined by the last three social primary goods: powers and prerogatives associated with professional positions, income and wealth, and the residual social bases of self-respect. We can call these *index goods*, because an index of these basic goods is to be used for comparing representative socioeconomic positions (see *TJ* §15 and *CP* 456, where *index* is used in the sense it has in economics, for a way of aggregating heterogeneous data). Rawls is prepared to expand the list of index goods should it turn out that he has missed important components. Following a suggestion by R. A. Musgrave, he has considered including leisure time defined as the residual of time worked (*CP* 455). One may also want to take account of the quality of work—recognizing time spent on dull or dirty work as a greater burden, for example.

Although Rawls speaks of an index, he gives no indication how the underlying goods are to be quantified and how such quantities are to be aggregated into a single index number for each person. Bypassing this problem, he gives simplified examples in which income serves as a proxy for index goods.

A popular objection to the difference principle is that it gives too much weight to the worst position. To illustrate the point for a simple two-class society: The objection contends that it makes no sense to prefer a design of socioeconomic institutions producing a $<15,12>$ distributional profile over another producing a $<100,11>$ profile. Rawls rejects this sort of counterexample as unrealistic. If a design of socioeconomic institutions with a $<100,11>$ profile is practicable, then there will be some practicable modification of it that would raise the least advantaged position to above 12 without thereby lowering the more advantaged position to 15 or below. One cannot simply make up such numbers, but must be able to give a credible explanation of how a society in realistic circumstances might actually be confronted with an institutional design choice involving the profiles in question.

Let us do this with a simple example. Imagine a group of people cultivating an island, with division of labor. Leaving other index goods aside, we use the wage rate (income per hour of work) as a proxy for individual shares of index goods. In this way, we take account of leisure time indirectly: A person who has twice as much income as another because she chooses to work twice as many hours counts as being equally well off, socioeconomically.

It may at first appear that the difference principle would favor a design of socioeconomic institutions (D_0) in which all participants are paid at the same hourly rate; after all, above-average wages for some are possible only at the cost of below-average wages for others. This argument holds, however, only if productivity is fixed or, at any rate, cannot be raised through wage differentials. And this prerequisite will rarely hold. Take, for instance, an alternative design D_{20} in which 20 percent of the total product is used for bonuses given to the most productive workers. Only the remaining 80 percent is distributed among all workers in the form of a uniform hourly wage. The least advantaged in D_{20}—those who win no bonus—then receive as an hourly wage only 80 percent of the average production per hour, as compared with the 100 percent everyone receives under D_0. The difference principle would nonetheless favor D_{20} over D_0 if the bonus incentive raised overall productivity by more than 25 percent. In that case, 80 percent of the higher average hourly production under D_{20} would be more than 100 percent of the lower average hourly production under D_0.

The preference of the difference principle for D_{20} over D_0 in this case is hard to contest, as all hourly wage rates under D_{20} are higher than any under D_0. The preference follows from the Pareto condition alone, without any special concern for the lowest socioeconomic position.

Judgments based on the difference principle become more controversial, however, once we ask how far our island society should take the bonus system. One could distribute 40 percent or even 60 percent of the total product as bonuses for the most productive workers, not to speak of the various possible ways of dividing up the bonus pool. According to the difference principle, the answer depends on empirical facts—on how variations in the bonus system affect average hourly productivity. The following table presents arbitrary, but nonetheless plausible, assumptions about these facts. The first two columns give the percentage of production to be set aside for bonuses (here the D_n label signifies a design of socioeconomic institutions in which n percent of the social product is used for bonuses). The third column gives the representative minimum share: the percentage of average production per work-hour earned by individuals who receive no bonus. Obviously, this percentage is $100 - n$. The fourth column gives social productivity in dollars per work-hour, and the fifth calculates the lowest hourly wage by multiplying the figures in columns three and four.

Design	Bonus Share	Minimum Share	Productivity	Lowest Wage Rate
D_0	0%	100%	10.00 \$/h	10.00 \$/h
D_{20}	20%	80%	20.00 \$/h	16.00 \$/h
D_{24}	24%	76%	21.50 \$/h	16.34 \$/h
D_{25}	25%	75%	21.80 \$/h	16.35 \$/h
D_{26}	26%	74%	22.00 \$/h	16.28 \$/h
D_{30}	30%	70%	22.70 \$/h	15.89 \$/h
D_{40}	40%	60%	25.00 \$/h	15.00 \$/h
D_{50}	50%	50%	27.00 \$/h	13.50 \$/h

Based on these empirical facts and estimates, the difference principle would select the D_{25} design of socioeconomic institutions on the ground that it produces the highest achievable socioeconomic position for the least advantaged (here symbolized by the highest achievable minimum wage rate). In our example, the difference principle favors a socioeconomic order that generates only modest inequality: the wage rate of the least advantaged is fully 75 percent of the average wage rate. But, on different empirical assumptions, the difference principle could demand socioeconomic institutions that generate vastly greater inequalities. In fact, there is no firm limit on the degree of socioeconomic inequality the difference principle might favor. Any arbitrarily large inequality is justifiable by the difference principle when no institutional alternative would reduce this inequality without also reducing the lowest index position in absolute terms. (Very large inequalities may be inconsistent with the fair value of the basic political liberties or fair equality of opportunity.)

Rawls proceeds from the assumption that practicable designs of socioeconomic institutions are related to one another in something

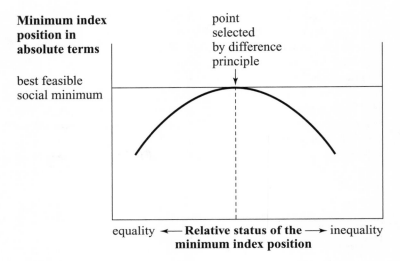

Figure 6.1. Impact of Inequality on the Lowest Index Position

like the way represented in the table. Through gradual modification, perhaps of tax rates, the design can be continuously adjusted and ought then to be shaped so as to optimize the economic distribution, that is, so as to raise the lowest absolute index position as high as possible. Rawls expresses this idea in a diagram (Figure 6, *TJ* 66), which I reproduce here (figure 6.1), slightly modified for greater generality.

6.2 The Difference Principle in Detail

Three further specifications are necessary for a more precise understanding of the difference principle. First, index positions are defined in terms of the index goods available to individuals over their whole lifetimes. The lowest index position is therefore determined by the lowest lifetime access to index goods. So the lowest income position, for instance, is occupied not by those with the lowest wage rate at a given moment in time, but rather by those who face the lowest wage rates over their whole lifetimes. Thus, a person able to earn only $10 per hour all his life is considered less advantaged than another who can earn only $9 in her younger years but then has her income rise throughout her life well beyond $10 per hour. In order to identify the least advantaged under each basic structure design and in order to compare these positions across such designs, the difference principle focuses then on persons over a complete lifetime rather than on time-slices of such persons.

The focus on lifetime shares requires a method of intertemporal aggregation within each life, which Rawls has not attempted to work out. Such aggregation faces at least three difficulties which necessitate significant complications of the initially appealing idea that a person's lifetime income score should be computed by averaging the wage rates she faced in the various years of her life. One difficulty is that the temporal composition of wage rates matters. It may be preferable, for instance, to face real hourly wage rates that rise gradually from $9 to $15 over one's lifetime than to face hourly wage rates that fall gradually from $15 to $9, even if the trajectories are exact mirror images of each other. And it may be preferable to face a smooth wage rate trajectory than one that displays wild fluctuations, even if the latter is higher on average.

Another difficulty is that people die at different ages. Averaging over time, one may implausibly consider one to be more advantaged than another merely because the former died sooner: Both have exactly parallel careers with declining real hourly wage rates, but the one dies early while the lifetime average of the other continues to be further eroded.

The last difficulty arises from the fact that some people choose a lower paying job even while they could easily earn more. Thus consider Ann and Bob working as clerk and gardener with hourly wage rates of $12 and $9, respectively. There is no good reason to consider Bob less advantaged if he chooses to be a gardener while knowing that he could also work as a clerk at the $12/hour rate. The difficulty arises when people's work options are affected by their earlier career choices. Suppose, for example, that clerks receive seniority pay increases while gardeners remain at a real wage of $9 per hour. In later years, Bob may still have the option of switching to being a clerk, but he would then be paid less than Ann, who was a clerk all along. In such cases, one might judge Bob to be less advantaged over his lifetime because of his lower earning opportunities later in life. Or one might judge them to be equally advantaged on the ground that Ann's superior lifetime wage-rate trajectory had been accessible to Bob at the beginning of his professional life. The latter judgment may seem plausible if Bob made his decision while complete information about its long-term consequences was easily available to him. In any actual society, however, such information about future wage rates in various careers, if available at all, is likely to be of dubious reliability.

Any method of intertemporal aggregation within lives thus embodies difficult choices about how to aggregate wage-rate data and about how to revise the profile of wage-rate trajectories a basic structure would actually generate to take account of superior wage rates that persons could have had if they had made different choices. The latter question is especially important for the assessment of socioeconomic institutions that are, as it were, unforgiving by allowing missed opportunities early in life to result in pitiful wage rates subsequently. To what extent, if at all, should applications of the difference principle revise such pitiful wage rates upward on the ground that better paying career paths were available?

Proceeding to the second specification, the minimum index position does not signify the lifetime index position of a determinate individual. For one thing, it is impossible to ascertain which person is least advantaged under a given actual or possible design of socioeconomic institutions: How could one possibly identify *the* person with the worst lifetime index position in the United States today? Moreover, the worst socioeconomic position, if indeed one could identify it for actual and possible designs of socioeconomic institutions, is bound to be influenced by many contingencies and therefore unsuitable to serve as the basis for judging entire such designs. Rawls therefore understands the difference principle so that the lowest index position generated by a given design of socioeconomic institutions is that of a *representative group*. I assume he would then define the lowest socioeconomic position generated by a basic structure as the arithmetic (or better: geometric) mean within this group of the least advantaged, but Rawls gives no more detail on this point.

Rawls also does not commit himself to a uniform way of identifying the representative group of the least advantaged. The suggestions he makes—half the median income, unskilled worker or below (*TJ* 84)—entail that the size of this group may vary across candidate institutional designs and may even be zero in some cases. But such variations are implausible. To see this, consider two alternative designs, D_x and D_y, generating lowest representative index positions of 21 and 20, respectively. The preference of the difference principle for D_x is implausible, if "21" represents the mean for the bottom 3 percent of the population under D_x, while "20" represents the mean for the bottom 1 percent of the population under D_y. Applied in this way, the difference principle can even violate the Pareto condition (as the socioeconomic position of the bottom third of the least advantaged under D_x may easily fall below 20), which is clearly contrary to Rawls's intent (TJ §12). To avoid this problem, it seems best to define the least advantaged group in terms of a fixed percentage of the population—for example, in terms of the lowest 2 percent of lifetime index positions.

Proceeding to the third specification. That the difference principle selects the design of socioeconomic institutions that would generate the highest possible lowest index position holds only as a first approximation. It may be possible for a society to raise its lowest index position through institutional prohibitions of research, nature conservation, various luxury products and leisure activities, or state support for the arts. Would the difference principle demand such prohibitions? Not necessarily. The difference principle demands only that social and economic *inequalities* be to the benefit of the least advantaged members of society. Thus it constrains only those aspects of institutional design that produce index inequalities—or better: those that affect the distributional profile of *relative* index positions. (On this point, Rawls's formulation of the difference principle may be misleading. D_0 generates no socioeconomic inequalities at all and thus seems to satisfy the difference principle trivially. But Rawls interprets the difference principle so that it not merely permits but actually demands inequalities that are to the benefit of the lowest socioeconomic position; e.g., JFR 59–63.)

By organizing itself to devote resources to research, natural parks, or museums or to protect the environment or to incentivize capital formation, a society reduces the lowest index position below what it would otherwise be. But if this design decision reduces other index positions proportionately, then it does not entail social or economic *inequalities* and is therefore not covered and prohibited by the difference principle.

Capital formation is constrained, however, by another principle, that of *just savings*. The parties in the original position are to institute a savings plan that determines an appropriate minimum rate of savings for each level of prosperity. In doing so, they take account of the interests of all generations—while they know that those they represent belong to the same generation, they do not know which generation this is (PL 273–74). Rawls does not say what savings plan they would agree to, except to suggest that, once a modest level of social prosperity sufficient for assuring the basic rights and liberties has been attained, no further economic growth is demanded by his public criterion of justice (*CP* 275–78, *JFR* 159–60).

In comparing alternative designs of socioeconomic institutions, one must hold constant any aspects not addressed by the difference principle. The relevant question in comparing various tax systems, for instance, is which of them would produce the best minimum index position if rate of savings, environmental protection, and other such factors are held constant.

Institutional design decisions that affect all index positions equally are unconstrained by the difference principle. This may well be plausible for societies that are affluent and where, with the difference principle satisfied, inequality is low. Such societies produce a comfortable minimum index position whose occupants will not be more severely affected than others by decisions that reduce or increase all positions by a uniform percentage. But things may be different in societies that are poor and where, with the difference principle satisfied, inequality is very high. Here, a 5 percent wage-rate reduction may be easily bearable for the more affluent and yet a real hardship for the poorest (seriously affecting their nutrition, for example). This reflection suggests that—contrary to the difference principle, which here seems too permissive—decisions about economic growth and environmental protection can pose a problem of socioeconomic justice even if they affect all index positions proportionately. We will revisit this important point later.

There is another way in which such decisions could affect different strata of society differentially. It might easily be the case, for instance, that tax-funded support for the arts is of less real benefit to the less advantaged—who may not be able to afford even highly subsidized opera tickets, for example. In such a case, it would seem to be in the spirit of the difference principle to disallow state support for the arts on the ground that it lowers the index position of the least advantaged not only in absolute but also in relative terms.

Here we run up against a more general problem. The alternative practicable designs of socioeconomic institutions need not lie on a continuum of the kind suggested by the previous diagram. There may be discontinuities, for instance, across different economic systems or across distinct methods of taxation. As discussed in section 6.6, Rawls believes that his public criterion of justice might be satisfied by either a property-owning democracy or liberal socialism, and he suggests entirely replacing income taxes by consumption taxes. In our simple example of an island society, we compared only socialist institutional

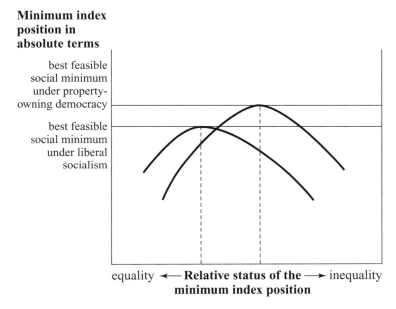

Figure 6.2. Impact of Different Ways of Instituting Inequality on the Lowest Index Position

designs, in which the total social product is distributed to the producers rather than also to owners of land, buildings, and machinery. Were we to take capitalist institutional designs into account as well, we might arrive at a more complicated diagram, one with several bell curves, such as in Figure 6.2.

Rawls suggests that the difference principle here mandates the optimal capitalist design of socioeconomic institutions as offering the highest attainable minimum index position (*JFR* 69–70). This question is further discussed in section 7.4.

6.3 Advocating the Difference Principle in the Original Position

Would the parties in the original position really agree on the difference principle as a public standard for evaluating alternative designs of socioeconomic institutions? One serious impediment to such an agreement has already been discussed (section 4.3): Insofar as they employ the maximin rule, the parties want the public criterion they adopt to lead to the implementation of basic structure designs under which the lowest level of fundamental interest fulfillment is as high as possible. But the degree to which citizens' fundamental interests (especially the third) are fulfilled depends not merely on their access to social goods but also on their natural endowments. The lowest prospects for fundamental interest fulfillment are had by citizens who are among the (naturally) less gifted *and* among the (socially) least advantaged. The parties may hope to avoid such low prospects by agreeing on a public criterion that requires citizens with poor natural endowments to be compensated through suitable social advantages. As we have seen, it may be possible to overcome this impediment with pragmatic arguments, adducing the substantial costs associated with making the public criterion, and presumably the basic structure designs it justifies, sensitive to citizens' measured natural endowments.

If the parties follow Rawls in attending to the distribution of social goods alone, they focus especially on the lowest socioeconomic position. But they may hesitate to agree to a principle that assesses the lowest index position exclusively in absolute terms. To be sure, it is important how much the poorest can buy. But is it not also important how much *less* they can buy than other citizens?

Rawls defends his exclusive concern for the absolute value of the lowest index position with the claim that envy is irrational. It is irrational for the poor to want a lesser share merely for the sake of reducing the distance between themselves and the more affluent (*TJ* 123–25, §§80–81). But envy is hardly the only reason for being concerned with one's relative index position. One might reasonably be concerned for one's access to various *positional* goods—for whether one can afford to have a house by the sea, to be treated by the better doctors, or to buy one's children the toys other children have—when access to such goods depends more on one's relative than on one's absolute financial position.

Rawls could accommodate this point through his third index good, counting a person's relative income and wealth (measured perhaps as a percentage of the average) as one social basis of self-respect. He could then say that what the difference principle demands, the highest feasible lowest index position, is not simply equivalent to the highest feasible minimum income rate. The difference principle could permit lower income rates when for the least advantaged position the financial loss is outweighed by a gain in the residual bases of self-respect. Working out this response would require a more precise specification of the residual social bases of self-respect, showing how these can be quantified and then be integrated into the index.

These two complications notwithstanding, the difference principle fits well with the maximin rule the parties are said to employ in the original position (*TJ* §26). This good fit helps convince the parties to make the difference principle part of their agreement. But it is of little help to Rawls's effort to convince his compatriots if they find implausible both his maximin contractualism and his difference principle. Coming to understand that this is in fact the case (*JFR* 132–33), Rawls de-emphasized the connection in his later writings and sought to support these two pieces of his theory on independent grounds as much as possible: He continued to highlight the close connection between the maximin rule and the popular *first* principle of justice, whose adoption protects citizens against a variety of intolerably bad outcomes (*JFR* 104–5). And he increasingly emphasized that the parties have strong reasons to adopt the difference principle even when they consider standpoints other than that of the worst off—to the point of flatly denying that the reasoning for the difference principle relies on the maximin rule in any way (*JFR* 95).

Rawls facilitates this expositional shift by tightly confining his advocacy in the original position to defeating only two competing candidates. In the first pairwise comparison he considers, Rawls seeks to show that the parties would prefer his two principles of justice over the principle of average utility (which requires social institutions to be designed so as to maximize average happiness). In this argument, the maximin rule plays an important part: Average utilitarianism can lead to wholly intolerable worst-case scenarios. The parties can protect their clients against such outcomes by agreeing on Rawls's proposed public criterion, which uncompromisingly requires the basic structure to be designed so that it protects certain basic liberties and access to basic necessities for all citizens. The parties are confirmed in their rejection of the principle of average utility by its being much less capable of clear and transparent public application than Rawls's two principles and therefore less suitable as a public criterion.

In the second pairwise comparison, Rawls seeks to show that the parties would prefer his public criterion over *restricted utilitarian* (RU) criteria. Such criteria accept some or all of the priority requirements of the public criterion Rawls proposes: that basic needs must be met, the first principle, and (formal and fair) equality of opportunity. But RU criteria include the principle of average utility, instead of the difference principle, in a subordinate role (*JFR* §§34–39; cf. *TJ* §49). The point of the second pairwise comparison is then to support particularly the difference principle by displaying the reasons the parties have for incorporating it into their agreement.

Because RU criteria incorporate Rawls's priority requirements, they do not involve intolerable worst-case scenarios. At least it is not obvious that they do. It is then disputable that it would be rational for the parties to rely on the maximin rule in making the second pairwise comparison. Rawls therefore presents his case to the parties by arguing that, if a society is organized by his proposed public criterion, both its more and its less advantaged members are better off than their counterpart groups would be if this society were organized by RU. This form of argument allows Rawls to show that the difference principle has important supports that are independent of the maximin rule.

A first important consideration is that, as part of a public criterion of justice, the difference principle beats the principle of average utility in regard to clear and transparent public applicability. Happiness, however understood, is difficult to measure and even harder to estimate, as must be done in the comparison of alternative basic structure designs. The difference principle, by contrast, works with a primary goods index that, once defined, permits precise measurements and more solid estimates. Moreover, the difference principle is informationally less demanding: To compare alternative basic structure designs, one need aggregate well-being information only about the least advantaged, not about all citizens. The identification of the least advantaged does require information about the other citizens, to be sure. But here simple ordinal data suffice. For the vast majority of the population, one does not need to know how well off they are but only that they are better off than the least advantaged.

Transparent public applicability reduces errors in application, of course. More important, it also limits the frequency and importance of disagreements which can lead to mutual distrust and can prevent widespread moral allegiance to the social order (stability). Utilitarian arguments for and against all sorts of institutional reforms are easy to formulate and easy to deny. Those making or denying such arguments would therefore easily arouse the suspicion that they are really (consciously or unconsciously) motivated not by the general happiness but their own. Such suspicions threaten the stability of an institutional order, because citizens have less reason to show moral deference to democratic decisions when they do not fully trust the motivations of the majority.

In the second consideration, stability concerns move center stage. Moral allegiance must not be overly demanding psychologically. Those in the lowest socioeconomic positions will often find it very hard to give willing support to socioeconomic institutions that produce such low positions—even if they believe RU to be just and understand how it justifies those institutions. Apathy and disloyalty are more likely to arise among citizens the more disadvantaged they are. And because the apathy and disloyalty of some run counter to the interests of all, everyone has an interest in moderating disadvantage. The difference principle goes furthest in this direction by demanding the highest feasible lowest index position. An average criterion, by contrast, might justify positions that are far lower than necessary.

Moreover, the more disadvantaged citizens of a society governed by RU may not even be convinced that RU is just. They would be told: "You are indeed more disadvantaged than anyone need be, but your loss is outweighed by others enjoying greater happiness than would otherwise be possible." But the disadvantaged may not find the greater happiness of others a compelling reason. They may well feel that, given how badly off they are, their happiness should be weighted more heavily than that of others who are so much better off.

This difficulty is avoided when, pursuant to the difference principle, socioeconomic institutions are designed to optimize the lowest socioeconomic position. Those least advantaged under the existing basic structure design can then more easily accept their position on the ground that under any practicable alternative design there would be people as disadvantaged as, or even more disadvantaged than, they are. This ground is much more compelling: The basic structure of society must be designed in one way or another, and, if it had a different design, then the least advantaged under that design would have at least equally strong grounds for complaint. Rawls says that the difference principle does, whereas the principle of average utility does not, specify an attractive notion of reciprocity between the worse off and the better off: The worse off accept the greater advantages of the better off, and the better off accept that such inequality is allowable only insofar as it raises the position of the worse off in absolute terms.

A third consideration makes a related point. It seems somewhat mysterious at first why Rawls should speak of a social *contract* when the parties all deliberate identically on the basis of identical information. Why should there even be more than one representative in the original position? Rawls describes his original position with many representatives because he wants it to result not merely in the selection of, but in an agreement on, a public criterion of justice. Agreement involves the extra element of commitment. The parties can agree to a public criterion only if they can be confident that their clients can live up to this agreement by supporting the resulting social order. The parties cannot have this confidence in RU, which may lead to socioeconomic positions that are very low in absolute and relative terms and generate excessive *strains of commitment* on those who occupy these positions. These citizens would be prone to disaffection and noncompliance to the detriment of all.

Proponents of RU could strike back at the difference principle with analogues of the last two considerations. They could argue that the difference principle compromises stability and is liable to engender excessive strains of commitment, because it constrains too tightly the socioeconomic prospects of the more gifted and affluent citizens (cf. *JFR* 127). The difference principle demands that, insofar as it influences relative index positions, the basic structure should be arranged so as to optimize the lowest index position. But such an institutional design cannot be maintained without the willing support of the more advantaged citizens. Can they realistically be expected to exercise their political influence on the design of socioeconomic institutions (e.g., the tax system) exclusively for the sake of optimizing the lowest index position? Doesn't this demand of complete disregard for the interests of those in their own socioeconomic position put their loyalty under excessive strain, thereby threatening the stability of a Rawlsian social order? The next chapter explores whether Rawls has satisfactory answers to these questions.

6.4 The Opportunity Principle

Let us now consider the opportunity principle (as I call it) and its lexical priority over the difference principle. Imagine a basic structure design that makes it difficult for highly talented and motivated persons born into poor households to receive a good education and to attain leadership positions. The difference principle, considered by itself, might permit or even demand such a design when it can be expected to raise overall productivity and hence the lowest index position. Of course, in one way such a design lowers productivity by giving leadership positions to less talented people from more affluent households, wasting some great talents among those effectively excluded. But this loss may be small when the more affluent families produce enough talented offspring to avoid the need of placing untalented people into important positions. (Such placement of untalented people is still bound to occur occasionally, of course, from other causes.) And such a small loss may be outweighed by the economic gains from family privilege: The lowest index position is raised when the cost of the higher education system is borne privately by the more affluent rather than by society at large and when citizens are incentivized to work harder by the fact that their children's opportunities crucially depend on their own socioeconomic position. The difference principle alone might well then support such a discriminatory design of socioeconomic institutions. Such discriminatory designs are disqualified as unjust by subordinating, within the second principle of justice, the difference principle to the constraints of the opportunity principle.

Alternative designs of socioeconomic institutions differ with regard to the distributional profile they generate and also with regard to how they regulate access to higher index positions. The difference principle assesses the distributional profile of index goods a given design of socioeconomic institutions is estimated to produce. The opportunity principle assesses the mechanisms that regulate access to the higher index positions. Because variations in these mechanisms affect the distributional profile, the constraints of the opportunity principle can have a negative impact on the distributional profile and on the lowest index position in particular.

The opportunity principle mandates that the basic structure be designed so that any social and economic inequalities they generate are attached to positions and offices *open to all* under conditions of *fair equality of opportunity*. The first constraint of *formal equality of opportunity* or *careers open to talents* requires that "all have at least the same legal rights of access to all advantaged social positions" (*TJ* 62). Rawls means not only that the law must not discriminate but also that it must forbid discriminatory rules imposed by other agents, such as a company policy of hiring only men. No one must be barred from competing for an educational or employment opportunity. Moreover, formal equality of opportunity is also meant to rule out discrimination in regard to the competition for positions. All citizens must not merely be entitled to apply for positions but must be entitled to compete for them on equal terms. Thus, formal equality of opportunity is violated when firms reserve a certain percentage of management positions for women or when blacks are given an advantage in gaining admission to universities. Rawls believes, however, that such affirmative action can nonetheless be justified temporarily as the best way of dealing with the effects of past unjust discrimination.

Formal equality of opportunity does not mandate that positions be filled by lot. The qualifications of candidates should, of course, be taken into account. Formal equality of opportunity also does not rule out high access fees (tuition) for higher education, which skew the competition against the poor. Finally, I believe Rawls understands formal equality of opportunity as not prohibiting "age discrimination." Rules barring those older than thirty-five from admission to medical school, excluding those under forty from the presidency, or requiring people to retire at age seventy—such rules do not entail unequal *life* chances. The inequalities such rules create can be expected to advantage and disadvantage all citizens equally over the full course of their lives. (Here we must, once more, consider those who die early, for whom advantages and disadvantages may not balance out over a lifetime.)

Formal equality of opportunity applies to firms, cooperatives, trade unions, guilds, associations, universities, and the whole public sector, constraining all personnel decisions and thus the selection of colleagues, suppliers, customers, members, students, and so on. It surely does not apply to religious associations—it can be legal to discriminate against Buddhists, homosexuals, and women in filling a position of Catholic bishop. Private clubs and societies—at least those in which business connections are forged only rarely—are presumably also exempt. Rawls has not addressed these questions in detail.

Even when the rules of the competition do not formally disadvantage anyone, members of some groups or social classes may not learn about certain attractive educational or employment opportunities, as such information is available only to insiders who pass it along to friends and relatives. This, too, is a violation of the career open to talent idea, and we should understand formal equality of opportunity as including the requirement that information about openings in education and employment must be widely available.

Even if all are eligible to apply for, and can easily find out about, all educational and employment opportunities, the competition itself can be unfair. For example, children of poor parents may be kept away from universities, and from the leadership positions these make accessible, by high tuition, and women by cultural barriers and prejudice in selection. Such social impediments are addressed by the constraint Rawls calls *fair equality of opportunity*: "those who are at the same level of talent and ability, and have the same willingness to use them, should have the same prospects of success regardless of their initial place in the social system. . . . Chances to acquire cultural knowledge and skills should not depend upon one's class position, and so the school system, whether public or private, should be designed to even out class barriers" (*TJ* 63; cf. *JFR* 44).

Children born into higher socioeconomic classes tend to receive more attention and stimulation in their home, and this may give them, from their very early years onward, an edge in abilities and motivation over their similarly endowed peers born into poorer families. The first quoted sentence suggests that Rawls wants to allow this edge to influence professional success: It is only among those with the same level of ability and the same willingness to apply themselves that (statistically) equal prospects of success are demanded. But the second quoted sentence suggests the opposite: that the socioeconomic class into which people are born should not affect professional success at all (not even through differential impact on motivation and abilities). It is unclear which of these is Rawls's considered view. The latter reading fits better with his presenting the opportunity principle as "eliminating the influence of social contingencies" (*TJ* 64). But it does lead to an informationally very demanding prescription: To check whether a society satisfies fair equality of opportunity, one must estimate to what extent citizens' abilities and their willingness to use them are themselves influenced by their initial socioeconomic class.

Rawls distinguishes four kinds of factors that explain inequalities in citizens' chances to occupy leadership positions: natural factors (talents), social factors (family and social class during one's formative years), personal qualities (motivation, ambition, initiative), and luck (later added by Rawls—*CP* 259). Fair equality of opportunity demands that the basic structure be designed so that social factors do not influence access to careers. Whether and how strongly factors of the other kinds should be allowed to influence professional success is to be settled by the difference principle. Socioeconomic institutions may be designed so that they give superior life prospects to those who are more talented, diligent, or lucky if and insofar as allowing such inequalities tends to raise the lowest index position.

We have already seen that it is difficult to separate social factors and personal qualities in a clear and plausible way, because the former have a formative influence on the latter. The interrelations between social and natural factors also call for clarification. Skin color and gender seem, at first glance, to be solely natural factors. But when blacks or women are disadvantaged, this is due not to their skin color or gender alone, which as such do not affect their professional prospects. Decisive here is the social factor of racist or sexist disrespect, which makes admissions and employment decisions sensitive to those natural factors. Fair equality of opportunity demands that the basic structure be designed to prevent these social factors from having causal impact. It forbids not merely the class-correlated inequalities Rawls mentions but also race- and gender-correlated inequalities in opportunity.

Rawls's explication of fair equality of opportunity pays little attention to race and gender, despite their great historical and ongoing importance. One reason, as with the fair value of the basic political liberties, is that Rawls works within ideal theory, where race and gender have no special salience (*JFR* 65). There are millions of possible personal characteristics that might, merely on account of prevalent negative attitudes, diminish professional prospects: all kinds of physical characteristics, sexual preferences, marital status, religious and political convictions and affiliations, and so on. Moreover, the difference principle presumably suffices to rule out basic structure designs that allow such discrimination, which is bound to reduce economic efficiency and thereby the lowest index position. Rawls is then focusing on class-correlated inequalities of opportunity in particular, because socioeconomic stratification would exist even in the fully just society he envisions and because the difference principle, left unconstrained, might well justify them. To be sure, class-correlated inequalities diminish economic efficiency insofar as people with less talent and motivation from more privileged families win leadership positions over people with more talent and motivation from less privileged backgrounds. But this economic loss may be outweighed by a greater gain: The incentive effects of given pay differentials depend on what money can buy. The more things money can buy, the greater are these incentive effects and the greater also the gain for overall productivity and the lowest index position achievable through them. When citizens know that money can buy not only ordinary goods and services but also a great head start for their children, many will try harder to be productive in order to earn more. In this way, an unconstrained difference principle could justify financial barriers to higher education.

One might think that a justification is available also for social institutions that allow race or gender or religion to have a discriminatory impact when prevailing attitudes are such that blacks or women or Catholics make less effective leaders. But this justification is unlikely to work in ideal theory. Rawls assesses each basic structure design by estimating not how it would function with persons as they are now (with attitudes shaped by the existing institutional design), but how it would function with persons whose attitudes were shaped by the design under examination. Now there are surely practicable institutional designs that would generate no or minimal disrespect based on personal characteristics (gender, ethnicity, religion, etc.) that, but for such disrespect, would have no relevance to performance. Under such designs, people with these characteristics would not make less effective leaders. The difference principle clearly favors such designs because they better coordinate the talents of all citizens, thus raising overall productivity and thereby the lowest index position.

In some cases, attitudes toward personal characteristics may persist regardless of institutional design. Consider height and good looks, for instance, which are currently highly correlated with professional success because citizens are more willing to be led by tall and handsome people. This fact may be due in part to innate dispositions and aesthetic preferences, hence not wholly social. It is likely that the tall and attractive make at least somewhat more effective leaders under any practicable institutional design. If so, then the points I have made about gender, race, religion, and the like do not work here. Then height and good looks have special salience even in ideal theory, and the difference principle may favor allowing the tall and attractive to have better chances to occupy leadership positions. And we face then a real question whether the opportunity principle should be understood as prohibiting height- and looks-correlated inequalities in professional prospects and hence as overruling the difference principle here. If yes, then social institutions must be designed so that citizens' (innately) greater readiness to be led by the tall and attractive does not affect professional prospects. But this may entail that key positions are occupied by less effective leaders, which in turn tends to reduce overall productivity and the lowest index position.

I conjecture that Rawls would have understood fair equality of opportunity as narrowly focused on socioeconomic class alone. This conjecture contrasts with the one I ventured regarding the fair value of the basic political liberties. The contrast would be explained by two relevant differences: Rawls attached far greater importance to the avoidance of gross inequalities in the political sphere, where citizens are deliberating as equals about justice and the common good, than in the socioeconomic sphere, where they are anyway distinguished by many differences and inequalities. And it is far easier and less costly for social institutions to achieve—for the short and less attractive, say— *roughly* equal chances, as required by the fair value of the basic political liberties, than the *same* prospects of success, as demanded by fair equality of opportunity.

6.5   Advocating the Opportunity Principle in the Original Position

In Rawls's proposed public criterion of justice, the opportunity principle is lexically prior to the difference principle. By agreeing to it, the parties would allow some socioeconomic inequalities that would be to the benefit of the lowest index position to be prohibited. What reasons can the parties be given to allow this, to constrain the difference principle by this prior equality of opportunity demand?

The parties have good reasons to constrain the difference principle by the requirement of formal equality of opportunity. The social cost of implementing this requirement is low, and surely much lower than the social cost of qualified people being excluded when formal equality of opportunity is violated or opportunities are not widely advertised. In ideal theory, anyway, the difference principle supports this requirement in nearly all imaginable circumstances because having more qualified applicants and therefore a better matching of people to positions enhances economic efficiency and thereby raises all index positions. Rather than rely on the difference principle, however, the parties have reason to adopt the requirement because they can thereby achieve a clearer and better-defined criterion of justice while incurring no real risk to the lowest index position. In particular, they eliminate the danger of specious disagreements over whether, in given circumstances, the difference principle implies this constraint or not. By exempting the requirement from the complex weighing the difference principle demands, the parties improve the transparent public applicability of the public criterion.

It is much harder to see why the contracting parties should agree to constrain the difference principle by the demand of fair equality of opportunity. Employing the maximin rule, why should they accept a worse minimum index position for the sake of equalizing the statistical career prospects of various social groups? The difficulty can be illustrated by a simple example.

Imagine a society whose basic structure satisfies the first principle and formal equality of opportunity and is otherwise governed by the difference principle. This society has two classes: the upper class (U) and the lower class (L). Individuals are born into one of these classes and also belong to one of them in their adult life. There are, then, four possibilities: UU, UL (born into the upper class but belonging to the lower class as an adult), LU, and LL. Natural abilities, ambition, and luck are roughly equally distributed among the children of both classes. But in the lower class only very few children are educated at their parents' expense. Nonetheless, enough people are born into the upper class, and educated at their parents' expense, to keep competently occupied all upper-class positions—including leadership positions, which demand a lot of talent and hard work in addition to a good education. Given this fact, it is then not economically worthwhile to divert resources toward educating additional lower-class children. Doing so, in the name of fair equality of opportunity, would not appreciably *raise* the lowest index position (would not raise overall productivity by channeling more-competent people into the higher positions). But doing so would substantially *lower* the lowest index position (LL): It would divert part of the social product toward educating lower-class children. And, by eliminating the ability to buy an educational head start for one's children, it would reduce the rewards of affluence and hence the incentive effects of these rewards. Under such circumstances, the class-specific inequality of opportunity would—without the demand of fair equality of opportunity—be justified.

The institutional design described, D_1, might be represented in the following table:

D_1	Lifetime Index Position	Percentage of Population
UU_1	180	9%
UL_1	110	1%
LU_1	170	1%
LL_1	100	89%
Weighted Average	108	

Clearly, D_1 does not secure fair equality of opportunity. Those born into the lower class have a much worse chance of belonging to the upper class later in life than those born into the upper class do (1 in 90 versus 9 in 10).

It would be possible to eliminate this inequality of opportunity by providing the children of the lower class with education and training similar to that available to children of the upper class. This reform would foster social mobility, enlarging the LU group (and the UL group as well). But it would also incur substantial social costs, which would worsen all index positions, including the lowest (LL). The reformed design of socioeconomic institutions, D_2, might then look like this:

D_2	Lifetime Index Position	Percentage of Population
UU_2	162	1%
UL_2	99	9%
LU_2	153	9%
LL_2	90	81%
Weighted Average	97.2	

D_2 does secure fair equality of opportunity. Those born into the lower class, just like those born into the upper class, have the same 1-in-10 chance of belonging to the upper class later in life.

Insofar as the contracting parties employ the maximin rule, they assume that they are representing someone who—however socio-economic institutions are designed—will occupy the lowest index position: LL. Rationally representing such a client, they would opt for a public criterion that favors D_1 over D_2. The reason is that D_2 reduces the lowest lifetime index position by 10 percent for the sake of an opportunity equalization that is of no use to the least advantaged (who, even with access to education, will not rise into the upper class). Is there an incoherence, then, between Rawls's incorporation of fair equality of opportunity into his public criterion of justice and his endorsement of the original position?

One might reply that while the index position of the LL group is indeed lower in D_2, this group is also smaller than its counterpart in D_1. But this fact does not help, for the index position of UL_2 is also below that of LL_1. Taking LL_2 and UL_2 together, we have a group in D_2 that is both larger and less advantaged than LL_1.

Another reply asserts that lifetime index positions should be estimated *ex ante* rather than *ex post*: the lowest index position produced by D_2 should then be understood as the *expected* lifetime index position of someone born into the lower class. But Rawls explicitly rejects this suggestion: "the least advantaged are, by definition, those who are born into and who remain in that group [who have the lowest index of primary goods] throughout their life" (*CP* 364). And it cannot, in any case, solve the problem: in D_1, the lowest expected index position is $(170 \times 1\% + 100 \times 89\%) \div 90\% = 100.78$. In D_2, the lowest expected index position is $(153 \times 9\% + 90 \times 81\%) \div 90\% = 96.30$. This shows that the proposed reform would lower even the lowest *expected* lifetime index position.

Here is a better reply. Education and training, and the qualifications they bring, have a value in themselves, even if one does not get a chance to use them professionally and to achieve a higher index position by means of them. The impact of the proposed reform is, then, more complex. One impact is negative: The index position of LL is reduced. Another impact is positive: The members of LL are better educated and qualified for more positions. Even if they attain no such position, they still have better opportunities. To justify giving the opportunity principle lexical priority over the difference principle, it would help to be able to say that the positive impact always, or almost always, outweighs the negative. In order to be able to say this, Rawls must postulate an additional social primary good that the parties have reason to deem much more important than the index goods.

In *TJ*, we do indeed find such a good—opportunities—on the official list of social primary goods (*TJ* 54, 79). But does it really make sense for the parties, in view of their clients' three fundamental interests, to adopt a public criterion that ranks this good so much higher than the index goods? Why should opportunities be so important when all they amount to is merely *being qualified for* (as opposed to actually attaining) higher positions? In response, attaching great importance to education and training can be defended on the ground that "the value of education should not be assessed solely in terms of economic efficiency and social welfare. Equally if not more important is the role of education in enabling a person to enjoy the culture of his society and to take part in its affairs, and in this way to provide for each individual a secure sense of his own worth" (*TJ* 87). And Rawls concludes on this basis that "resources in education are not to be allotted solely or necessarily even mainly according to their return as estimated in productive trained abilities, but also according to their worth in enriching the personal and social life of citizens, including here the less favored" (*TJ* 92).

The recognition of opportunities (understood as education and training) as a social primary good leads, however, to other difficulties. Thus it is unclear why such a good should be distributed equally (across social classes) even when its unequal distribution would raise access to education for the least educated members of society. Rawls actually concedes this point at two places, writing that, in order to justify inequalities of opportunity, one must be able to "claim that the attempt to eliminate these inequalities would so interfere with the social system and the operations of the economy that in the long run anyway the opportunities of the disadvantaged would be even more limited" (*TJ* 265; cf. 266).

Moreover, if education and training are really so much more important (for fundamental interest fulfillment) than index goods, shouldn't the parties then prefer a public criterion of justice that would require a large part of the social product to be devoted to this good? Here one could reply that what matters is not citizens' absolute but their relative access to education (measured perhaps as a percentage of the average). The key interest of prospective citizens is to avoid having a substantially worse education than most others. This reply requires, of course, that we give up Rawls's idea that "an inequality of opportunity must enhance the opportunities of those with the lesser opportunity" (*TJ* 266)—for it is logically impossible to increase the smallest *relative* share of opportunities by allowing departures from an equal distribution of this good.

And there is a further problem with this reply. Parties greatly concerned for their clients' relative access to education would favor a public criterion that requires this good to be distributed equally—not merely statistically across social classes, but strictly equally across all citizens. But this demand is at variance with Rawls's proposed criterion, which allows educational inequalities to arise from natural factors, personal qualities, or luck, if and insofar as these inequalities satisfy the difference principle (cf. *TJ* 86–87).

Probably aware of these difficulties, Rawls jettisons in later work "opportunities" as a separate primary good, replacing it on the official list with "freedom of movement and free choice of occupation" (*PL* 76, 181; *JFR* 58), though these are also included among the basic rights and liberties (*PL* 228, 335). But he never attempts to provide a new original-position rationale for constraining the difference principle by a prior demand of fair equality of opportunity. I suspect no such rationale can be provided. Representing prospective citizens, the parties care how well individuals would do under the basic structures that citizens might come to construct under the guidance of the various candidate public criteria of justice. They pay attention, therefore, to the distributional profile each such basic structure would generate. But they pay no attention to the causal mechanisms through which such distributional profiles come about. The parties would find it wholly irrational to agree that citizens' life prospects must not be affected by their family background (or race or gender), even when meeting this demand makes citizens at all percentiles worse off. Insofar as they employ the maximin rule, the parties would find it wholly irrational to accept a worse fate for those in the worst position in exchange for the assurance that class background (and race and gender) play no role in determining its occupants.

Our intuitive sense of justice, however, opposes such indifference. Most do find it unjust that persons' class background and especially their race and gender affect their education and employment opportunities. And our discussion reveals then a tension between our considered judgments and the thought experiment of the original position: We regard fair equality of opportunity as an important component of socioeconomic justice even while the parties would rationally agree that this demand should *not* detract from the demands of the difference principle.

This tension is a problem for Rawls, who wants his contractualist theory to account for our considered moral convictions. How well a society does in terms of fair equality of opportunity cannot be read off from the distributional profile of individual well-being, however defined. Rather, it is a matter of how individuals get distributed over the various index positions and how socioeconomic success therefore correlates with social factors, natural gifts, and motivation. For this reason, the intuitive badness of, say, women being underrepresented in leadership positions cannot straightforwardly be cashed out as bad for any specific individuals as represented in the parties' deliberations.

It may nonetheless be possible to incorporate a concern for such holistic features into a contractualist conception. One might claim that a disadvantaged social position is much harder to bear when one knows all along that, because one is a child of working-class parents or female or black, one has a lesser chance of rising above the lowest socioeconomic position. When working-class children know from the start that they will never be able to attend university, or when women and blacks know that they will never reach a managerial position, they feel relegated to the status of second-class citizen and gravely damaged in their sense of self-worth.

I doubt that this line of thought can resolve the tension, because it would seem to hold for natural factors as well. Would not one's sense of self-worth be gravely damaged if one realized all along that one's limited natural talents give one no chance at being admitted to higher education (because admitting the less talented would reduce the lowest index position)? In fact, is not one's self-respect damaged more when one is excluded from higher education on account of one's lack of intelligence than when one is excluded on account of one's race or gender or the poverty of one's family? If the damaging awareness by the untalented of their lesser chances can be sufficiently taken into account through the difference principle (the residual bases of self-respect), then why cannot the damaging awareness by blacks, women, and working-class children of their lesser chances be taken into account in the same way? Unless exclusion based on *social* factors can be shown to be substantially more damaging to individuals than exclusion based on natural factors, then the special injustice we see in restrictions of opportunity based on social factors cannot be reaffirmed within a contractualist framework.

This problem need not be a flaw in the contractualist approach. It might also be a flaw in our intuitive sense of justice. This shared sense of justice is surely shaped in large part by the more intelligent and better educated citizens, who sympathize more readily with intelligent persons who are excluded from higher education by their poverty, gender, or skin color than they do with individuals who, despite high motivation, are excluded by their lack of native intelligence and other natural talents. A less biased sense of justice might demand that access to education should depend on motivation alone, so that everyone willing to work hard could achieve optimal educational opportunities. This broader demand of fair equality of opportunity could be justified in contractualist terms, if one postulated a further primary good, *opportunities*, with lexical priority over the index goods and then defined opportunities (in contrast to Rawls's original approach) in *relative* terms. This broader demand would mandate that equally motivated citizens, regardless of their talents, race, class, or gender, should to the same degree have access to support for acquiring the knowledge and skills available in their society. The education system would have to devote equivalent resources to untalented as to talented individuals (of equal motivation)—though the latter would still excel the former in respect to knowledge and skills acquired.

I conclude that the parties in the original position would not agree to Rawls's fair equality of opportunity as a constraint upon the difference principle. If they are assumed to believe that inferior opportunities are especially damaging to individuals' sense of self-worth, they might agree on a broader constraint that would extend the demand of fair equality of opportunity from social factors (which Rawls includes) to natural factors as well. With more plausible assumptions about the actual social bases of self-respect, the parties would probably

THE SECOND PRINCIPLE OF JUSTICE

do away with fair equality of opportunity altogether and agree to take account of any damage inferior opportunities might do to individuals' sense of self-worth under the heading of "residual bases of self-respect" within the difference principle.

6.6 A Property-Owning Democracy

In *JFR* (136), Rawls distinguishes five types of regime or social order: laissez-faire capitalism, welfare-state capitalism, state socialism with a centrally controlled economy, property-owning democracy, and liberal (or democratic) socialism. The first three types of regime cannot satisfy his criterion of justice. A laissez-faire capitalist basic structure (cf. the system of natural liberty, *TJ* 57, 62) is unjust because it secures neither the fulfillment of basic needs, nor the fair value of the basic political liberties, nor fair equality of opportunity, and furthermore violates the difference principle. The second and third of these injustices are also found, to a lesser degree, in capitalist welfare states as they exist in the United States and other affluent countries. State socialism with a one-party system violates the first principle, notably the political liberties and free choice of occupation. Only the remaining two types of regime are capable of satisfying Rawls's criterion.

Rawls concentrates here on a property-owning democracy (first described by the British economist James Edward Meade) and how it differs from a capitalist welfare state. Both types of regime provide for private ownership in the means of production. In a capitalist welfare state, however, economic power—and therefore also political power—is highly concentrated, so that a small elite dominates the political process. A property-owning democracy sustains a much broader distribution of wealth. To this end, a high and progressive inheritance tax—levied on the inheritor rather than (as is currently the case in the United States) on the decedent's estate—would be essential. Rawls also proposes replacing income taxes with expenditure taxes (*TJ* 246–47), like the "value added" taxes common in Europe. This reform would engender a tendency for wealth to concentrate in households with high savings rates—something Rawls seems willing to accept on the assumption that inheritance taxes effectively ensure that large family fortunes are not passed on across generations.

Another important difference consists in the fact that a capitalist welfare state tends to engender a permanent underclass of welfare recipients who, even if they receive adequate benefits, are excluded from any real role in their society's social and economic life. A property-owning democracy avoids this problem. Rather than alleviate the most severe poverty—after the fact, as it were—through public assistance, its design preempts the very emergence of an underclass in need of public subsidies. The aim is to enable all citizens to meet their own socioeconomic needs out of their own earned income. Here educational institutions play a crucial role. All citizens are to be educated in such a way that they can participate, fully and as equals, in the economic and social life of their society and are motivated to do so by their secure sense of being, and being seen and treated as, equal citizens. In such a society, there would be much less need for welfare payments, though they could hardly be wholly eliminated.

Rawls gives only a brief description of liberal socialism. The basic idea is that the members of production units, those who work together in a firm or farm, should govern this unit together democratically. The economy would then consist of such autonomous production units in competition with one another. In other respects, a liberal socialist regime would be similar to a property-owning democracy. It would feature a multiparty democratic political process and an education system designed to develop as many citizens as possible into full, equal, and self-supporting participants in the social and economic life of their society.

Seven

A RAWLSIAN SOCIETY

I N order to understand and appraise a conception of justice, we need a concrete picture of the kind of society that would implement this conception. But such a concrete picture alone is not enough, according to Rawls. For it could be that this concretely imagined society would simply not work, with actual people, in the real world. In this case, the conception of justice would need to be modified to the point where its implementation is realistic: where it envisions a society that could maintain itself long term (cf. *PL* 65–66). Pragmatic concerns are thus deeply embedded in Rawls's thinking. We have already seen how his public criterion of justice assesses alternative basic structure designs by the effects each would have on the distributional profile of social primary goods and how his thought experiment of the original position assesses alternative public criteria of justice by the effects each would have on citizens' fundamental interest fulfillment. Now we find that Rawls wants to make the acceptance of an entire conception of justice dependent upon the effects this conception *itself* would have: To be acceptable, a conception of justice must be able to contribute to its own realization and endurance by inspiring and sustaining citizens' willingness to organize their society in accordance with it.

This may seem shocking. We are familiar with the thought that moral judgments should take account of empirical circumstances and that it may sometimes—when disaster threatens—be permissible to do things that are normally strictly forbidden. In this thought, the permissible exception is, so to speak, built into morality as a permanent part of its content. This familiar thought is therefore entirely different from Rawls's view that morality itself may need to be revised in light of empirical conditions: If a society structured according to our conception of justice turns out to be unrealizable, then we are to revise this conception until we have one that envisions a realizable social order.

Rawls's view is not quite as dramatic as this last remark may make it seem. For he would certainly not have let such revisions go on without limit. He was open to the possibility that in our world, even with human beings as ideal social institutions might shape them, a just social order is unrealizable—even if we are willing to make reasonable revisions in our conception of justice so as to meet empirical realities partway. Were we to reach this conclusion, it would show that, in this important respect, ours is not a good world.

Moreover, Rawls is not prepared to revise his conception in the face of practical obstacles of all kinds. He is primarily concerned with internal obstacles, ones that interfere with a just society sustaining itself, *as* a just society, long term. For instance, should it emerge that Rawlsian societies tend to produce a powerful class of wealthy citizens who reject the difference principle and seek to undermine the prevailing order, one may have to revise this principle. No such revision is required by the fact that many affluent citizens in the United States today would reject the difference principle and would block the institutional reforms needed to satisfy it (*CP* 251–52). It is a more serious matter, as the next chapter discusses, that the difference principle has "little support in our public political culture at the present time" (*JFR* 133). Still, even in the face of this obstacle, one may hope that such support will grow over time—partly as a consequence of reflections on justice becoming more prominent in the public culture (*JFR* 121n42). Rawls offers, in general terms at least, an account of how the historical development toward a just society has proceeded and might realistically continue to proceed. So he does want to show that his conception of justice accommodates not only the permanent conditions of human nature and our planet but also the actual historical possibilities of (especially) the United States—though not its political balance of power and political mood in some particular period.

Let us examine in more detail how Rawls envisions a just society that is historically within our reach. This society is organized by his conception of justice. We can bring this society more sharply into view by exploring four independent features of Rawls's vision, which is that of a society *well-ordered* by a *political* conception of justice that, in its substantive content, is both *liberal* and *egalitarian*. The chapter returns, at the end, to the question of the realizability of justice.

7.1 A Well-Ordered Society

A conception of justice should be able to well-order a society. A society is *well-ordered* by such a conception if and only if the following three conditions are satisfied and publicly known to be satisfied (cf. *CP* 466, *PL* 35, 201–2):

> The conception's public criterion of justice is accepted, and known to be accepted, by all citizens.
> Citizens have good reason to believe, and it is in fact the case, that their society's basic structure satisfies this public criterion.
> Citizens have a normally effective sense of justice and thus are willing and able to follow their shared public criterion of justice and to comply with the institutional order it justifies.

These three conditions leave the substantive content of the conception of justice wide open, and Rawls in fact recognizes as well-ordered certain decent hierarchical societies whose conceptions of justice—or, as Rawls prefers, conceptions of decency—are neither liberal nor egalitarian nor democratic nor political (*LP* 4, 63). Let us examine the significance and presuppositions of the three conditions of well-orderedness and what these conditions contribute to a full understanding of Rawls's realistic utopia.

If citizens are to agree that their society's basic structure satisfies their shared public criterion of justice, then they must have a shared way of judging whether this is in fact the case. They need shared application guidelines that can help them determine when and how their criterion is relevant to their institutional design decisions. A well-ordered society is therefore one in which such guidelines exist and are publicly known to be accepted by its citizens. Such guidelines play an especially important role in the case of criteria of justice that (like utilitarian ones or Rawls's) pay much attention to the effects of social institutions. A shared criterion without shared guidelines of public inquiry and rules for assessing evidence would be, Rawls says, "to no effect" (*PL* 139). For this reason, the parties in the original position must include such application guidelines in their agreement (*PL* 62, 225).

These guidelines must enable citizens to answer together (hence in a transparent way) three questions about any design decision they face: Which empirical judgments need to be made in order for the criterion to be brought to bear on this decision? What data are relevant to making these empirical judgments, and how should such data be collected and evaluated? Once the needed empirical judgments are on hand, which solutions to the institutional design problem does the criterion permit or require? It may turn out, of course, that the public criterion of justice does not constrain some given design decision at all.

Even if the public criterion of justice is supplemented by clear and complete guidelines, its application to institutional design decisions will often be complex and difficult. Such application then requires that citizens have certain capacities. They must be able to collect and process data, to understand and analyze arguments, and to combine the considerations relevant to a given decision into one overall judgment. A criterion whose collective application presupposes capacities that most ordinary citizens cannot develop, even with the benefit of a strong and inclusive education system, is unsuitable as a public criterion. For this reason, Rawls deems utilitarian conceptions of justice—at least those featuring a public criterion that involves interpersonal comparisons of happiness—incapable of well-ordering a society.

Citizens must not merely be *able* to apply the public criterion in accordance with the guidelines; they must also be *willing* to apply it conscientiously. Such willingness cannot be taken for granted. Any conception of justice often requires design decisions that go against the interests of some individuals and groups, possibly against those of a majority. A *political* conception of justice, like Rawls's, moreover assumes that citizens have diverse comprehensive worldviews, which may generate strong moral or religious reasons for opposing political decisions that this conception permits or requires. A well-ordered society therefore presupposes certain *political virtues* that stabilize adherence to the shared political conception of justice in the face of countervailing citizen interests and values. Faced with political disagreement, citizens must be willing to deal fairly with one another, to argue on the basis of the merits, and to be responsive to others' arguments. They must show one another trust, respect, and tolerance and must be prepared to meet others partway. They must be committed to keeping their efforts toward eliminating perceived injustices within the accepted framework of the political process. In a society well-ordered by a political conception of justice, these virtues take on a specific character through their connection with the duty of civility.

The substance of this duty, in turn, is determined by the idea of *public reason*.

7.2 A Political Conception of Justice

Rawls postulates the *fact of pluralism*: In a free society, there can be no enduring agreement upon a comprehensive moral, religious, or philosophical worldview—such values will always be controversial. He explains this fact by appealing to various impediments, the *burdens of judgment*, that arise in connection with the justification and balancing of values. This explanation is meant to show that the fact of pluralism does not depend on the presence of irrationality or malice (*CP* 475–79, *PL* 54–58). Rawls speaks therefore of the fact of *reasonable* pluralism (section 2.3).

In order to accommodate this fact, Rawls envisions his ideal society as one that seeks agreement on a *political* conception of justice (*PL* 11–14). A conception of justice is political if and only if it has the following three features:

It limits itself to addressing the design of society's basic structure.
It is *freestanding*, that is, does not presuppose, hence can be presented as independent of, any comprehensive moral, religious, or philosophical worldview.
It is constructed around certain fundamental ideas available in the society's public political culture (to be discussed in chapter 8).

These three features, like the three conditions of well-orderedness, leave the substantive content of the conception of justice wide open. A wide variety of very different political conceptions of justice are conceivable—each with its own ideal of public reason and its own specification, based on this ideal, of the duty of civility.

If citizens who disagree deeply in their comprehensive worldviews can nonetheless agree on a political conception of justice, then fully legitimate government is possible. To attain such legitimacy, the exercise of political power must satisfy a principle of legitimacy, which Rawls formulates for the special case of liberal political conceptions of justice as follows: "political power is proper and hence justifiable only when it is exercised in accordance with a constitution the essentials of which all citizens may reasonably be expected to endorse in the light of principles and ideals acceptable to them as reasonable and rational" (*PL* 217). Like the application guidelines earlier discussed, this *liberal principle of legitimacy* is an integral part of the agreement Rawls proposes to the parties in the original position (*PL* 225).

Legitimacy presupposes that citizens exercising political power honor their *duty of civility* (*JFR* 92): At least with regard to political decisions that affect the design of the basic structure itself, they orient the exercise of their political power as citizens, in good conscience and to the best of their knowledge and ability, exclusively according to their shared public criterion as applied in light of the shared guidelines and empirical data accessible to all. This duty does not typically apply within specific organizations such as churches, universities, trade unions, and the like. But it applies in public spaces where citizens argue and vote, and also often deliberate and decide in one or another public role or office. The duty of civility requires citizens, in such public spaces, to forgo reliance on their own more comprehensive worldview or on empirical data whose validity depends on such a view (e.g., the "fact" that some particular decision would displease God or lead to the corruption of souls).

The duty of civility is specific to political, or perhaps more broadly to freestanding conceptions of justice. Respect for this duty is among the political virtues in societies organized by such a conception and part of the sense of justice its citizens must develop if their society is to be well-ordered by a political conception of justice.

When majorities honor their duty of civility and exercise their political power legitimately, then minorities can accept and honor decisions reached through a political process they regard as just, even when such decisions conflict with their deeply held moral, religious, or philosophical values. The duty of civility requires reciprocal self-restraint: to govern legitimately and to comply with legitimate government.

It may seem that the duty of civility places many citizens in a paradoxical situation—those citizens whose acceptance of a political conception of justice is motivated by a more comprehensive moral or religious worldview, which they are now asked to set aside in their political discourse. When such a person endorses a political conception and therefore seeks to fulfill her duty of civility, she is setting aside the very values that ground her endorsement of the shared political conception.

This apparent paradox can be used to clarify the duty of civility. Rawls is not hoping that citizens will, so to speak, forget their religion in certain contexts. His hope is, rather, that they will interpret their religious duties so that these permit—or even require—respect for citizens with deeply different views. Someone about to speak or act in a relevantly public context might then perhaps reason as follows: "I know which political outcome would be pleasing to God. But I cannot demonstrate this knowledge to my fellow citizens in a way that is accessible to them. Forcing the correct decision on them without being able to show them why it is correct—this would not be a service to God but would, on the contrary, negate their God-given freedom. Urging them to accept this truth without being able to show them its grounds would deny them the respect they are due as equally endowed with reason by our Creator. In public political discourse, I should therefore appeal to the values and facts all citizens can acknowledge together and should support whatever political decisions seem most reasonable on this basis. Some such political decision will go against religious truths. But, from the divine standpoint, this is a lesser evil than denying other citizens the respect due them as creatures endowed with reason and conscience."

This fictional reasoning is merely an example to illustrate how one can understand as fairly undemanding the duty of civility and the setting aside of comprehensive moral, religious, or philosophical worldviews it requires. This possibility makes Rawls's hope seem more realistic: We can envision that religious believers respect the duty of civility for the sake of their religion, not in spite of it. But is it realistic to hope that existing religions and other comprehensive worldviews will evolve as envisioned? One must admit that, in the United States today, the envisioned attitude is hardly widespread among religious believers. This should not be surprising, however, seeing that this attitude is not easily accessible to common sense but presupposes considerable philosophical reflection. Thus there is room for hope that, once its possibility is more widely appreciated, this attitude will become more widespread.

In the years preceding publication of *PL*, Mario Cuomo, then governor of the State of New York, contributed considerably to the public awareness of this possibility. As a devout Catholic, Cuomo accepts premises that lead to a strict moral condemnation of abortion and shares the conviction that abortion is wrong. He nonetheless believed that, in his role as governor, he should not allow his official conduct to be affected by this conviction, because the grounds on which he held it were inaccessible to many of his fellow citizens and therefore grounds they could reasonably reject as the basis of legislation binding upon them. Cuomo therefore politically opposed some laws and policies supported by his own worldview, because he felt himself bound by something like Rawls's duty of civility. Aware of

Cuomo's views (*CP* 607n83), Rawls writes that "it is vital to the idea of political liberalism that we may with perfect consistency hold that it would be unreasonable to use political power to enforce our own comprehensive view, which we must, of course, affirm as either reasonable or true" (*PL* 138). Here *political liberalism* refers to any political conception of justice that is also liberal in content.

This duty of civility can be only a moral duty, not a legal one. Its practical effect depends, therefore, on the extent to which it is internalized by citizens. Here the duty of civility should not be viewed as one reason for action competing on a par with many others, such as ethical and religious duties and personal interests. It should instead be regarded as a higher-order reason for completely disregarding some reasons in decisions about certain issues. We can illustrate this model with an example of someone who acts as trustee for an orphan child. She takes it to be her duty (first-order reason) to manage the child's property well. She may regard this duty as one that competes on a par with her other duties, values, and interests—for instance, her duty of charity, her value of supporting local businesses, or her interest in raising the worth of her own stock portfolio. In this case, her management of the child's property may be influenced by these other reasons. Alternatively, she may believe that she ought to manage the child's property without regard to her other duties, values, and interests (a second-order reason). She is likely to do this only if she attaches to her trusteeship the kind of significance that requires her to separate her duties in this role from her other first-order reasons for action. Many roles—such as those of legal counsel, doctor, and investment advisor, in contrast to those of manager or salesperson—are often viewed as having this sort of significance.

In the United States, the role of citizen is rarely so viewed. Voting on the basis of one's own economic interests or values, or for whatever reasons one likes, is seen as normal and unobjectionable. Even legislators are not above trading their votes in exchange for political support from colleagues or financial support for their reelection campaigns. Rawls, in contrast, compares the role of a citizen affecting decisions about the basic structure with that of a judge on the highest court, who must publicly justify decisions solely on the basis of publicly accessible constitutional principles (*PL* 219–20, 235–40). Were such a judge to take her or his own personal values or interests into account, she or he would be hypocritical—distorting a judge's official weighing of the publicly accessible reasons bearing on the case in order to replicate, in the published opinion, the decision that was actually influenced by personal values or interests.

In exercising public reason, citizens should ideally proceed in something like the way judges do, at least when important institutional questions are concerned ("something like" because the duty of civility varies in stringency and demandingness as it applies across judges, members of the legislative and executive branches, bureaucrats, and ordinary citizens). In the reasons they give one another, citizens, like judges, should appeal only to such facts and empirical regularities as are publicly recognized or supported by publicly recognized methods or experts. As regards values and norms, there is a substantial difference: Judges may appeal only to values and norms that—relying here also on legal precedents and the works of recognized legal scholars—can be shown to be contained in the laws or constitution. Citizens may appeal only to values and norms that can be shown to be contained in their political conception of justice. Rawls does not object to citizens' publicly presenting and endorsing their religious or other world-views—even in the context of decisions about important institutional questions. This may be useful for enabling other citizens to gauge the integrity and sincerity of their moral commitment to the shared political conception of justice (*JFR* 90). (The duty of civility is stricter for judges, who must not introduce their comprehensive worldviews in any way.) But even if citizens may, like Martin Luther King Jr., expound their religious beliefs in public spaces, they must then *justify* their political decisions on political grounds, that is, by recourse to the shared political conception of justice, the constitution, and possibly other generally accepted norms and values.

As contrasting with political conceptions of justice, Rawls discusses *comprehensive* conceptions of justice that presuppose, and are an integral part of, a deeper and broader moral, religious, or philosophical world-view. A Catholic conception of justice, for instance, is part of a comprehensive conception of the good which seeks to cover all moral questions and to assign all values their proper place (breadth) and which is derived from theological premises rooted in Holy Scripture and the teachings of the Church Fathers (depth). Utilitarian conceptions of justice are usually understood along the same lines: as local applications of a deeper and universally applicable insight into the nature of value (i.e., that happiness is the source of all value). Such a deeper justification cannot achieve predominant acceptance in a modern democratic society (the fact of reasonable pluralism), and those who reject it cannot find acceptable a conception of justice dependent on it, nor a society organized by such a conception of justice.

Rawls seeks to offer a conception of justice that all members of a pluralistic society can accept. He wants this conception not to depend on some deeper justification but rather to be *freestanding* (*CP* 482, *PL* 10). This does not exclude deeper foundations. In fact, they are invited. Rawls's conception, with its internal and relatively superficial justification, is compatible with diverse deeper foundations. It is compatible, for instance, with the utilitarian rationale that a society well-ordered by Rawls's conception would tend, as far as one can tell, to produce a lot of happiness—more happiness, anyway, than if it employed a utilitarian public criterion of justice. Although these deeper foundations may well be mutually incompatible, their proponents can nonetheless jointly acknowledge *justice as fairness* and live together in a Rawlsian society on the basis of shared moral principles reflecting an overlapping consensus.

7.3   Political versus Comprehensive Liberalisms

It is surprising that Rawls, in his pursuit of a political conception of justice, is keen to distance himself from all major variants of liberalism—those of Kant, John Stuart Mill, Ronald Dworkin, and Joseph Raz, for example. After all, these other liberalisms also seek social institutions that are morally acceptable to adherents of diverse comprehensive worldviews and could allow them to live together in mutual tolerance. For Rawls, these liberalisms are nonetheless too *deep* (and too *broad*). Being themselves comprehensive, they needlessly conflict with certain comprehensive doctrines that Rawls wants his conception to accommodate. They therefore allow too little space for the great variety of diverse worldviews that, as experience shows, tend to flourish in a free modern society. Dworkin, for instance, imagines a society whose members want to realize sophisticated ambitions that fully exercise their natural capacities. This model allows space for a great variety of such ambitions but presupposes that a valuable life must be one dedicated to such sophisticated ambitions. More relaxed ways of life are permitted in such a liberal society but are regarded as inferior. In Rawls's view, this unnecessarily limits the acceptability of Dworkin's conception and moreover imports an ethical value that has no place in a political conception of justice (*PL* 211n42).

Seeking to avoid any appeal to such controversial values, Rawls offers only political grounds for accepting the three fundamental interests central to *justice as fairness*: Citizens can be fairly confident of the survival of their particular comprehensive doctrine, and can thus confidently abide by the rules of the political process, if they know that their fellow citizens have an effective sense of justice, as well as the interest in preserving a wide variety of competing comprehensive worldviews. Rawls need not characterize these two interests as themselves ethically valuable, but can instead justify them politically, by appeal to their essential role in maintaining widespread moral allegiance to a shared conception of justice on the part of citizens who differ deeply in their moral, religious, and philosophical worldviews.

Rawls also accuses older liberalisms of relying on an ethical ideal of the good life—in Mill's case the value of individuality (to the point of eccentricity), in Kant's case the value of autonomous thought and action (*PL* 78, 98–99). (It is undeniable that Kant held such an ideal, but it is far from obvious that he meant this ideal to play any role in his political thought as developed in his *Rechtslehre*, the first, political part of his *Metaphysics of Morals*). Rawls also criticizes those other liberalisms (*PL* xxvi–xxvii) for assertions like the following three: (1) The question of how one should live can be answered not only by a few individuals, such as clerics, but rather by any reasonable person who conscientiously considers it. (2) Moral values have no external, for example, divine source but arise instead out of human nature and the requirements of living together in society. (3) Human nature is such that we can comply with our duties even without divine or governmental threats or inducements. As a political conception, *justice as fairness* remains uncommitted with regard to these and similar assertions and is thus compatible with comprehensive doctrines that deny them.

But Rawls is committed to these three assertions within the political sphere. He dismisses as unjust, for instance, theocratic social orders under which all questions of value are to be decided by religious leaders, and he dismisses as unreasonable any view that demands such a social order (*CP* 483). He does not thereby embrace assertion 1. Rather, he merely affirms that citizens should be left free to reach their own judgment about the truth or falsity of this assertion and should therefore neither be coerced to follow the guidance of religious leaders nor be prevented from doing so. Even those who hold assertion 1 to be false can accept this sort of liberty. They could think, perhaps: "Indeed, religious leaders are the only ones who can reliably answer ethical questions. But we cannot demonstrate this fact to many of our reasonable fellow citizens. It is better to seek peacefully to convert such citizens than to try to force them to accept this fact. We can therefore accept a conception of justice and correlated basic structure under which conversion is permitted but coercion is not."

A political conception of justice should thus be able to surpass other liberalisms—to require even less depth and breadth or, as Rawls says, to push even further the *method of avoidance* of potentially controversial presuppositions and implications. This should make possible a society in which an even greater variety of competing comprehensive doctrines can coexist on equal terms, thanks to their joint acceptance of a political conception of justice whose presuppositions are compatible with each of these doctrines. Rawls regards the capacity to facilitate the equal coexistence of a large variety of reasonable worldviews as an important virtue in a conception of justice.

A comprehensive doctrine is *reasonable* if it meets the demands of theoretical and practical reason—is at least coherent and intelligible—and stands in a tradition that, if it develops at all, does so in a comprehensible and internally plausible manner (*PL* 59). Rawls seems to believe in the possibility of a society in which no reasonable view is suppressed: "It is unreasonable for us to use political power, should we possess it, or share it with others, to repress comprehensive views that are not unreasonable" (*PL* 61). This should not, however, be taken to mean that every reasonable view would endure in such a society (by gaining sufficient numbers of new adherents). A social order influences the values and interests of its members, with the result that many reasonable ways of life would not survive. This is not repression, however, but a universal sociological fact obtaining in every conceivable social order (*PL* 195–200). So long as a great variety of reasonable ways of life *can* endure in a free social order, the demise of some is not a valid basis for criticizing it.

One may have to qualify Rawls's claim that no reasonable comprehensive doctrine would need to be repressed. First of all, this claim can include only worldviews that can support the going political conception of justice, which facilitates and organizes the equal coexistence of many such comprehensive worldviews. Rawls may hope, of course, that comprehensive doctrines will evolve to become supportive in this way of *justice as fairness*. But this evolution may take much time in some cases and may never happen in others. Any political conception of justice would therefore have to authorize the repression of comprehensive doctrines that refuse to tolerate other such doctrines. If liberal, it would also have to repress comprehensive doctrines that deny their adherents the right to exit as well as doctrines that reject formal equality of opportunity (demanding racial segregation in the workplace, for example, or enjoining its adherents to found, join, and patronize only "pure" firms whose employees, suppliers, and customers are all white). Recognizing that such doctrines can be reasonable in the thin sense first defined (*PL* 59), Rawls narrows this sense to exclude them as unreasonable (*PL* 64, *LP* 177). He took his conception to permit, I believe, that doctrines of these kinds may be repressed.

More difficult is the question of whether a legislative majority should be entitled to outlaw the practice of reasonable doctrines that offend the interests or values of the majority. Rawls's negative answer to this question seems obvious in the abstract but can lead to shocking surprises. Followers of some doctrines would merely cause noisy disturbances at night or annoy travelers with religious begging chants. But other doctrines may involve the practice of polygamy, pederasty, incest, necrophilia, sex with animals, eating of the dead, or even human sacrifices—without thereby failing to be reasonable in Rawls's sense. The adherents of such doctrines may be willing to tolerate all other reasonable worldviews and willing also to practice their own on a strictly voluntary basis (so that sex with a minor requires the consent of the child and her parents, for instance, and human sacrifices the consent of the person to be killed). The question is then whether citizens may be legally prevented from living in accordance with such doctrines. Rawls's answer would surely have been in the affirmative: The practice of such doctrines, though presumably not their advocacy, may be outlawed by the majority. But can each of the doctrines listed be shown to be unreasonable in Rawls's sense (cp. *LP* 173)? If not, then Rawls must either admit the reasonable ones or else make the weakened claim that his *political* liberalism would offer *more* space for the equal coexistence of a *larger* variety of reasonable doctrines than other, more comprehensive liberal conceptions of justice would.

Still, the distinction between his and traditional liberal conceptions is not simply a matter of degree—that Rawls's conception makes fewer presuppositions and offers more space. It also has to do with the basis of the presuppositions made. Rawls wants to justify his presuppositions in as purely political a way as possible: from the purpose of a conception of justice (to sustain a stable social order in which citizens can successfully fulfill their interests) and from certain generally accepted normative ideas that he believes to be present in the political culture of his society. He sees this as the only way of ensuring that, from the standpoint of the shared conception of justice, all permissible comprehensive worldviews have, and are recognized as having, genuinely equal status.

7.4 An Egalitarian Liberal Conception of Justice

While stressing how his political liberalism is different from other, (more) comprehensive liberalisms, Rawls also emphasizes the commonalities in substantive content that the word "liberal" suggests. He defines a *liberal* conception of justice in terms of three features (*PL* 6, 223):

> It specifies certain basic rights, liberties, and opportunities familiar from constitutional democracies.
> It assigns a special priority to these basic rights, liberties, and opportunities being secured for all.
> It demands measures assuring all citizens of sufficient all-purpose means to make effective use of their basic rights, liberties, and opportunities.

These defining features of liberalism are compatible with a range of liberal conceptions of justice. Rawls identifies his own conception as distinctive among these in virtue of being the most egalitarian (*LP* 14). He supports this claim by listing three important elements that render *justice as fairness* egalitarian in ways other liberalisms are not: its fair value requirement for the political liberties, its demand of fair equality of opportunity, and its difference principle (*PL* 6–7). Here one might add—but perhaps all good things must come in threes—that Rawls's conception contains a fourth distinctively egalitarian element: the highest-priority requirement that basic needs be met.

Understanding his conception of justice as a political one, Rawls envisions that citizens honor their duty of civility when they apply this conception. In debates about features of their society's basic structure that engage their shared public criterion of justice, citizens rely solely on this criterion with its associated application guidelines and the empirical evidence these guidelines single out as relevant. For the special case of liberal political conceptions (of which Rawls sees his own as the sole extant instance), Rawls seeks to define two classes of such features: *constitutional essentials* and *matters of basic justice*. Constitutional essentials, but not matters of basic justice, are to be codified in law—possibly prioritized, and even entrenched, through a written constitution—and thus justiciable in the courts.

Rawls offers four separate considerations on the basis of which features of the basic structure are to be sorted into constitutional essentials and matters of basic justice (*PL* 230, *JFR* 49): (a) Features of the political-order part of the basic structure should be classified as constitutional essentials, and features of the socioeconomic order as matters of basic justice; (b) features that are more urgent to settle should be classified as constitutional essentials, the others as matters of basic justice; (c) features of which it is easier to tell whether or not they are realized should be classified as constitutional essentials, the others as matters of basic justice; and (d) features that it is easier to achieve agreement on should be classified as constitutional essentials, the others as matters of basic justice. These considerations obviously do not all support exactly the same division, but, taken together, they are supposed to provide sufficient support for the division Rawls arrives at in regard to his own public criterion of justice.

Rawls holds that features of the basic structure qualifying as constitutional essentials are of two kinds (*PL* 227). Constitutional essentials of the first kind fix the general structure of government and the political process: relations among legislative, executive, and judicial organs, further territorial and functional divisions of governmental powers, processes for filling governmental positions. Constitutional essentials of the second kind fix the basic rights and liberties of citizens as constraints on government and the political process. In a society well-ordered by *justice as fairness*, the constitutional essentials of the second kind would define, in terms of individual legal rights, a particular specification of the following *three requirements* of Rawls's public criterion of justice: the requirement that basic needs be met, the first principle, and formal equality of opportunity. The remaining *two demands* of Rawls's public criterion—fair equality of opportunity and the difference principle—do not give rise to corresponding constitutional essentials of the second kind (*PL* 228–29; the expressions "three requirements" and "two demands" are my shorthand).

The first principle requires a scheme of equal basic liberties that is fully adequate in three dimensions: *extent, security,* and, specifically for the basic political liberties, (fair) *value*. One may wonder whether Rawls meant the latter two dimensions to be reflected in constitutional essentials of the second kind. He seems to leave them out when stressing how straightforward it is to specify the basic rights and liberties required by the first principle into constitutional essentials (*PL* 228). But on the whole, his writings seem to me to support the opposite answer—most plainly his chastisement of *Buckley v. Valeo*, which refers to the fair value of the political liberties as a constitutional requirement (*PL* 362; cf. *JFR* 48). So I read Rawls as envisioning the constitutional essentials of the second kind to be individual legal rights that guarantee full adequacy also in the security dimension and (for rights guaranteeing basic political liberties) in the fair-value dimension.

To be sure: no legal text can ensure that the rights it formulates are actually fully adequate in the latter two dimensions. That depends on the actual quality of the police and the court system, on the conduct of ordinary citizens, and much else. But a legal text can make security and fair value justiciable. This is what I think Rawls envisions: a constitution that not merely permits but also commands all branches of government to ensure, for all citizen groups, the security of the constitutionally guaranteed basic liberties and the fair value of the constitutionally guaranteed basic political liberties. In addition, the envisioned constitution also commands all branches of government to ensure that citizens' basic needs be met. These three commands are embedded in citizens' constitutional rights and enforceable by them through the court system.

Do the four considerations Rawls provides support this way of separating constitutional essentials from matters of basic justice? All three commands are clearly supported by the consideration of urgency (b), which stands out as both clear and compelling. Citizens' fundamental interests are gravely threatened when they cannot meet their basic needs, are insecure in their guaranteed basic liberties, or marginalized in the political process. A constitutional essential that citizens must be able to meet their basic needs goes against consideration (a), but this may not count for much because this consideration does not seem relevant (and Rawls does not explain why it should be) to separating constitutional essentials and matters of basic justice. The application of consideration (c) is more difficult because there are many different ways of formulating the required constitutional text. The question is then whether there is at least one way of incorporating the three commands into the constitution so that courts can reliably judge whether they are implemented or not. If this can be done, then consideration (d) is likely to support the constitutionalization of the three commands as well. Here a constitutional command to ensure the fair value of the constitutionally guaranteed basic political liberties is the most problematic: It would be not only highly controversial in the United States today but also presumably unwelcome to some degree in any imaginable society by citizens whose natural endowments and socioeconomic position would otherwise afford them greatly superior political influence.

Let us turn next to the two demands of fair equality of opportunity and the difference principle of which Rawls writes that they, unlike the three requirements, are not constitutional essentials (*PL* 228–29). This way of putting the contrast may be misleading. It would indeed be a bad idea to enshrine fair equality of opportunity and the difference principle in the constitution (*PL* 337)—most obviously because the courts could not transparently and reliably apply these principles (consideration (c)). But the same is true, for the same reason, of the first principle of justice, and Rawls does not want its text to be copied into the constitution either. Instead, he envisions clear and applicable constitutional articles that detail one particular fully adequate scheme of equal basic rights and liberties as required by his first principle. The parallel question is then whether one could formulate clear and applicable constitutional articles that would help realize fair equality of opportunity and the difference principle. This seems entirely possible along lines Rawls has himself suggested (cf. *TJ* 245–48): The constitution might provide, for instance, that there is to be a branch of government that—much like the central banks of many countries today—does not report to the executive and is charged with making revenue-neutral adjustments to the tax system with the sole end of realizing the two demands and the fair value of the basic political liberties. Except in gross cases, the courts would not be competent to assess whether this *distribution branch* is operating successfully. But they would be competent to judge in a transparent and reliable way whether the branch is properly set up and kept free of political interference.

The example shows how the two demands, like the three requirements, are relevant to settling constitutional essentials of the first kind. The key difference is then that, unlike the three requirements, the two demands do not give rise to corresponding constitutional essentials of the second kind: to individual constitutional rights. Nonetheless, the two demands may still affect how constitutional essentials of the second kind are settled. With regard to the first principle of justice, Rawls writes that "the basic rights and liberties ... can be specified in but one way, modulo relatively small variations" (*PL* 228). This is true perhaps of the specification of a scheme of equal basic liberties that is fully adequate in *extent*. But Rawls envisions that the constitution specifies this scheme in two further dimensions as well: The constitution must guarantee that all basic liberties it guarantees are fully adequate in *security* and that all basic political liberties it guarantees are fully adequate in their (fair) *value*. In regard to these latter two dimensions, the two demands may well be relevant to specifying the first-principle requirement of *some* fully adequate scheme of equal basic liberties into the particular such scheme laid down in the constitution.

To illustrate. Citizens with greater talents and higher social status will inevitably be able to exert more influence within the political process. Insofar as they are tempted to abuse this influence to benefit themselves, they are best able to do so by furthering interests they as a social class have in common. The shared private interests of those with greater talents and higher social status threaten to subvert especially the egalitarian elements of a conception of justice. Being highly egalitarian, *justice as fairness* is highly vulnerable to this danger. Its egalitarian requirements regarding basic needs and the fair value of the basic political liberties can be made fairly safe through clear individual legal rights that count as constitutional essentials. But its egalitarian demands regarding fair equality of opportunity and the difference principle could be highly vulnerable to subversion through political decisions properly arrived at. This danger can be reduced through an appropriate design of the general structure of government and the political process. And it can be further reduced through a fitting specification of the individual constitutional rights protecting the fair value of the basic political liberties: The constitutional protection of this fair value should be specified with an eye to ensuring that the whole output of the democratic political process will be as supportive as reasonably possible of fair equality of opportunity and the difference principle.

If the two demands are relevant to settling the constitutional essentials, there may be a danger of "frequent controversy over the structure of government" (*PL* 228) and other fundamental features of the basic structure—for example: over how to structure the system of government in terms of functional and territorial (e.g., federalist) divisions of power; over whether its legislative seats are filled through a first-past-the-post system or through proportional representation; over whether there should be a written constitution and, if so, whether some or all of its provisions should be entrenched in one of various ways (*PL* 234–35); over property-owning democracy versus liberal socialism; and over the precise legal formulation of basic individual rights.

Rawls wisely suggests that efforts to keep the difference principle satisfied should confine themselves to a few policy instruments, such as the amount of income or consumption exempt from taxation (*JFR* 161–62). It would be impossibly complex and divisive, hence counterproductive, to bring the difference principle to bear on every institutional design decision that might affect relative index positions.

But the way some constitutional essentials are settled has such a profound effect on how well the difference principle is likely to be satisfied that it is implausible to exclude the difference principle from its (subordinate) role in settling these constitutional essentials.

The best way to balance these two countervailing concerns may be to give substantial weight to constitutional essentials already in place. Such fundamental features of the basic structure should be revised only if there is a substantial preponderance of reasons in favor of revision. A substantial preponderance is much easier to achieve in regard to constitutional violations of the three requirements, of which it is generally relatively obvious whether they are fulfilled or, if not, what is lacking. A substantial preponderance is harder to achieve in regard to the two demands, where arguments must rely on empirically grounded speculations about how feasible revisions of the constitution would tend to affect the distribution of opportunities and the distributional profile of index positions.

To be sure, the demand for substantial preponderance cannot be a legally enforceable one. With enough clout in the political process, a political party can make any constitutional revisions it likes. The demand would thus be a moral one, understood to be part of the liberal principle of legitimacy: Those in power are to refrain from revising constitutional essentials unless they can connect the revision to the shared public criterion in a convincing way. Only if they can show this connection is their revision a legitimate exercise of political power. Other groups, whose political influence may be diminished by the revision, should be able to appreciate its moral importance and should be able to have well-grounded confidence that it is not merely a ploy to enhance the political influence of those in power.

7.5 A Society Well-Ordered by Rawls's Conception

To be able to well-order a society, a political conception of justice, with its application guidelines and the empirical evidence these guidelines draw in, should be *complete*, that is, should suffice transparently to support definite answers to all or nearly all questions regarding the design of the basic structure (*PL* 225). Definite answers need not be unique answers. It may turn out that presidential and cabinet government are both fully acceptable choices for a society's structure of government. That is a definite answer, though it leaves the choice to the political process unconstrained. And definite answers could also take the form that there is no substantial preponderance of reasons in favor of institutional revision. An existing settlement need not be derivable from Rawls's criterion; it suffices that there is no alternative that would do better in terms of justice and legitimacy.

Appeals to the two demands involve empirically grounded speculations that may be complex and contestable. The completeness of *justice as fairness* is not that of an algorithm. In the end, some judgment is required, and some disagreement among reasonable people is to be expected. Still, the public criterion, application guidelines, and empirical evidence should suffice to guide the decision, to assemble and order the considerations relevant to it, and to make clear what needs to be argued on one side and the other to win out.

Even with these cautions attached to the notion of completeness, Rawls may be too easily convinced that *justice as fairness* is complete. This is most evident perhaps in regard to the first principle of justice, where the special difficulties facing implementation of the two demands do not apply. How are we to judge whether present democracies satisfy the first principle and, if not, how they fall short? To provide definite answers, Rawls's conception must allow us to judge not merely whether the rights and liberties legally guaranteed in some society are fully adequate in extent but also whether they are sufficiently secure, and whether the guaranteed political rights have their fair value, for every relevant group of citizens.

If Rawls indeed meant to classify such security and fair value as constitutional essentials (section 7.4), then it is easy to judge that most existing democracies fail to satisfy the first principle by giving insufficient legal protection to these two dimensions of the basic liberties. Yet, to know how to remedy this defect, some guidance is needed from the first principle with regard to these two dimensions of a fully adequate scheme of equal basic liberties. Take the security of physical integrity, for example: How is one to judge whether this component of the first principle is realized by some given society? What kinds of physical harms are relevant—beatings and torture by the police, certainly, but what about victimization by violent crimes, traffic and work accidents, avoidable illnesses, and premature deaths (high infant mortality)? How is an adequate level of security defined (cf. section 5.1)—presumably the statistical risk of physical harm must be below a certain level, but how high is this level to be set? Is the statistical risk of physical harm calculated on the basis of aggregate data only or on the basis of disaggregated data as well and, if the latter, which kinds of disaggregations (by gender, skin color, locale, income level, etc.) are relevant, and how fine-grained do they need to be (e.g., are the relevant locales states, counties, or neighborhoods)?

The great importance of these questions is evident from experience: Many women are battered by their husbands, boyfriends, fathers, and brothers with impunity, even while they have a legal right not to be so abused. Poor people are at the mercy of criminals in their impoverished and poorly policed neighborhoods. Prisoners and suspects are beaten and raped in understaffed jails. People with serious medical problems are turned away from hospital emergency rooms because they have no way of covering the cost of treatment. These are real and serious threats to the physical integrity of citizens, and it would be important to know what Rawls's first principle requires in regard to them. Without a hint as to what security means here, citizens cannot assure themselves and one another in a public, transparent way that their society's basic structure satisfies Rawls's first principle. In this regard, Rawls's proposed public criterion does not fill the role for which it was intended.

Things look better with regard to the fair value of the legally guaranteed political rights. Here Rawls says clearly and forcefully that the United States falls short (section 5.3). And he provides some guidance by requiring that "citizens similarly gifted and motivated have roughly an equal chance of influencing the government's policy and of attaining positions of authority irrespective of their economic and social class" (*JFR* 46). Still, this guidance is hard to apply: The formulations "similarly gifted and motivated," "roughly an equal chance," and "economic and social class" leave much room for interpretation. And it remains unclear whether only the chance of success must be roughly equal or also the influence exerted and position attained if one succeeds. These questions, too, are important because citizens with greater talents and higher social status tend, and are often believed, to favor an interpretation of the first principle that enfeebles its fair-value requirement. If this requirement is not clear and specific, and much is thus left to the discretion of the political process, then, in this regard as well, citizens cannot publicly ascertain in a transparent way that their society's basic structure satisfies the first principle of justice.

Despite these gaps, it may be premature to conclude that *justice as fairness* is incomplete. For this conception features not merely a public criterion, its application guidelines with the empirical evidence these guidelines draw in, and the ideal of public reason Rawls has sketched. It also features the justificatory thought experiment of the original position, which, providing a unified rationale for the preceding features, is supposed to inform citizens' efforts to interpret their public criterion and to apply it to novel conditions as may be triggered by environmental, technological, or cultural changes (section 2.3). The original position could conceivably also be invoked to adjudicate among alternative ways of filling the gaps just discussed. The question would then be which specification of Rawls's public criterion the parties in the original position would find it most rational to agree on.

The answer to this question depends to some extent on what general empirical facts and regularities the parties are given to work with. These empirical facts and regularities determine, for example, how difficult and how costly it would be to achieve one or another specific security threshold for constitutional rights guaranteeing this or that basic liberty or to safeguard the fair value, on one or another specification thereof, of constitutional rights guaranteeing the basic political liberties. These general facts and regularities should always correspond to the state of the social and natural sciences in the society in question—they may be modified when necessary to reflect progress in these sciences (so long as such innovations are essentially uncontroversial among experts and independent of any particular comprehensive doctrine).

In addition, Rawls's readers and citizens in the well-ordered society he envisions could further draw on the arguments that justify the hypothetical-contract model and Rawls's specification of it (the original position). All these arguments should be understood and accepted by all citizens, or at least understandable and acceptable to all (to allow for some citizens not wanting to take their philosophical reflections quite this far—*PL* 67). This intellectual background ought to be a universally recognized part of the public culture, available to help overcome difficulties of interpretation and application. And this intellectual background is part of what citizens of Rawls's well-ordered society feel morally bound by in their sincere efforts to design, maintain, and adjust the basic structure of their society in accordance with *justice as fairness* to the best of their abilities.

7.6 A More Realistic Vision

Having explored in some detail Rawls's idea of a society well-ordered by *justice as fairness*, we are assailed by the question: How is this supposed to be realistic? Rawls seems to have worried about this himself. He refers to this idea as "highly idealized" (*PL* 35) and to the society it envisions as "the limit of the practical best" (*CP* 466). Because it is doubtful that this limit can be reached, we must ask: Which elements of this ideal are really indispensable, and which might be relaxed if necessary?

One concession is already built into the very notion of a well-ordered society: It is sufficient that citizens should have a *normally* effective sense of justice. Sometimes a citizen's competing motives, arising from personal interests or values, will simply be too strong or too overwhelmingly immediate. We must therefore realistically expect that, even in the best possible society, some citizens will occasionally violate the law. This fact calls for an institutionalized penal system but, with such a system in place, poses no genuine danger to the survival of a just society. We must also realistically expect some violations of the ideal of public reason. Thus, some citizens may, on the basis of their comprehensive worldview, press for a broad legal ban on abortions, which, Rawls believes, is clearly ruled out by the political values implicit in *justice as fairness* (*PL* 243n32). So long as such objectors are not numerous enough to prevail politically at important junctures, they would also pose no genuine threat to the justice, legitimacy, and stability of the social order.

Rawls's ideal must be weakened somewhat more. It is unrealistic to expect that literally *all* citizens will have a normally effective sense of justice. There will always be egoists and sociopaths—people who pay no more than lip service to a conception of justice or else have no such conception at all. Such people are likely to be relatively rare in a Rawlsian society, and their conduct, too, could be adequately controlled through penal sanctions.

The most serious question about Rawls's ideal is whether we can realistically hope for a society whose citizens endorse only *one* conception of justice. Why should reasonable pluralism, which Rawls views as an ineliminable characteristic of free societies, neatly exempt the political values essential to the construction of a social order? There are various points Rawls might make in defense of his hope for an overlapping consensus converging on *justice as fairness*. He can say that many competing conceptions of justice are vulnerable to serious philosophical or pragmatic objections. He can add that many competing conceptions are not genuinely incompatible with his own; utilitarians, for instance, might come to see that their own principle is unsuitable as a public criterion of justice and might then accept Rawls's conception as the one best suited for producing happiness (cf. *PL* 170).

And he can claim that general acceptance of his conception, if it could once be achieved, would perpetuate itself without repression.

There are traces of these thoughts in his writings, but they did not in the end satisfy Rawls. There will always be worldviews whose adherents refuse to accept one or another of the basic rights and liberties while pressing for their abolition (*PL* 65). Furthermore, "it is inevitable and often desirable that citizens have different views as to the most appropriate political conception; for the public political culture is bound to contain different fundamental ideas that can be developed in different ways. An orderly contest between them over time is a reliable way to find which one, if any, is most reasonable" (*PL* 227). This passage suggests that it would not be an unmitigated loss if a society well-ordered by *justice as fairness* turned out not to be fully achievable.

In the same context, Rawls envisions a society of another sort, which he deems more realistic. This is a society whose members share an ideal of the public use reason but one that is not tied to one particular shared conception of justice. Citizens of this society would, conscientiously and to the best of their ability, each adopt some political conception of justice (which may be revised on due reflection) and would then be guided solely by this conception in all political decisions about the social order (*PL* 226–27, 241). Even if citizens are guided by diverse political conceptions of justice, they may still be able to resolve their differences about institutional design through civil discussion. Still, such discussion would go well beyond questions of how one shared conception of justice should be applied to given political decision problems.

The citizens of such a society would embrace the same political virtues and the same duty of civility. But the substance of this duty is relativized. It would require that citizens, in public deliberations about the design of the basic structure, set aside their personal interests and values in favor not of *one* (Rawls's) but in favor of *their own* respective conceptions of justice. This duty would require, in addition, that citizens understand their conceptions of justice as *political* ones: ones that can be developed and supported on the basis of values available in the public political culture, without appeal to controversial comprehensive doctrines.

Rawls understands, of course, that citizens, civility notwithstanding, will tend to select, from those political conceptions of justice supportable in their culture, one that closely matches their own personal values or can be expected to promote their personal values or interests. People with similar economic interests and similar conceptions of the good will also tend to have similar conceptions of justice (*PL* 164).

Rawls hopes that in such a society only a few liberal political conceptions of justice would endure. These conceptions would largely coincide in their implications for the constitutional essentials, and their political rivalry would thereby be much mitigated. (There would be no need to fear that the proponents of some conceptions of justice would use their political clout to entrench themselves by revising the electoral system or basic political or other rights.) And a society of this kind would thus come close to the ideal of a society well-ordered by *justice as fairness*.

And yet, one of Rawls's constitutional essentials might be controversial in such a society: According to some liberal conceptions of justice, a just social order need not ensure the fair value of the basic political liberties for all citizens. Moreover, because different liberal conceptions of justice would provide different justifications for the remaining constitutional essentials, there is also the possibility of conflict over how these constitutional provisions are to be interpreted in difficult cases and applied, and possibly adjusted, when circumstances and conditions change. Finally, such a society would probably engender conflicts over matters of basic justice. Rawls came to doubt that general agreement on fair equality of opportunity and the difference principle would ever be reached.

Perhaps one can say that Rawls came to see a society well-ordered by his conception of justice as the possibly unattainable end point of a progressive historical process of broadening and deepening an existing constitutional consensus. Broadening this consensus involves achieving agreement on ever more constitutional essentials and matters of basic justice. Deepening it involves achieving ever more agreement on the principles and ideals, empirical facts, and assumptions on which the general acceptance of an institutional order is to be based. Such broadening and deepening is limited, of course, by the concept of a *political* conception of justice: No attempt should be made to broaden the consensus beyond the design of the basic structure or to deepen it through incorporating ultimate philosophical or religious foundations tied to some particular comprehensive doctrine.

Even if no conception of justice can achieve its ideal—a society well-ordered by this conception—such ideals are nonetheless an important part of these conceptions. An ideal of this kind allows us concretely to examine whether we can really accept the conception of justice that gives rise to it. And such an ideal also gives concrete direction to our striving toward a more just world. So long as we are convinced that a stable society in the vicinity of the ideal can be achieved, working toward its realization is (in a sufficiently strong sense) realistic.

Eight

ON JUSTIFICATION

W<small>E</small> have explored five elements of *justice as fairness*. We began with its public criterion of justice (the two principles with the two priority rules), the guidelines for the application of this criterion, and the political virtues (the ideal of public reason and the duty of civility). These three elements led us to the fourth, namely, the ideal of a society well-ordered by Rawls's conception, which ideal might be further specified through additional information about a society's specific conditions (e.g., its natural environment, culture, and level of technological and economic development). These four elements are supposed to guide the political conduct of citizens—not only of the hypothetical citizens of the ideal society but also of the actual citizens here and now. For this, a fifth element is also required: the justificatory device of the original position, which citizens can draw on in two ways: This thought experiment helps citizens understand how to apply the first four elements to new institutional design problems. And it may sometimes also guide them in adjusting these four elements in light of new empirical knowledge and insights, typically incorporated into the thought experiment by modifying the information the parties are presumed to have.

The justification of the first four elements through the device of the original position is an internal justification, one that itself is part of Rawls's conception of *justice as fairness*. We should ask then how this conception itself, as a whole, is to be justified—from the outside, as it were. This question again arises from two perspectives: the citizens of a society well-ordered by Rawls's conception must have reasons for believing their society to be just in virtue of the fact that it realizes precisely *this* conception, and we, here and now, must have reasons for evaluating and reforming the basic structure of our society by reference to precisely *this* conception of justice. I will concentrate on the second, more difficult problem: What external justification can Rawls offer to those of his fellow citizens who are not yet convinced by his conception and perhaps even reject important elements of it, such as the fair value of political liberties, fair equality of opportunity, or the difference principle?

8.1 Reflective Equilibrium

Rawls proceeds from the assumption that his readers, much like himself, want to develop a conception of justice. The thought process that had led him to his conception might therefore be of interest to them as well. Such reflection must begin with something one already accepts, from existing convictions of relevance to the topic of justice. But a collection of diverse convictions is not yet a conception of justice. With respect to a given decision problem, there will often be several different convictions that imply mutually incompatible solutions. A conception of justice, by contrast, should yield definite solutions. When several considerations bear on an institutional design decision, such a conception will therefore set priorities or assign weights so as to facilitate a definite solution. (It may yield two equal-best solutions, of course. But it must not give us two solutions of which each is better in one respect and worse in another, without offering any basis for an overall judgment.) Moreover, a conception of justice should be complete within its domain, in contrast to a mere collection of convictions which may imply nothing at all about some pertinent design decisions.

The task is then, beginning from one's initial convictions, to go beyond them toward a conception of justice. This effort is presumably itself motivated by a moral conviction—the conviction, perhaps, that one should eliminate contradictions, gaps, and biases in one's justice judgments and should therefore develop a complete conception of justice. Toward this end, Rawls suggests the following method: One concentrates on those convictions in which one is especially confident, which one has not had reasons to doubt for some time. Rawls calls these *considered* judgments, *fixed* and *settled*. Convictions of many kinds may qualify: moral and religious convictions, other kinds of normative convictions (in logic, decision theory, etc.), and empirical and philosophical convictions. Such convictions may exist at any level of generality: from the concrete conviction that a particular policy is unjust and could not have been adopted in a just society, to the more abstract conviction that all adults should have equal political rights, to the still more abstract conviction that it is a desirable feature in a conception of justice that the members of the society it regulates would themselves agree to it beforehand. One tries, then, to relate these firm convictions so as to check them against one another and to forge them into a complete conception of justice.

The basic idea is that it is reasonable to increase the plausibility one ascribes to some firmly held conviction if one finds it to cohere with other firmly held convictions—and, conversely, to reduce the plausibility one ascribes to it if one finds that it cannot be reconciled with the others. We are familiar with analogous thoughts in other domains. A jury member, for instance, ascribes a certain initial credibility to the testimony of each witness and then adjusts these credibilities on the basis of critical comparisons. If two material witnesses give independent and matching descriptions of events, each of their testimonies becomes more credible than it would have been on its own. Conversely, if two witnesses contradict one another, this immediately reduces the credibility ascribed to each of their testimonies—though the credibility ascribed to one may be raised again when further evidence corroborates it or indicates that the conflicting testimony was false. Appreciating this analogy, we should note this difference: While the jury member proceeds on the assumption that, independent of the witnesses' reports, there is a fact of the matter concerning what actually happened, Rawls leaves open the question of whether there is a moral reality or moral truth independent of our convictions. The overlapping consensus he aims at is meant to solve a practical problem, to achieve justly ordered coexistence. Attempts to broaden such consensus to encompass claims about moral realism or objectivity would unnecessarily complicate this task. Rawls therefore excludes such issues from the envisioned overlapping consensus, leaving citizens to judge them individually according to their respective worldviews.

How is one to relate different convictions to one another when they have nonintersecting spheres of application—so that they do not agree or disagree about any particular cases? One can try to find a single principle underlying several more concrete convictions. Confirmed by the latter, such a principle would gain its own credibility, and one could then relate it to other more concrete convictions for the purpose of mutual testing. Rawls makes use of this strategy, explicitly comparing it with procedures used in linguistics (*TJ* 41). Our intuitive sense for our native language allows us to classify many expressions as definitely grammatical or definitely ungrammatical. Still, there are certain expressions about which we are unsure. In this situation, we can try to glean from the most definite cases more general grammatical rules, on the basis of which we can then decide more doubtful cases. This process of reflection is likely in turn to influence our linguistic intuitions. When a dubious expression is authorized by a rule that is confirmed by many definitely grammatical expressions, then the initially dubious expression will, in time, come to seem grammatically correct.

Rawls suggests that we can develop our sense of justice in analogy to this way of developing our intuitive linguistic sense. Here, however, the recourse to ever more general convictions can be carried much further than in linguistics. Rawls tries to develop a universal procedure for solving pertinent decision problems, which procedure would then be specified and corrected by recourse to more concrete convictions. The idea of a hypothetical social contract provides such a procedure: "The original position serves as a mediating idea by which all our considered convictions, whatever their level of generality . . . can be brought to bear on one another" (*PL* 26). This mediating idea is itself a highly abstract conviction to the effect that judgments of justice in the real world can be modeled on judgments of rational self-interest in a fictional situation. The just way of solving a given decision problem is the way citizens themselves would have endorsed prudentially, before their birth, as it were, in ignorance of their personal characteristics and the social class of their birth. This very abstract idea mediates among all our pertinent convictions by relating any one of them to any other.

Some of these convictions concern the procedure itself: the fictional contract situation that we must be able to accept, in all its details, as fair and adequate to its modeling function. After all, the procedure should have so much credibility that we will be prepared to accept its results, whatever they may turn out to be. In other words, we should be able to accept the original position as a case of *pure procedural justice* (*TJ* 104, *PL* 72–73).

Other convictions bear upon the fictional agreements of the hypothetical contracting parties. We must be able to accept their agreements as matching our own judgments of justice. This qualifies the idea of pure procedural justice. We have full confidence in the procedure only when we see that its output matches our considered convictions—much as we fully trust a consultant or umpire only after having closely observed her performance for some time.

The hoped-for harmony of all our convictions can therefore not be expected right away. One will go back and forth in one's deliberations and reach some dead ends: One will, for instance, explore various hypothetical contract situations that will ultimately prove unacceptable because they result in agreements that are at variance with our firmly held convictions about justice. After much trial and error and consequent fine-tuning, one may finally arrive at a specification of the contract situation such that the fictional agreements reached by the parties coincide with one's firm convictions in the great majority of cases. Such coincidence may give so much credibility to the contractualist thought experiment that one begins to doubt those very few convictions that militate against its output and feels prepared to revise those convictions so as to conform them to what the parties would agree to.

If such a process of reflection can really cause a person's convictions to adjust to one another, a coherent system of convictions may result: a unified and complete conception of justice. Rawls says that this person then reaches a state of *reflective equilibrium*. There is a harmonious balance between the procedure she accepts and her more concrete convictions—and therefore also harmony among all her convictions as each of them confirms the process and is in turn confirmed by it.

Such a state of reflective equilibrium is not necessarily permanent. One may encounter experiences that shake up one's most firmly held convictions. Or one may become aware, through moral writings or discussions, of new possibilities for systematizing one's convictions. Referring to this latter possibility, Rawls distinguishes between narrow and wide reflective equilibrium (*CP* 289–90). A reflective equilibrium that arises through reflection on merely one's own prior convictions is *narrow*. A process of reflection that also pays careful attention to the moral conceptions advanced by others—in one's own and in foreign intellectual traditions—and thereby gives these a chance to influence one's own convictions and systematizations results in a *wide* reflective equilibrium.

Ideally, one might even think of a wide reflective equilibrium as incorporating various narrow reflective equilibria. Here one might take various unifying ideas competing with that of a hypothetical social contract and then work out the most convincing critical reconstruction of one's considered convictions within each such framework (*critical* reconstruction, because each such account would propose revisions of one's considered convictions insofar as these cannot be made to fit the framework perfectly). One would then reach a plurality of narrow reflective equilibria—best systematizations one can give of one's considered convictions within various frameworks: within the framework of a fictional impartial observer equally concerned with the well-being of each individual (as deployed by Adam Smith), within the framework of a republican state that guarantees its citizens mutually consistent equal domains of external freedom (as developed by Kant), within the framework of a recursive, historical justification of social institutions (as proposed by John Locke and Robert Nozick), within a perfectionist framework that revolves around an account of human excellences, and so on. Developing and comparing these competing best critical reconstructions, one would in the end feel drawn toward the one that best fits one's (now more educated) considered convictions on the whole. One would then embrace this conception in wide reflective equilibrium, in full view of the alternative systematizations one has worked up and then found less convincing.

The content of any reflective equilibrium will naturally depend on the convictions with which one begins one's process of reflection. This might be seen as a problem. A person's initial convictions may be shaped by her society's prevailing ideology, by the views of her parents, and by any number of other prejudices. Even confrontation with conceptions from other cultures and epochs will not be able to neutralize the influences entirely. Rawls can concede these points and yet deny that they constitute an objection to his method. By aiming for wide reflective equilibrium, we do all that we can do to free ourselves from biases and prejudices. There is no external and independent touchstone of justice against which we could check our convictions. To be sure, some people come to accept something as such an independent touchstone—some religious text, perhaps, or some theory about the developmental logic of human history. But such acceptance, if it has a reasonable basis at all, must again be grounded in one's antecedent convictions, through which one recognizes a text or person as divine or a theory of human history as compelling.

While Rawls's reflective equilibrium is focused on social justice, on the terms on which one is to live with others in society, this equilibrium itself is defined as a state of a single individual. Rawls's aim is to "characterize one (educated) person's sense of justice" in a systematic way (TJ 44). This may seem like an excessively monological undertaking. Each individual is supposed to systematize his relevant convictions into one unified, plausible conception of justice. To attain wide reflective equilibrium he must, to be sure, engage with the thoughts and systematizations of others. But the judgment how to assess these engagements and how to adjust his own reflections in response to them is once more his alone. When he finally arrives at a set of convictions about justice that support one another well in a wide reflective equilibrium, this achievement has justificatory force. It satisfies him that he has firmly grounded his convictions, perhaps as firmly as he could, and renders his unified convictions highly credible to him. But this achievement has no justificatory force for others and will not render his convictions any more credible to them.

But the project is not quite so monological as it seems. Other people do not merely enrich my moral thinking by showing me alternate possibilities of reflection and systematization that challenge my convictions and reasoning. Others also furnish an important motive for seeking wide reflective equilibrium. I develop a conception of justice not merely as a guide for conduct but also to show others that I am genuinely concerned with justice and hence willing to act and willing to restrain my conduct in accordance with firmly held and enduring principles. To fulfill this function, my conception of justice must also be coherent, unified, and comprehensible, so that others can clearly see what it requires of me and of anyone in diverse realistic circumstances.

There is an even deeper qualification to be added. It is one of my initial considered convictions that I should give weight to the considered judgments of others. When people whose intelligence, integrity, and life experience I have learned to respect think that some of my judgments are wrong, I myself must remain less than fully satisfied with these judgments. This convergence-promoting thought has wide appeal—in physics and religion as much as in matters of justice. And Rawls has at least hinted at it through his idea of a *general* reflective equilibrium, defined as involving convergence among citizens (*JFR* 31). Only with such convergence would a public conception of justice be justified *fully* in some society.

To facilitate such convergence, citizens must not merely be open to being convinced by others but also be willing to try to convince them. There are many reasons for citizens to want to influence others' convictions and reflections toward a shared conception of justice: One may want to improve their reflections or have one's own validated by their approval; one may need their help in implementing some policy measure; one may want them to appreciate one's conduct as just; or one may want to promote an overlapping consensus. In order to be convincing to others, one's conception of justice must not merely be coherent, unified, and comprehensible but also be capable of being presented and justified in such a way that one's fellow citizens can accept it. One therefore has reason to exclude from such presentation and justification those among one's considered convictions that depend upon one's own religious, moral, or philosophical worldview and to invoke instead only such considered judgments and factual premises as are widely accepted and at least implicitly part of the society's public culture. This is a counsel of political prudence, especially to those committed to a comprehensive worldview that is not shared by most of their fellow citizens. But, more important, it is also a duty—a specific application of the duty of civility—that Rawls places upon citizens, including actual ones here and now, and that he has himself observed in addressing his fellow citizens through his writings and teachings.

At this point we come across a new difficulty. Some of the firm convictions with which individuals begin their process of reflection are likely to be dependent on their respective comprehensive worldviews—in regard to which, Rawls believes, the citizens of a modern democratic society unavoidably diverge. These particular convictions are not excluded from the reflective process and are bound to affect its result. For instance, the reflections of art lovers more than those of other citizens are likely to equilibrate toward a conception of justice that permits state support for the arts. And the reflections of Catholic men are more likely than those of non-Catholic women to equilibrate toward a conception of justice that permits a broad legal ban of abortions. This phenomenon impedes progress toward an overlapping consensus.

But there is a still deeper difficulty. Rawls asks that citizens who invoke a conception of justice in public should justify this conception without appeal to any elements of their comprehensive worldview. And this may be asking too much. Consider a citizen who holds, in wide reflective equilibrium, a conception of justice whose content is substantially influenced by various unmistakably Catholic convictions that she holds very firmly. How is she to justify her conception of justice in public? If she relies on her Catholic convictions, she runs afoul of her duty of civility. If she appeals only to the remainder of her firmest convictions, her reflective commitment to *this* conception of justice is likely to remain mysterious—the best systematization of *all* her considered convictions is unlikely also to be the best systematization of the subset she may invoke in public justifications. And if she replicates the upshot of her wide reflective equilibrium by mis-representing her own reflection—by replacing the Catholic considered convictions she holds but cannot appeal to with other convictions she can appeal to but does not hold, perhaps, or by misstating the weight and importance she actually attaches to the convictions she can appeal to—she comes to exemplify the problem of the hypocrisy mentioned earlier. How then is such a citizen to conduct herself in public dis-cussions of justice?

This is a difficulty internal to Rawls's theory, a difficulty for his ideal of a society whose members observe the duty of civility. And it is also a difficulty for Rawls himself as he is, after all, trying publicly to convince his fellow citizens of his conception of justice. He intro-duces this conception to them as the one that best systematizes all his considered judgments about justice. In justifying this conception, however, he appeals only to those convictions that have a place in the political culture of his society or are very widely shared by his fellow citizens, and he is silent about any remaining firm convictions, which are dependent on his comprehensive worldview. Perhaps Rawls had no such remaining firm convictions dependent on some compre-hensive conception of the good. But if he did have such convictions, they would very likely have affected the content of his conception of justice. And Rawls would then have to have fudged his justification of this conception a bit: interpreting, weighting, and bending the con-sidered judgments he is permitted to appeal to so that they uniquely support the conception of justice that best corresponds to the totality of his considered judgments.

One might think that this problem can be solved by envisioning the reflective process as drawing on only those firm convictions that also have a place in the public political culture of one's society. But this solution is unworkable. Were one to set aside some of one's initial considered convictions from the start, then one could easily end up with a conception of justice that one would oneself feel compelled to reject in light of the totality of *all* one's most deeply held convictions. By envisioning citizens' reflection in this way, Rawls would moreover have jettisoned the hope that their publicly accessible convictions would, over time, transform their doctrine-dependent ones so as to render the latter ever more accepting and even supportive of the idea of a political conception of justice sustained by an overlapping con-sensus. These drawbacks would dash the hope for an overlapping consensus among citizens wholeheartedly committed to a common conception of justice. And it thus makes good sense for Rawls to insist that each citizen's process of reflection should take account of *all* of her firm convictions—so that at the end of the process she will fully embrace its result. Of course, this leaves the problem still unsolved.

At this point, Rawls can still express the hope that doctrine-dependent convictions will only rarely affect the outcome of a citizen's effort toward reflective equilibrium. This is so because there are likely to be, in a given society at some given time, only a few political conceptions of justice that are serious candidates—that is, sufficiently unified, coherent, and credible in terms of their content—for citizens whose convictions were formed in this society (*TJ* 44). Rawls observes that in most societies there are only a few live theoretical traditions—traditions that are continually being perfected through internal innovations and mutual critique. If a random citizen of the United States, for example, were to think about justice in a serious way, she would most likely reach a wide reflective equilibrium whose content corresponds roughly to the contemporary libertarian, liberal, or utilitarian school. On this supposition, doctrine-dependent convictions may indeed be unlikely to make a difference to the upshot of a citizen's reflective equilibration. But then the supposition downplays the fact that each of the grand traditions contains several variants and that the substantive discrepancies among these variants are often of great consequence.

8.2 Fundamental Ideas

When developing a conception of justice, one is to draw upon all of one's firm and well-considered convictions so that one can then morally commit oneself to this conception wholeheartedly. But when one presents one's conception to others and justifies it to them, one is to appeal only to generally accepted convictions: "Since justification is addressed to others, it proceeds from what is, or can be, held in common; and so we begin from shared fundamental ideas implicit in the public political culture in the hope of developing from them a political conception that can gain free and reasoned agreement in judgment" (*PL* 100–1). Let us examine how Rawls envisions such a justification to others.

As the quote shows, such a justification should appeal to *ideas* that are part of the public political culture. Rawls uses the word "idea" in a deliberately vague sense that covers everything from *concept* to *conception* (*PL* 14n15). We want to elucidate this spectrum of meanings through the example of the "idea" of justice. In a very weak sense, I have an idea of justice when I possess the concept—when I know what the word "justice" means. I know, then, that justice is a property of social institutions, one that they have if, and only if, they regulate the interactions of their participants in a morally acceptable manner. In a very strong sense, I have an idea of justice when I am able to specify very precisely how social institutions must be designed in order to be just. An idea in this strong sense is a conception of justice. Of course, there are many such conceptions, but their respective proponents can disagree materially only if they agree on the concept. Rawls need not take on someone who thinks of justice as a property of dogs, say, and then offers a specific "conception of justice" on this basis.

We can distinguish here two stages of specification. The first one specifies a concept through a definition (perhaps with the help of illustrations and examples). This specification is complete as soon as the conceptual elements introduced in the definition are collectively sufficient to delineate the concept precisely. Then a second specification can begin, one in which the content of the concept in question is narrowed down further by reference to potentially controversial values or purposes. In the case of evaluative concepts like *justice*, this second specification involves substantive claims about how the positive and negative assessments expressed in using the concept are to be assigned: How should we judge which social institutions merit the label *just* and which the label *unjust*? In the case of nonevaluative concepts like *society*, the second specification introduces values in light of which societies should be assessed and designed—values that allow us to envision a society as it ought to be. In both cases, the second specification draws on substantive value judgments that go beyond the meaning of the word and thereby specifies a concept of something into a conception of it.

In the case of an evaluative concept of X, it is always clear what is meant by a conception of X. In the case of a nonevaluative concept, this may be unclear. Sometimes such talk brings nothing to mind: We may have no clue, for instance, how to conceive oxygen as it ought to be (gaseous?). Sometimes such talk brings to mind too much: We may conceive human beings as they ought to be in terms of physique, talents, moral character, and more.

When Rawls talks of fundamental ideas being involved in justification to others, he is not thinking of fully worked-out conceptions, for these are supposed to be controversial in the public political culture of a democratic society. Nor is he thinking of concepts, for these are likely to be common ground already and, in any case, have little justificatory potential (political debates are rarely decided by looking up words in even the most excellent dictionary). The ideas at issue here are then *partial conceptions*—partially specified conceptions that, though specific enough to entail some value judgments, nevertheless remain vague. Let us henceforth use the expression "idea of X" in this narrower Rawlsian sense for something that is more specific than the concept of X but less specific than a conception of X. In a given society, there may then be a widely accepted idea of justice that entails various value judgments such as, for example, that it is unjust for citizens' basic rights to depend (as in feudalism) on their descent. Entailing such value judgments, this idea is more specific than the concept of justice: Denial of the value judgments ("it is just for nobles to be assigned more extensive basic rights than commoners") is not self-contradictory. Yet this idea is also less specific than a conception of justice insofar as it lacks the determinacy and completeness Rawls requires from something meriting this title.

Now it is likely that most of the conceptions of justice seriously held in a society are compatible with the idea of justice contained in its public political culture. It will hardly be possible, therefore, to justify the choice of one candidate conception solely by appeal to that idea. Still, the public political culture may contain various other widely accepted ideas, which entail additional value judgments. And it may then be possible to justify the choice of one candidate conception of justice by showing that it provides the most plausible interpretation and development of a whole set of ideas. This is the justificatory strategy Rawls is pursuing.

The two most important ideas Rawls claims to find in the public political culture of his society are those of *society* and *citizen*. These ideas go beyond the mere concepts toward an idea of society "as a fair system of social cooperation between free and equal persons viewed as fully cooperating members of society over a complete life" (*PL* 9). In a society in whose culture this normative idea is implicitly contained and in which it is generally accepted, the task of political philosophy can be summarized in the following question: "What is the most appropriate conception of justice for specifying the fair terms of social cooperation between citizens regarded as free and equal, and as fully cooperating members of society over a complete life, from one generation to the next?" (*PL* 3).

Rawls wants to show that his conception is the one best suited to do this, and he tries to present it as such a specification. His conception of justice specifies ideas in the public political culture of his society by relating them to one another partly through further ideas Rawls develops. Thus, the idea of society is specified through the fundamental ideas of *society as a fair system of cooperation* and *a well-ordered society*. The idea of citizen is specified as the fundamental idea of *citizens as free and equal*. And these specifications are supported and connected by the fundamental ideas of the *basic structure*, the *original position*, and *public justification*, which are further connected to the ideas of *reflective equilibrium* and an *overlapping consensus*.

In the characterization and further specification of these ideas, more and more other ideas come into play—some explicitly so called, others not. A list of such ideas cannot be complete, but here are the more important ideas, not yet identified as such, which Rawls incorporates into his conception of justice: *person, the rational, goodness as rationality, primary goods, conception of the good, (reasonable) comprehensive doctrine, mutual advantage, reciprocity, cooperation, impartiality, equality, fairness, social contract, justice as fairness, pure procedural justice, legitimate expectations, responsibility for ends, basic needs, social minimum, freedom, basic rights and liberties, democracy, equality of opportunity, constitutional essentials, strains of commitment, stability, priority of right, legitimacy, practical reason, (free) public reason, reasonable pluralism, reasonable disagreement, method of avoidance, the domain of the political, a political conception of justice, political liberalism, political constructivism, autonomy, self-respect, fundamental interests, moral powers, sense of justice, burdens of judgment, political virtues, tolerance, civility, community*. Of the great majority of these ideas, Rawls can claim that they are implicit in the public political culture of his society—at least in rudimentary form, and not always under the name Rawls gives them—while of some (e.g., *original position, fundamental interests, primary goods, method of avoidance*) he would be able to claim only that they emerge as by-products of the work of developing and specifying the former.

I will not attempt here to give an exhaustive account of how Rawls builds his conception of justice from these ideas in a process that also specifies each of these ideas further by determining more precisely its role and significance in relation to all the others. Insofar as space allows, this has already been done in earlier chapters. Here the task is to clarify what Rawls's achievement has to do with justification. Rawls can claim to have given the best reconstruction of his society's public political culture. Backed by his mighty theoretical edifice, this claim has a certain weight and gives rise to a burden of proof.

An opponent must either challenge Rawls's reconstruction or else produce a similarly weighty competitor. One can challenge Rawls by showing, for example, that he has misunderstood certain ideas implicit in the public political culture or that he has left out certain other important ideas that cannot be made to fit with his conception. One can compete with Rawls by developing a conception of justice that systematizes, in a similarly convincing and elegant way, the ideas implicit in the public political culture of the same society.

Developing such a competing conception is surely possible: One might specify the ideas Rawls appeals to somewhat differently, relate them to one another in other ways, assign less weight than Rawls does to some and more to others, exclude some ideas Rawls draws on, and include some ideas Rawls ignores. In these ways, with ingenuity and patience, it should be possible to develop a theoretical edifice whose unity and power make it as appealing a reconstruction as Rawls has produced. But this work must actually be performed and be delivered for inspection. Citizens should not be impressed with a mere indeterminate possibility. They need to make judgments of justice, here and now, about decisions on the political agenda, and in the absence of a convincing alternative, it makes sense for them to base these judgments on the best-articulated credible conception of justice available to them.

If this makes sense, then Rawls can claim to have provided his fellow citizens with a justification of his conception. It is not a definitive justification, to be sure. But in a modern pluralistic society, there can anyway be no definitive justification, according to Rawls. The best that can be done in such a society by way of justification is to provide a fully elaborated conception of justice that gives a more convincing and better articulated reconstruction of this society's public political culture than any of its competitors does. This is something that Rawls can be said, with some plausibility, to have achieved. If so, then his conception is the best basis we can have on which to make legitimate political decisions.

8.3 Truth and Reasonableness

Providing justification in the sense discussed belongs to the business of philosophy: "The real task [of political philosophy when it presents itself in the public culture of a democratic society] is to discover and formulate the deeper bases of agreement which one hopes are embedded in common sense" (CP 306). This quote may suggest cultural relativism: A conception of justice is justified for a given society if, and only if, it accounts for the ideas contained in the public political culture of this society in a more credible and unified way than any competing conception. Analogously, the idea of reflective equilibrium may suggest individualism or subjectivism: A conception of justice is justified for an individual if, and only if, it accounts for the totality of this person's firm and considered convictions in a more credible and unified way than any competing conception.

The suspicion of relativism solidifies when Rawls continues, "I should emphasize that what I have called the 'real task' of justifying a conception of justice is not primarily an epistemological problem. The search for reasonable grounds for reaching agreement rooted in our conception of ourselves and in our relation to society replaces the search for moral truth" (*CP* 306). Is Rawls then a relativist, who denies the existence of universally valid moral norms? No. Embracing relativism would undermine Rawls's hope of making his conception of justice the focal point of an overlapping consensus, as many comprehensive doctrines emphatically reject relativism. Other worldviews, whose support Rawls would also like to win, accept some version of moral relativism, however. And so Rawls once more follows his *method of avoidance* (*CP* 434). A political conception of justice that is to be respected and applied by people with diverse worldviews need not either affirm or deny that its norms have universal validity. For it to be justified against competing conceptions, it need merely be the most reasonable one for us, the best available reconstruction of our public political culture. Many who support this conception of justice on the basis of a deeper and more comprehensive worldview will also hold this conception to be true and valid universally. But they need not be disturbed if some of their fellow citizens regard it not as true, but only as reasonable for us or fitting in our culture—so long as these fellow citizens feel morally bound by it.

Discussing those more comprehensive worldviews found in a free democratic society, Rawls often uses the qualifier "religious or moral or philosophical." The inclusion of "philosophical" alludes to philosophical controversies outside Rawls's concern of settling the substantive content of a shared political conception of justice. Such controversies may be over subjectivism, relativism, objectivism, and realism with respect to moral values, for example. Rawls treats such controversies as he treats those about ethics, morals, and religion: Settling them definitively in a publicly demonstrable way is probably impossible and, more important, is unnecessary for achieving general agreement on a conception of justice and basic structure design. Political philosophy as Rawls practices it thus strives to remain largely independent, not only of comprehensive moral and religious views but also of other areas of philosophy—to stay "on the surface, philosophically speaking" (*CP* 395).

Rawls's method of avoidance runs into a problem, however. Those who believe in moral truth, or even in a moral reality independent of human beings, may have very different ideas about how a conception of justice should be grounded and justified. They may complain that Rawls, though he eschews commitment to any meta-ethical position, is actually grounding and justifying his conception like someone who does not believe in the existence of moral truth.

Rawls would, I believe, answer this complaint as follows: As far as justification to oneself is concerned, there is no reasonable alternative to the quest for reflective equilibrium. Thus even intuitionists, for whom correct moral judgments are expressions of the truth about an independent order of moral values (*PL* 112), will want to distinguish between moral judgments that merely seem intuitively correct to someone and those that actually are correct. In drawing this distinction, they have no other guide than this: Can the judgment in question be reconciled with others within the framework of a *single* conception? Now there may be intuitionists who see no reason for doubting their moral perceptions unless they encounter conflicts among them. They may hold that, while it would be nice if the moral truth were as simple and elegant as Newtonian physics, if it turns out to be messy and complicated, we will just have to put up with that. Such intuitionists would be less inclined toward critical examination, revision, and theory building than Rawls is. But this preference has nothing to do with their intuitionism: Nonintuitionists, too, may be averse to theorizing, perhaps because they lack a strong conviction that their various convictions about justice should be systematizable into a consistent and complete conception. And intuitionists, too, may be strongly disposed toward theorizing, perhaps on account of a clear and powerful intuition that the moral truth must be unitary and elegant. So Rawls indeed cannot expect others to be as keen as he is on revising their initial convictions for the sake of greater systematic unity. But he can certainly insist that his model of reflective equilibrium is equally acceptable to adherents of many meta-ethical positions and therefore at right angles to their disputes (*PL* 95–96).

As far as justification to one's fellow citizens is concerned, it may seem that someone who believes himself in possession of the moral truth has much less reason to observe the duty of civility than someone who ascribes no truth value to moral convictions. Why shouldn't one *impose* the moral truth upon one's fellow citizens, when one can, even if one cannot justify this truth to them by appeal to ideas available in the public political culture? And why shouldn't one resist demo-cratically instituted laws when they flagrantly run counter to the moral truth? Two possible answers are: (1) because one cannot be sure that what one now firmly believes to be the moral truth really is the moral truth, and (2) because one believes the liberal principle of legitimacy and the duty of civility to be part of the moral truth. Some objectivists might reject both answers, and they would then stand outside the overlapping consensus Rawls seeks. But the mere possibility of these two objectivist answers shows that Rawls's model of justification to others is also meta-ethically noncommittal. It does not implicitly deny (or affirm) that moral statements have truth value.

Nine

THE RECEPTION OF *JUSTICE AS FAIRNESS*

I T is a commonplace that Rawls's *A Theory of Justice* brought political philosophy back to life, inspiring a flood of many thousands of articles in the journals of philosophy, political science, economics, and law. It is also well known that this work has been translated into twenty-eight languages, has sold some four hundred thousand copies in English alone (it holds the record at Harvard University Press), and has also found many supporters in the developing world. I mention these facts only in passing to concentrate instead on three important substantive debates in which Rawls's conception of justice has become involved.

9.1 Rawls and Libertarianism

Merely three years after the publication of *TJ*, another Harvard philosopher, Robert Nozick (1938–2002), published his counterproposal: *Anarchy, State, and Utopia*. Nozick's critique of Rawls centers around three main points that are still much debated.

Nozick objects, first, to the fact that Rawlsian judgments of justice are oriented in a consequentialist manner to distributional profiles. He finds two problems with this: In order to institute any distributional profile, one must override already existing property rights. And, even after such a thoroughgoing intervention, further redistributive interventions will be needed in order to preserve the desired distributional profile. Nozick concludes that a conception of justice like Rawls's requires an exceedingly interventionist government that, as is typical in the welfare-state era, continually meddles with free agreements among citizens. Whoever respects human freedom must reject all conceptions of justice committed to some distributional profile.

As an alternative to such conceptions, Nozick advocates a *historical* conception of justice. According to such a conception, the justice of a distribution depends not on the extent to which it approximates some ideal profile, but rather on whether it evolved in a morally acceptable way. One cannot tell from the shape of a distributional profile whether or not it is just. For every possible distributional profile could have evolved in a just way—for instance, through a series of voluntary poker games in which no one cheats. Nozick applies this idea not only to the distribution of property but also to that of basic rights. In his view, slavery is unjust only when people become slaves through force or deception, not when they freely give up their liberty—in exchange for help in an emergency, for example.

This criticism, which has gained some popularity in the United States, involves a fundamental misunderstanding. *Justice as fairness* is not about how government officials, or others, should interfere with transactions under established rules so as to improve the distribution of primary goods these produce. Rather, Rawls's conception addresses the design of these rules themselves. By raising this issue, Rawls denies what Nozick's criticism presupposes, namely, that we already know which rules should govern social cooperation and which existing property holdings are morally justified. Rawls proposes that we choose these rules—the design of our society's basic structure—on the basis of the distributional profiles the various practicable sets of rules would tend to produce. Once these rules are in place, they are to be treated as an instance of pure procedural justice, exactly as Nozick would like: The rules are known in advance, and whatever distribution they generate counts as just and is therefore protected against ad hoc government interference or *re*-distribution. Rawls's conception uses information about distributional profiles for assessing and structuring a society's social institutions—never for interfering with their operation.

Rawls can then respond to Nozick that we can accept the outcomes of free interactions among citizens under existing rules (rather than "correct" these outcomes through government meddling) and still avoid the horrendous outcomes Nozick is willing to countenance. We avoid such outcomes not through interference or redistribution, but through careful formulation of the rules that govern citizen interactions and thereby condition the resulting distribution. An institutional order designed on the basis of the distributional profile it tends to produce will not produce the horrendous outcomes Nozick condones.

What rules are best for some particular society in some particular period is, for Rawls, partly an empirical question. These rules may involve built-in taxes and subsidies and may assign the government an important role in economic life. In a property-owning democracy, for example, education is likely to be publicly funded so as to ensure universal access. Through taxes, wealthy citizens will then contribute more, and poor ones less, to such an education system than they get out of it. And is not such redistribution, even if built into the rules, still redistribution?

It is easy here to fall for the illusion that there are two distinct sets of rules operating in such a society: the rules that give people what they deserve, their gross incomes, and the corrective rules that redistribute. However, this distinction is artificial, and the notion that gross incomes reflect what people deserve in some deeper sense is false. Both points are illustrated by the fact that the tax system has a feedback effect on gross incomes. This is so because, in making career decisions, people are sensitive to the *net* incomes they could earn in various professions. People attracted to a medical service career, for instance, will use the ratio between the net income of a doctor and that of a nurse to decide whether to undertake the more arduous training required to be a doctor. Thus, the more progressive the tax system is, the greater will be the ratio of the two gross incomes that would emerge in a market system. To illustrate: Under a no-tax or flat-tax regime, a 2:1 ratio of gross incomes results in a 2:1 ratio of net incomes, which, let us suppose, produces an efficient mix of doctors and nurses. If a steeply progressive tax regime is employed instead, the 2:1 ratio of gross incomes results in a much lower ratio of net incomes, which would produce an inefficient mix of mostly nurses. This mix would, however, not actually come about, because the medical labor market would adjust to the steeply progressive tax regime through a gross income ratio above 2:1, which would raise the net income ratio closer to 2:1. It would be a mistake, therefore, to take the gross income ratio under a steeply progressive tax regime as indicative of how much doctors are contributing relative to nurses.

Gross incomes are also affected by many other features of a society's institutional order that have nothing to do with the "true value" of the contribution they pay for: The gross incomes of professionals depend in part on how accessible their career path is to citizens from all social strata. The gross incomes of landlords depend on rules governing ownership of real estate. The gross incomes of heirs are influenced by inheritance rules and taxes. And gross incomes available in various industries (tourism, gambling, prostitution, entertainment, hospitality, financial, etc.) are influenced by how these industries are regulated and policed.

Reflection on all these institutional options gives rise to yet a third sense of *redistribution*. Endorsing some particular institutional design, one might complain that, relative to it, some existing institutional order is redistributive by engendering lower incomes for investment bankers and better schooling for children of the poor, say. But this complaint can have no force because it can be adduced in behalf of every conceivable institutional design against any other. Every institutional design "redistributes" things relative to how they would be distributed under some other design. So understood, the charge of redistributive interference loses all critical power. To make progress, we must then focus on precisely the question Rawls has posed: How can one justify the choice of one institutional design over the remaining possibilities? Rawls has proposed to do this by reference to the distributional profiles each candidate design would tend to produce. This proposal is not vulnerable to the charge that it involves redistribution.

But Nozick presses a second criticism against it which again is meant to show that his own rather extreme laissez-faire design is superior. In one variant, this second criticism invokes the idea that (as far as possible) every member of society should receive the value of his or her contribution. This principle stands in need of justification, of course. But first of all, its meaning must be explicated. What exactly is the value of a person's contribution? Should we say, for instance, that those who cannot work throughout their lifetime contribute nothing, or should we say that they contribute a fraction of the natural resources (ultimately owned by all human beings in common) that are used in production? There are plainly many competing ways of explicating the principle, and this fact alone greatly undermines the suggestion that the idea of contribution can furnish a natural or obvious competitor to Rawls's conception of justice.

One may think that this indeterminacy can be overcome through appeal to a version of the social contract idea. In this variant of his second criticism, Nozick contends that, if it is to be plausible to endorse the design of the social order that its participants would have agreed to ahead of time, then this hypothetical agreement must be conceived very differently. The agreement presented by Rawls is one-sided and unfair: The untalented get the design that is best for them, while the talented must put up with this design even if they could do much better on their own (excluding the untalented). Against this, Nozick—and others, notably David Gauthier (section 3.2)—maintain that, if both groups are to cooperate within one social order, their cooperation ought to be beneficial to both. To ensure this, one should conceive the hypothetical contract situation as one in which the parties are aware of their natural endowments. This would protect the interests of the talented by enabling them to refuse cooperation when their proposed share of the cooperative product is smaller than what they could produce on their own. The interests of the untalented are similarly protected, albeit at a much lower level. And the negotiations between the two sides would then be only over the cooperative surplus, the excess over what the two groups could have produced separately.

Rawls could respond to this counterproposal by probing the imagined condition of noncooperation which is supposed to provide the threat potential in the negotiations. Is this a fictional situation without any moral restrictions, in which one group could threaten the other with murder or enslavement? If so, then it seems offensive to attach to the agreements rational parties would make against such a baseline any *moral* significance for how we ought to structure our coexistence. Or is it a fictional situation in which certain moral rules (constraining the use of force and the appropriation of natural resources, perhaps) are observed? If so, then these rules would need to be formulated and justified—which means that the thought experiment, proposed to deliver a conception of justice, is presupposing that a rudimentary conception of justice is already on hand.

Moreover, even if the fictional situation were more fully described, it would still be impossible to work out, even very approximately, how well the talented and the untalented would do in it. The relevant subjunctives are simply too remote. Finally, Rawls could also point out that it is arbitrary to conceive the hypothetical contract as between these two groups. Why should they be the only groups for which justice demands that each should fare no worse than it would fare on its own? All sorts of other groupings in the proposed alternative thought experiment could also form a coalition demanding that it should fare no worse than it would fare on its own. And if each conceivable such demand puts a constraint on the agreement, then (quite apart from the problem of remote subjunctives) it becomes impossible to work out what agreement would be reached, because the number of possible coalitions is simply too large. To see this, take an extremely small society of 100 people, and consider only scenarios where these people are divided into two groups of exactly 50 members each. Even with these extreme simplifications, we would have about 100 billion billion billion possible coalitions of 50 to consider.

Nozick's third significant criticism of Rawls—one that has also been taken up by the communitarian Michael Sandel—has to do with a misleading formulation Rawls has given of the difference principle. This principle represents in effect, writes Rawls, "an agreement to regard the distribution of natural talents as in some respects a common asset" (*TJ* 87), "a social asset" (*TJ* 92), or "a collective asset" (*TJ* 156). This sounds as if Rawls is proposing to regard natural endowments as common property—as if he is in favor of redistributing organs and in favor of conscripting talented individuals for forced labor or at least of imposing especially heavy taxes upon them. Nozick claims that Rawls, in order to be consistent, must support such measures, or at least permit them, given that he holds that "the initial endowment of natural assets . . . [is] arbitrary from a moral point of view" (*TJ* 274) and that "we do not deserve our place in the distribution of native endowments" (*TJ* 89).

In reply to this objection, we should first recall that Rawls's public criterion of justice focuses exclusively on the distribution of social primary goods while disregarding all information about natural endowments (though we have also seen, in section 4.3, how difficult it is for Rawls to justify this focus against the background of his appeal to the three fundamental interests). His public criterion thus provides no direct support for a redistribution of organs. It might provide indirect support in contexts where schemes of organ redistribution, or forced labor, facilitate economic gains that raise the lowest socioeconomic position. But such schemes would nonetheless be prohibited as violations of the (lexically superordinate) first principle of justice. The same goes for a "head tax" on especially talented adults, which Nozick thinks Rawls's theory would support. Such a tax would force the talented into more productive careers and might thereby raise the lowest socioeconomic position. But it would violate their free choice of occupation as guaranteed by the first principle of justice (*PL* 228, 335) and violate formal equality of opportunity by denying talented people access to low-paying careers that are open to others.

If his public criterion clearly rules out the institutional arrangements Nozick contemplates, how can we explain Rawls's curious comments about the difference principle? A main point about the cited formulations is that a society should benefit from the distribution and diversity of talents among its members (*JFR* 75–76). In order to do so, the economic order may be designed so that the talented are better rewarded than the less talented for the same expenditure of effort and so that those with rare or especially productive talents are better rewarded than those whose talents are middling, common, or of little economic use. Nozick would completely agree with this claim, which is widely accepted. Virtually every economic order we know of allows such variations in reward, often through market mechanisms, which are useful for eliciting the productive employment of diverse talents. Rawls's view is distinctive in demanding that such variations in reward should be structured to the maximum benefit to the lowest socioeconomic position. This means, roughly, that the net income rates for various types of work should be influenced, through taxes and subsidies, for example, in such a way that the lowest net income rate is as high as possible.

How some specific kind of work is rewarded in a Rawlsian society depends, then, on many empirical factors. How many citizens have the talents necessary to do similar work? How inclined are these citizens to do this work in preference to other kinds of work? What impact could various possible taxes and subsidies have on the number of citizens choosing work of this kind and on the quality of their performance? What contribution does work of this kind make to the social product? The rewards offered for some particular talent will depend on these empirical matters concerning the kinds of work this talent enables its possessor to do.

One might say against such an economic order that certain talents confer a special value on their possessors, a value that must be reflected in the distribution of rewards. (Nozick would certainly not support such an objection, which targets his own laissez-faire economic order as well.) To this objection, Rawls replies that talents are morally arbitrary and undeserved. This does not mean that one has no right to one's talents, that talents may be confiscated or requisitioned for the common good. Nor does it mean that the exercise of special talents should not be rewarded. It means only that no talent gives its possessor a right to any special reward. Talents are morally inconsequential; they say nothing about the moral value of their possessor. And rewards for their exercise may then be structured in whatever way seems best designed to advance the common good, which the difference principle identifies with the lowest socioeconomic position.

9.2 Rawls and Communitarianism

Libertarianism builds upon the legacies of Locke and Hobbes and differs from Rawls's position primarily in supporting a laissez-faire market economy. United States communitarianism is a more diffuse intellectual movement that—influenced by Hegel, Aristotle, and the Scholastics—includes a number of diverse practical-institutional proposals. Some of the representatives of this movement (Alasdair Mac-Intyre) are on the political right, others (Roberto Unger, Benjamin Barber) on the left, while others (Michael Walzer, Charles Taylor, Michael Sandel) develop alternative versions of liberalism, not too different from Rawls's own.

Here I will confine my discussion to two points of communitarian critique addressed specifically to Rawls's view. The first point is the central claim of Sandel's critique of Rawls (also raised earlier, in a more general fashion, by Bernard Williams). Rawls's demand that societies should strive above all toward a just basic structure presupposes a particular "metaphysical" or "epistemological" conception of the human being that Sandel finds to be both false and morally repugnant. Sandel supports this claim by reference to the way in which Rawls derives his social ideal from the device of the original position:

> The original position is the fulcrum of the justificatory process in that *it* is the device through which all justification must pass. . . . What issues at one end in a theory of justice must issue at the other in a theory of the person, or, more precisely, a theory of the moral subject. Looking from one direction through the lens of the original position we see the two principles of justice; looking from the other direction we see a reflection of ourselves. (*Liberalism and the Limits of Justice*, 47–48)

The theory of the moral subject that Sandel finds to be implicit in Rawls's conception envisions people who want to coexist with others according to just rules and are willing, to this end, to curtail or abandon all of their other goals, ambitions, ideals, memberships, friendships, and commitments. Such people have no "constitutive" commitments—commitments whose abandonment would be unthinkable. They can always reinvent themselves, finding new goals, ideals, and loyalties.

One can hardly blame Sandel for rejecting this image of the moral subject. But Rawls is not committed to it. His public criterion of justice and the basic structure it justifies are no moody deity that might unpredictably command this or that sacrifice. Citizens of a just society can, of course, have constitutive commitments. They will, however, form such commitments with some thought: They will not become deeply involved with members of the Mafia, will not marry a professional assassin, and will understand any friendship so that the moral demands it might make upon them remains within the bounds of morality. Thus the ideal of a just society does not imply that of superficial, unconnected citizens.

Rawls does withhold from the parties in the original position all information about the particular commitments and deep ambitions of their clients. But this is not to suggest that such constitutive attachments do not matter much. Rather, the reason is twofold: Individuals acquire such attachments in a particular social context, one determined in large part by their society's conception of justice and by its institutional order as shaped by this conception. Because citizens' constitutive attachments develop within social structures whose nature is yet to be agreed upon in the original position, they cannot be presupposed as already known by the parties in their deliberations. The other reason is that Rawls seeks a public criterion of justice and matching social institutions that can be justified to persons with diverse constitutive attachments. He therefore models the choice of the public criterion as one that plainly does not depend on any particular such attachments.

Although the parties are ignorant of the particular attachments of those they represent, Rawls does inform them that people usually have such deep attachments that are essential to them: "citizens in their personal affairs, or within the internal life of associations, . . . may have attachments and loves that they believe they would not, or could not, stand apart from; and they might regard it as unthinkable for them to view themselves without certain religious or philosophical convictions and commitments" (*CP* 331–32). Rawls does not make this stipulation as a concession to his critics. He needs it in his justification of the lexical priority of the basic liberties, in particular, of the freedoms of conscience and association (*TJ* §32, *PL* 310–15, *JFR* 104–5). And so Rawls can reply to Sandel that his ideal society *does* leave space for citizens' deep commitments—more space, in fact, than its alternatives.

To be sure, there will be conflicts, even in the best liberal society, between a citizen's deep attachments and her or his duties of justice. And in some cases demanding resolution in favor of justice would be demanding too much. (This does not mean that one is then justified in violating one's duties of justice; some situations, as Williams says, lie beyond justification.) A just society can live with such conflicts. So long as the great majority of citizens honor their duties of justice by supporting its basic structure, its justice, legitimacy, and stability are assured.

Sandel wants citizens of the ideal society to be animated by a shared idea of the common good that is richer than a shared commitment to the justice of its basic structure. But he says little about the content of this idea. He evidently yearns for community—not for those partial communities within a society which Rawls accommodates (as "associations"), but for one community that encompasses all members of society. This ideal must run aground, according to Rawls, on the fact of reasonable pluralism. A democratic society engenders an abundance of competing and mutually incompatible values; a society whose members would all accept the same rich array of community values cannot be realized without substantial governmental regimentation and repression. A free societywide community is simply impossible in the modern era.

Another criticism, set forth in different ways by most communitarians, is based on an empirical sociological thesis. In a liberal society of Rawlsian provenance, partial communities and deep commitments simply would not thrive, regardless of how much space there is for them to do so. This thesis is supported by saying that, in modern liberal societies, there are no longer any real religious communities or deeply religious individuals. Friendships have become superficial, losing so much of their value that many prefer bowling alone. Marriages are fleeting partnerships of convenience, with people staying together as long as they get along, then seeking new partners when their interests and preferences change. We live today in societies in which people no longer really believe in anything, except perhaps in justice or, more likely, in rights of their own on whose enforcement they may insist always, no matter at what cost to others.

Because this critique of modern culture tends to be accompanied by a certain nostalgia, it should be pointed out that, though previous eras were different, they were not necessarily better. There were indeed fewer divorces a hundred years ago, but this meant that women often had to suffer unspeakably under their abusive husbands. There were indeed more deeply religious individuals, but these were often exploited and defrauded by their clergymen. This is not to deny that a liberal social order may involve some loss of values. As Rawls (following Isaiah Berlin) likes to point out, "there is no social world without loss" (*CP* 462). In every social world, some forms of life will be ruled out completely, and many others unable to thrive. In the face of this fact, we are forced to choose. Rawls holds that, on the basis of our current state of understanding, we should choose an egalitarian liberal social order at least for our Western societies.

This is not to concede that Rawls, in supporting this choice, is willing to accept even very large losses in valuable forms of life. Far from being an apologist for the status quo, Rawls is convinced that the society he envisions would do much better in terms of communal values than existing societies that call themselves liberal. By maintaining the fair value of the political liberties, his society would draw poorer citizens into joint public deliberations about justice and the common good. By maintaining fair equality of opportunity, it would greatly improve social mobility. By satisfying the difference principle, it would reduce existing wage-rate inequalities, thereby enhancing free time available, especially to the poorer strata of the population. With these principles properly institutionalized, Rawls can hope for a genuine sense of reciprocity and civic friendship among citizens, which in turn could sustain von Humboldt's idea of a social union of social unions (*TJ* §79, *PL* 320–23).

9.3 Rawls and Kant

Rawls's occasional attempts to present his conception of justice as importantly Kantian in character has attracted attention as well as some head shaking (especially among German scholars). Rawls has learned, and incorporated into his theory, a great deal from some of his eminent predecessors. Even among these, however, Kant occupies a special place. In his lectures and publications, Rawls discussed Kant more extensively than anyone else and has continually rethought and reformulated the relationship between his theory and Kant's.

Rawls has borrowed ideas from other predecessors by detaching them from their context in those authors: He took from Aristotle the Aristotelian principle, from Hobbes the idea of a hypothetical nonhistorical social contract, from Locke thoughts about liberal tolerance, from Hume the circumstances of justice, from Rousseau ideas about democracy and moral education, from Bentham and Marx the focus on social institutions and from Marx also the interest in the (fair) value of especially the political liberties, from Mill arguments for freedom of thought and conscience, from Sidgwick inspiration for the idea of a reflective equilibrium, and from Hart, finally, various important conceptual distinctions, in particular, that between natural duties and institutional obligations.

From Kant, however, Rawls did not merely learn and borrow. Kant's work—less the later *Rechtslehre*, interestingly, than Kant's moral philosophy presented in the *Groundwork* and the *Critique of Practical Reason*—decisively inspired Rawls's own project. Let us then take a closer look at several aspects of Rawls's relationship to Kant.

The first significant effort Rawls makes to specify his relationship to Kant is in §40 of *TJ*, where he suggests a "Kantian interpretation" of his own theory. The basic idea there is that the deliberations of the parties in the original position correspond to the deliberations of an individual with a good will who tests her maxims against Kant's categorical imperative. The correspondence is, of course, not exact. Kant describes monological reflections about how to act that lead to negative conclusions (the rejection of certain maxims). Rawls describes thinly collective deliberations about institutional design that lead to a positive conclusion (a particular criterion of justice ought to be satisfied). Nonetheless, Rawls attempted—with a larger technical apparatus and a correspondingly greater degree of precision—to show exactly what, on his interpretation, Kant had also wanted to show: how rational individuals *as such* reach moral decisions. Like Kant, he "begins with the idea that moral principles are the object of rational choice" (*TJ* 221).

What the Kantian interpretation is ultimately supposed to show is this: "The description of the original position resembles the point of view of noumenal selves, of what it means to be a free and equal rational being. . . . The original position may be viewed, then, as a procedural interpretation of Kant's conception of autonomy and the categorical imperative within the framework of an empirical theory" (*TJ* 225–26).

Rawls seeks to connect his device of the original position with Kant's idea of autonomy in two ways. "Kant held, I believe, that a person is acting autonomously when the principles of his action are chosen by him as the most adequate possible expression of his nature as a free and rational being. . . . Now the veil of ignorance deprives the persons in the original position of the knowledge that would enable them to choose heteronomous principles" (*TJ* 222). Moreover, "the motivational assumption of mutual disinterest parallels Kant's notion of autonomy" (*TJ* 223).

Rawls also seeks to connect his principles of justice to the categorical imperative: "The principles of justice are also analogous to

categorical imperatives. For by a categorical imperative Kant understands a principle of conduct that applies to a person in virtue of his
nature as a free and equal rational being. . . . The argument for the two
principles of justice does not assume that the parties have particular
ends, but only that they desire certain primary goods. These are things
that it is rational to want whatever else one wants. Thus given human
nature, wanting them is part of being rational. . ." (*TJ* 222–23).

As Oliver Johnson was the first to show, this analogy fails. This
becomes especially clear when Rawls writes: "My suggestion is that we
think of the original position as in important ways similar to the point
of view from which noumenal selves see the world. The parties qua
noumenal selves have complete freedom to choose whatever principles
they wish; but they also have a desire to express their nature as rational
and equal members of the intelligible realm with precisely this liberty
to choose. . ." (*TJ* 225). Rawls wants to say then that when we orient
our conduct toward the criterion of justice that would be chosen in the
original position, we show thereby that we are motivated and disposed,
like the parties themselves, as ideal-typical free and autonomous
noumenal subjects. But this claim does not fit with Rawls's description
of the parties' rationality as means-ends rationality in a narrow econ-
omistic sense (*TJ* 125). Wanting as many all-purpose means as possible
and wanting to express one's nature as a rational member of the intelligible world are not two variations on the same desire. Prudential
rationality in the pursuit of given ends is not what Kant means by
reason—though Rawls, in *this* passage, uses the predicate *rational* in
both senses. [Elsewhere in *TJ*, Rawls shows that he is well aware of the
difference and distinguishes clearly between rational and reasonable
(e.g., *TJ* 16–17).] The parties in the original position are rational
maximizers, not free and autonomous noumenal subjects.

One could try to get around this criticism through a modification
of the Kantian interpretation suggested by Stephen Darwall. Darwall
defends the conclusion of §40: "men exhibit their freedom, their
independence from the contingencies of nature and society, by acting
in ways they would acknowledge in the original position" (*TJ* 225).
But he does not endorse Rawls's way of arriving at this conclusion
and does not present the parties as free, autonomous, and *vernünftig*
(reasonable). Darwall's revision—adopted and further developed by
Rawls himself (*CP* 303–22)—distinguishes the merely rational autonomy of the parties from the full autonomy of actual citizens in existing
or ideal societies. Its basic idea is this: Guided by Kant in envisioning a
just society, we should not allow ourselves to be influenced by any

personal inclinations or interests. We can comply with this prohibition by asking ourselves how we would specify justice if we were ignorant of our own particular inclinations. Rawls can answer that we would then envision the just society as one that enables its members to fulfill their human interests (representable by the interest in being successful in terms of the particular conception of the good one has chosen).

But does this answer really save the connection with Kant? By specifying justice through the thought experiment of the original position, we do indeed, thanks to the veil of ignorance, disconnect our reflections from our inclinations and personal interests. But our reflections remain bound to the needs and interests of human beings in general, as reflected in the stipulated third fundamental interest and in Rawls's conception of primary goods. *Justice as fairness* can then be accused of exemplifying heteronomy in Kant's sense—not the heteronomy of the egoist, whose conception of justice is influenced by his personal desires, but the heteronomy of the consequentialist, whose conception of justice is shaped by the desires of all.

Three points can be made toward defending Rawls's conception against this charge of heteronomy. First, there is an important difference between an egoistic and an impartial concern for the fulfillment of needs and interests. Parties in the original position aim for a society in which all citizens do well because this is the only way each can ensure that she (or her client) fares well. One could thus say that the parties' motivation is egoistic (or particularistic). But the same cannot be said of us who are conducting the thought experiment. It is not from egoistic motives that we endorse the agreement the parties would reach in the original position. Rather, we endorse it—regardless of how it relates to our own situation—because it matches our considered convictions about justice by impartially taking account of the interests of all citizens and of the worst off in particular. And such impartial concern for the interests of others is something Kant endorses, for instance, by holding that we have a moral duty to promote the happiness of others and especially the happiness of those most in need of help. We are not offending Kant, then, when we ask ourselves, as we go about helping others, what sort of help would best satisfy their needs and interests—even if we pose this question as a "selfish" hypothetical: What would they rationally want us to do for them? Analogously, we are not offending Kant when we ask ourselves, as we go about organizing our society, which social order would best satisfy the needs and interests of its citizens—even if we pose this question as a "selfish" hypothetical: What would these citizens rationally want to get out of their society? As Rawls might have put it: Although the deliberators in our thought experiment have only rational autonomy, we who conduct this experiment and honor its result (regardless of our personal interests and values) in our conduct thereby show our full autonomy (*PL* 72–79).

Second, there is an important difference between a concern for the satisfaction of inclinations (happiness) and a concern for the fulfillment of needs and interests or for success in terms of a conception of the good. To be sure, some citizens may decide to devote the social primary goods at their disposal to the pursuit of their own happiness. But many citizens will pursue very different conceptions of the good, focused perhaps on knowledge and culture, on love, family, and friendship, on protecting the environment, on athletic success, on artistic achievement, or on some religious project. The point of a Rawlsian society is not then to satisfy citizens' inclinations, to make them happy, but rather to enable them to attain their freely chosen aims (for the content and quality of which they are themselves responsible). To say it with a single word, the point of a Rawlsian social order is not the happiness of individuals, but their freedom. This point is reflected in the basic liberties and their priority, of course, but it is served by the remaining social primary goods as well, which are conceived as all-purpose means to almost any ends citizens might freely choose to set for themselves.

Third, while it is true that the Rawlsian primary goods are geared to this human world rather than to any conceivable world of rational beings, one can readily defend them as instantiating a more abstract categorical imperative: Justice requires that the interactions among rational beings be organized through such institutional arrangements as best enable their participants to attain their freely chosen goals. This move—which Rawls himself would probably have shunned in service to his method of avoidance—would present his conception as an application of a more general conception of justice to the specific conditions of this human world.

Before we conclude that the Kantian interpretation is defensible after all, we must discuss one last important discrepancy, which was first highlighted by Otfried Höffe. Kant distinguishes in his practical philosophy between the doctrine of right (*Rechtslehre*), concerned with the proper organization of society, and the doctrine of virtue, concerned with the ethical conduct of individuals. In the latter domain, motives play a central role: They are criterial for whether an action has moral worth and for whether its agent has good will and autonomy. In the doctrine of right, however, motives are sidelined. Here the concern is solely with *external* freedom—more precisely, with ensuring that persons have mutually secure domains of external freedom. To ensure this, persons must comply with legal restrictions placed upon their conduct, but their motives for such compliance are legally irrelevant. The discrepancy is then that, whereas Kant excludes a discussion of motives from the doctrine of right, Rawls does discuss motives at length—specifically the question whether and how a conception of justice and the institutional order it justifies can produce in citizens an effective sense of justice and the political virtues.

Rawls is interested in motives because he sees it as the task of political philosophy to identify a social order that is not merely just but also capable of enduring in our world. I do not want to say that Kant was not interested in this question. But he did not give it much thought beyond the suggestion that an enduring social order would need to rely on the police power of the state, on the threat and use of force. Rawls finds this answer doubly insufficient: Reliance on force alone is empirically inadequate and morally objectionable.

The empirical inadequacy Rawls sees does not arise from ordinary criminal lawbreaking, against which he, too, is willing to rely on the police. The problem is rather that those who hold influential positions within a democratic society may seek to shape its institutional order in favor of their own interests and values—officially and legally, through the political process. With the benefit of an additional 200 years of historical experience, Rawls sees more clearly than Kant the danger that a rule-governed competition among political (including religious or philosophical) parties or coalitions might degenerate into an all-out power struggle over the rules of competition themselves.

In taking this danger more seriously than Kant did, Rawls may also be motivated by the fact that the egalitarian character of the society he envisions makes it especially vulnerable to the problem. Kant held—notoriously—that the equality of citizens he endorsed is perfectly consistent with the utmost inequality in income and acquired wealth and privileges. By contrast, Rawls calls for the institutional order to be designed so as to optimize the lowest socioeconomic position. More seriously than Kant, Rawls is then challenged by an endurance problem for his ideal society: Is not this society doomed to failure because of the fact that its politically most influential citizens—those advantaged in terms of natural endowments, education, and economic means—will use their superior influence to dilute and undermine the egalitarian elements of its social order (answering to the fair value of the basic political liberties, fair equality of opportunity, and the difference principle)? Rawls's negative answer relies on citizens having an effective sense of justice that morally commits them to *justice as fairness* and to the institutional order this conception selects.

Furthermore, Rawls finds it morally desirable that a just social order should maintain itself not merely by sanctions but also and primarily by a widespread sense of justice, animated by a shared conception of justice. This does not mean, of course, that such a sense of justice should be legally mandatory; those who pay their taxes merely from fear of punishment should not be punished for that. It means only that we have reason to prefer a society that maintains itself by inspiring a widespread and effective sense of justice among its citizens over one that is sustained through a clever system of threats and inducements. Perhaps there is—as Kant asserted in regard to his republican constitution—some acceptable design of the institutional order that would function well even in a society of devils. But it would be preferable to have a social order that does not need to function well with devils because it inspires in its citizens the moral desire to display justice, fairness, and civility in their political conduct.

Though Rawls has not himself discussed the alleged divergence from Kant, there is reason then to concede it and score it as a point in Rawls's favor. Rawls sought to offer a Kantian interpretation, not an interpretation of Kant. Such a Kantian interpretation succeeds if Rawls's conception can be shown to correspond to Kant's in important ways and, where it diverges, to do so for good reason.

After the appearance of *TJ*, Rawls has both played up and played down his relationship to Kant. Kant figures in the title of a paper from the 1970s and also in the title of his three John Dewey Lectures (which were Rawls's most important publication between *TJ* and *PL*). The later version of these Dewey Lectures, published in *PL*, excises Kant's name as Rawls moves from "Kantian" to "political" constructivism.

We can understand these changes as follows. On the one hand, Rawls wants to present the connection between his conception and Kant's practical philosophy as an asymmetrical one. He wants to convince good Kantians that his conception is an authentic and attractive development of Kantian values and methods. But he also wants to convince the rest of his audience that they can accept his conception without thereby becoming Kantians. There is a Kantian interpretation of Rawls's conception, but this does not mean that there can be no other authentic interpretations of it—a Catholic one, for instance. Rawls wants to remain noncommittal on two Kantian doctrines in particular: He does not want to affirm or deny that human beings should strive to achieve autonomy of the will. Such questions concerning what makes a human life worth living should be left to citizens to answer individually as they see fit. (To be fair, one must add here that Kant would say the same in the context of his political philosophy—a point Rawls fails to appreciate. Unlike Rawls, Kant has developed a moral philosophy in addition to his political philosophy. But this does not mean that the latter is dependent on, or an integral part of, the former.) Further, Rawls does not want to affirm or deny that moral values and principles have their source in human reason. His conception of justice should therefore be acceptable to citizens who hold that the best life is the one most pleasing to God or believe that moral values and principles are independent of us in their existence or validity.

On the other hand, however, Kant's practical philosophy is not for Rawls merely one more comprehensive worldview among many, but, for him personally, the most important among them. I would think that Rawls's own worldview was Kantian in a deeper and more comprehensive sense than his political philosophy.

CONCLUSION

R AWLS has inspired much admiration and emulation for his commitment to bring the philosophical study of justice down to earth. His theory of justice is meant to be appealing, upon reflection, not merely to his colleagues in political philosophy but also to his fellow citizens as an attractive specification of ideas they already hold about their society as a fair system of social cooperation and about themselves as free and equal members of it. Moreover, this theory is meant to be a guide that citizens can apply to the political decisions they face. We should bear these ambitions in mind as we continue his work.

I have indicated some of the work that remains to be done. We might work out a sharper understanding of what it means for a society to ensure the fair value of the basic political liberties, as well as the security of all the basic liberties it guarantees. With the war on terror upon us, especially, we also need a more precise understanding of what reductions in basic liberties are justifiable by reference to the basic liberties themselves. Rawls did not give us all the answers. But he left us a living theoretical framework within which we can debate and resolve the political questions we face. If it is not used in this way, it becomes one more well-arranged bouquet of abstract ideas and principles for display in the philosophical museum. Using the framework as intended, we preserve and enhance that in which Rawls himself saw its value: its capacity to guide and to motivate.

APPENDIX

A.1 Timeline

1921   February 21, birth of John Bordley Rawls in Baltimore, Maryland, as the second of five sons of William Lee and Anna Abell Rawls (née Stump).

1939–43   Studies at Princeton University concluded with an AB degree.

1943–45   Military training and service in the Pacific.

1946–50   Graduate studies at Princeton University concluded with a PhD in philosophy.

1947–48   Fellowship student at Cornell University.

1949   Marriage to Margaret Warfield Fox.

1950   PhD dissertation, *A Study in the Grounds of Ethical Knowledge: Considered with Reference to Judgments on the Moral Worth of Character.* Birth of his first child: Anne Warfield.

1950–52   Instructor in the Princeton philosophy department.

1952–53   Fulbright fellow at Christ Church, Oxford.

1953   Appointment as assistant professor of philosophy at Cornell University.

1954   Birth of his second child: Robert Lee.

1955   "Two Concepts of Rules," proposing to confine the principle of utility to the assessment of practices. Birth of his third child: Alexander Emory.

1956   Promotion to associate professor with tenure at Cornell University.

1957/58   "Justice as Fairness," introducing an early version of his two principles of justice, by which persons should agree to assess and reform their shared practices. Birth of his youngest child: Elizabeth Fox.

1959–60   Visiting professor at Harvard University.

1960   Appointment as professor at the Massachusetts Institute of Technology.
1962   Appointment as professor of philosophy at Harvard University.
1969–70 Fellowship at the Stanford University Center for Advanced Study in the Behavioral Sciences.
1971   *A Theory of Justice.*
1974   Appointment as John Cowles Professor.
1974–75 Sabbatical at the University of Michigan.
1977   Sabbatical (fall) at the Princeton Institute for Advanced Study.
1979   Appointment as James Bryant Conant University Professor, succeeding Nobel Prize winner Kenneth Arrow.
1980   John Dewey Lectures: "Kantian Constructivism in Moral Theory."
1983   Honorary doctorate from Oxford University.
1986   Sabbatical (spring) in Oxford.
1987   Honorary doctorate from Princeton University.
1991   Retirement.
1993   *Political Liberalism.*
1996   *Political Liberalism*, revised and expanded edition.
1997   "The Idea of Public Reason Revisited."
        Honorary doctorate from Harvard University.
1999   *Collected Papers.*
        The Law of Peoples.
        A Theory of Justice, second edition, incorporating revisions made in 1974 for the German and subsequent translations.
        Rolf Schock Prize in the Field of Logic and Philosophy, awarded by the Royal Swedish Academy.
        National Humanities Medal of Excellence.
2001   *Lectures in Moral Philosophy.*
2002   November 24, death at his home in Lexington, Massachusetts.

A.2 Literature

A.2.1 Works by Rawls

A Study in the Grounds of Ethical Knowledge, Considered with Reference to Judgments on the Moral Worth of Character, 1950, see Dissertation Abstracts 15, 1955: 608–9.

"Review of *An Examination of the Place of Reason in Ethics*, by Stephen Toulmin," *Philosophical Review* 60 (1951): 572–80.

A Theory of Justice, Cambridge, MA: Harvard University Press 1971.

"Reply to Lyons and Teitelman," *Journal of Philosophy* 69 (1972): 556–57.

"Themes in Kant's Moral Philosophy," in Eckhart Forster, ed., *Kant's Transcendental Deductions: The Three Critiques and the Opus Postumum*, Stanford, CA: Stanford University Press 1989.

"Roderick Firth, His Life and Work," *Philosophy and Phenomenological Research* 51 (1991): 109–18.

Political Liberalism (*PL*), New York: Columbia University Press [1993], 1996; second edition 2005.

"Reconciliation through the Public Use of Reason" (Reply to Jürgen Habermas), *Journal of Philosophy* 92 (1995): 132–80.

A Theory of Justice (*TJ*), revised edition, Cambridge, MA: Harvard University Press 1999.

The Law of Peoples, with "The Idea of Public Reason Revisited" (*LP*), Cambridge, MA: Harvard University Press 1999.

Collected Papers (*CP*), ed. Samuel Freeman, Cambridge, MA: Harvard University Press 1999 (contains 27 papers with original publication dates from 1951 to 1998).

Lectures on the History of Moral Philosophy (*LMP*), ed. Barbara Herman, Cambridge, MA: Harvard University Press 2000.

Justice as Fairness: A Restatement (*JFR*), ed. Erin Kelly, Cambridge, MA: Harvard University Press 2001.

Lectures in Political Philosophy (*LPP*), ed. Samuel Freeman, Cambridge, MA: Harvard University Press forthcoming.

A.2.2 Selected Secondary Works

A.2.2.1 Collections

Arneson, Richard, ed., *Symposium on Rawlsian Theory of Justice: Recent Developments*, *Ethics* 99 (1989): 695–944.

Blocker, H. G., and E. H. Smith, eds., *John Rawls's Theory of Social Justice*, Athens: Ohio University Press 1980.

Brooks, Thom, and Fabian Freyenhagen, eds., *The Legacy of John Rawls* (reprinted from *Journal of Moral Philosophy*), New York and London: Continuum 2005.

Canterbery, E. Ray, and Harry G. Johnson, eds., *Justice, Nozick, and Rawls: A Symposium*, *Eastern Economic Journal* 4 (1978).

Corlett, J. Angelo, ed., *Equality and Liberty: Analyzing Rawls and Nozick*, New York: St. Martin's Press 1991.

Daniels, Norman, ed., *Reading Rawls: Critical Studies on Rawls'* A Theory of Justice, New York: Basic Books 1974.

Darwall, Stephen, ed., *Equal Freedom: Selected Tanner Lectures in Human Values*, Ann Arbor: University of Michigan Press 1995.

Davion, Virginia, and Clark Wolf, eds., *The Idea of Political Liberalism: Essays on Rawls*, Lanham, MD: Rowman and Littlefield 1999.

Freeman, Samuel, ed., *The Cambridge Companion to Rawls*, Cambridge: Cambridge University Press 2003.

George, Robert, and Christopher Wolfe, eds., *Natural Law and Public Reason*, Washington, DC: Georgetown University Press 2000.

Goodin, Robert, and Philip Pettit, *Contemporary Political Philosophy: An Anthology*, Oxford: Blackwell 1997; second edition 2005.

Goodin, Robert, Philip Pettit, and Thomas Pogge, eds., *Companion to Contemporary Political Philosophy*, Oxford: Blackwell 2007.

Griffin, Stephen, and Lawrence Solum, eds., *Symposium on John Rawls's Political Liberalism, Chicago-Kent Law Review* 69 (1994): 549–842.

Höffe, Otfried, ed., *Über John Rawls's Theorie der Gerechtigkeit*, Frankfurt: Suhrkamp 1977.

Höffe, Otfried, ed., *John Rawls: Eine Theorie der Gerechtigkeit*, Berlin: Akademie Verlag 1998.

The Legacy of John Rawls, special issue, *Politics, Philosophy & Economics*, 4 (2005): 155–248.

Lloyd, Sharon A., ed., *John Rawls's Political Liberalism*, special double issue, *Pacific Philosophical Quarterly* 75 (1994).

Martin, Rex, and David Reidy, eds., *Rawls's* Law of Peoples*: A Realistic Utopia?* Oxford: Blackwell 2006.

Rawls and the Law, special issue, *Fordham Law Review* 72 (2004), 1381–2175.

Reath, Andrews, Barbara Herman, and Christine M. Korsgaard, eds., *Reclaiming the History of Ethics: Essays for John Rawls*, Cambridge: Cambridge University Press 1997.

Richardson, Henry, and Paul Weithman, eds., *The Philosophy of Rawls: A Collection of Essays*, in 5 volumes, New York: Garland 1999: Volume I: *Development and Main Outlines of Rawls's Theory of Justice*; Volume II: The *Two Principles and Their Justification*; Volume III: *Opponents and Implications of A Theory of Justice*; Volume IV: *Moral Psychology and Community*; Volume V: *Reasonable Pluralism*.

Stayn, Susan, ed., *Symposium on* Political Liberalism, *Columbia Law Review* 94 (1994), 1813–1949.

Symposium: A Theory of Justice, Journal of Philosophy 69 (1972).

Symposium: The Role of Religion in Public Debate in a Liberal Society, San Diego Law Review 30 (1993): 643–916.

Wellbank, J. H., Dennis Snook, and David T. Mason: *John Rawls and His Critics: An Annotated Bibliography*, New York: Garland 1982.

A.2.2.2 *Monographs*

Ackerman, Bruce, *Social Justice in the Liberal State*, New Haven: Yale University Press 1980.

———. *We the People,* Vol. 1: *Foundations*, Cambridge, MA: Harvard University Press 1991.

Alejandro, Roberto, *The Limits of Rawlsian Justice*, Baltimore: Johns Hopkins University Press 1998.

Barry, Brian, *The Liberal Theory of Justice*, Oxford: Clarendon 1972.

———. *Theories of Justice*, Berkeley: University of California Press 1989.

Baynes, Kenneth, *The Normative Grounds of Social Criticism: Kant, Rawls, and Habermas,* Albany: State University of New York Press 1992.

Beitz, Charles, *Political Theory and International Relations,* Princeton, NJ: Princeton University Press 1979; second edition 1999.

Berlin, Isaiah, *Concepts and Categories,* London: Hogarth 1978.

———. *The Crooked Timber of Humanity,* New York: Knopf 1991.

———. *Four Essays on Liberty,* Oxford: Oxford University Press 1969.

Bidet, Jacques, *John Rawls et la Theorie de la Justice,* Paris: Presses Universitaires de France 1995.

Brandt, Richard B., *The Good and the Right,* Oxford: Clarendon 1979.

———. *Morality, Utilitarianism, and Rights,* Cambridge: Cambridge University Press 1992.

Brink, David O., *Moral Realism and the Foundations of Ethics,* Cambridge: Cambridge University Press 1989.

Buchanan, James, *The Limits of Liberty: Between Anarchy and Leviathan,* Chicago: University of Chicago Press 1975.

Campbell, Tom, *Justice: Issues in Political Theory,* Humanity Books 1988; revised and updated second edition, Palgrave Macmillan 2000.

Cohen, G. A., *If You're an Egalitarian, How Come You're So Rich?* Cambridge, MA: Harvard University Press 2000.

D'Amato, Anthony, *Jurisprudence,* Dordrecht: Nijhoff 1984.

Daniels, Norman, *Just Health Care,* Cambridge: Cambridge University Press 1985.

———. *Justice and Justification,* Cambridge: Cambridge University Press 1996.

Dombrowski, Daniel A., *Rawls and Religion: The Case for Political Liberalism,* Albany: State University of New York Press 2001.

Dworkin, Ronald, *A Matter of Principle,* Cambridge, MA: Harvard University Press 1985.

———. *Sovereign Virtue: The Theory and Practice of Equality,* Cambridge, MA: Harvard University Press 2000.

———. *Taking Rights Seriously,* Cambridge, MA: Harvard University Press 1977.

Ely, John Hart, *Democracy and Distrust: A Theory of Judicial Review,* Cambridge, MA: Harvard University Press 1980.

Fellner, William, *Probability and Profit,* Homewood, IL: R. D. Irwin 1965.

Fishkin, James S., *Justice, Equal Opportunity, and the Family,* New Haven, CT: Yale University Press 1983.

Freeman, Samuel, *Justice and the Social Contract: On Rawls and Rawlsian Justice,* Oxford: Oxford University Press 2006.

Galston, William A., *Justice and the Human Good,* Chicago: University of Chicago Press 1980.

Gauthier, David, *Morals by Agreement,* Oxford: Clarendon 1986.

Gibbard, Allan, *Wise Choices, Apt Feelings: A Theory of Normative Judgment,* Oxford: Clarendon 1990.

Gutmann, Amy, *Liberal Equality,* Cambridge: Cambridge University Press 1980.

Habermas, Jürgen, *Moral Consciousness and Communicative Action*, Cambridge, MA: MIT Press 1990.

Hampton, Jean, *Political Philosophy (Dimensions of Philosophy Series)*, Boulder, CO: Westview 1997.

Hart, H. L. A., *The Concept of Law*, Oxford: Clarendon 1961.

Herman, Barbara, *The Practice of Moral Judgment*, Cambridge, MA: Harvard University Press 1993.

Hill, Thomas, E., *Dignity and Practical Reason in Kant's Moral Theory*, Ithaca, NY: Cornell University Press 1992.

———. *Respect, Pluralism, and Justice: Kantian Perspectives*, New York: Oxford University Press 2000.

Höffe, Otfried, *Ethik und Politik*, Frankfurt: Suhrkamp 1979.

———. *Kategorische Rechtsprinzipien*, Frankfurt: Suhrkamp 1990.

———. *Politische Gerechtigkeit*, Frankfurt: Suhrkamp 1987.

Kant, Immanuel, *The Metaphysics of Morals*, Cambridge: Cambridge University Press 1996.

Kersting, Wolfgang, *John Rawls zur Einführung*, Hamburg: Junius 1993.

Kohlberg, Lawrence, *The Philosophy of Moral Development: Moral Stages and the Idea of Justice*, San Francisco: Harper & Row 1981.

Koller, Peter, *Neue Theorien des Sozialkontrakts*, Berlin: Duncker & Humblot 1987.

Kolm, Serge-Christophe, *Modern Theories of Justice*, Cambridge, MA: MIT Press 1996.

Korsgaard, Christine M., *The Sources of Normativity*, Cambridge: Cambridge University Press 1996.

Kukathas, Chandran, and Philip Pettit, *Rawls's* A Theory of Justice *and Its Critics*, Stanford, CA: Stanford University Press 1990.

Kymlicka, Will, *Contemporary Political Philosophy: An Introduction*, Oxford: Oxford University Press 1990; second edition 2001.

———. *Liberalism, Community, and Culture*, Oxford: Clarendon 1989.

Larmore, Charles, *Patterns of Moral Complexity*, Cambridge: Cambridge University Press 1987.

Lyons, David, *Ethics and the Rule of Law*, Cambridge: Cambridge University Press 1984.

———. *The Forms and Limits of Utilitarianism*, Oxford: Clarendon 1965.

Macedo, Stephen, *Liberal Virtues*, Oxford: Clarendon 1990.

Mackie, John, *Ethics: Inventing Right and Wrong*, New York: Penguin 1977.

Mandle, Jon, *Global Justice*, Cambridge: Polity 2006.

———. *What's Left of Liberalism: An Interpretation and Defense of Justice as Fairness*, Lanham, MD: Lexington 2000.

Martin, Rex, *Rawls and Rights*, Lawrence: University Press of Kansas 1985.

Meade, James Edward, *Efficiency, Equality, and the Ownership of Property*, Cambridge, MA: Harvard University Press 1965.

Miller, David, *Principles of Social Justice*, Cambridge MA: Harvard University Press 1999.

Munoz-Darde, Veronique, *La justice sociale: le liberalisme egalitaire de John Rawls*, Paris: Nathan Universite 2000.

Nagel, Thomas, *Equality and Partiality*, New York: Oxford University Press 1991.

———. *The Possibility of Altruism*, Oxford: Clarendon 1970.

———. *The View from Nowhere*, New York: Oxford University Press 1986.

Nozick, Robert, *Anarchy, State, and Utopia*, New York: Basic Books 1974.

Okin, Susan, *Justice, Gender, and the Family*, New York: Basic Books 1989.

O'Neill, Onora, *Bounds of Justice*, Cambridge: Cambridge University Press 2000.

———. *Constructions of Reason*, Cambridge: Cambridge University Press 1989.

———. *Towards Justice and Virtue: A Constructive Account of Practical Reasoning*, Cambridge: Cambridge University Press 1996.

Parfit, Derek, *Reasons and Persons*, Oxford: Clarendon 1984.

Peffer, Rodney, *Marxism, Morality and Social Justice*, Princeton, NJ: Princeton University Press 1989.

Pogge, Thomas, *Realizing Rawls*, Ithaca, NY: Cornell University Press 1989.

Raz, Joseph, *The Morality of Freedom*, Oxford: Clarendon 1986.

Richards, David A. J., *A Theory of Reasons for Action*, Oxford: Clarendon 1971.

Sandel, Michael, *Liberalism and the Limits of Justice*, Cambridge: Cambridge University Press 1982; second edition 1998.

Scanlon, Thomas M., *The Difficulty of Tolerance: Essays in Political Philosophy*, Cambridge: Cambridge University Press 2003.

———. *What We Owe to Each Other*, Cambridge, MA: Harvard University Press 1999.

Scheffler, Samuel, *Human Morality*, New York: Oxford University Press 1992.

Sen, Amartya K., *Collective Choice and Social Welfare*, San Francisco: Holden-Day 1970.

———. *Inequality Reexamined*, Cambridge, MA: Harvard University Press 1992.

———. *The Standard of Living*, Cambridge: Cambridge University Press 1987.

Shue, Henry, *Basic Rights: Subsistence, Affluence, and U.S. Foreign Policy*, Princeton, NJ: Princeton University Press 1980; second edition 1996.

Soper, Philip, *A Theory of Law*, Cambridge, MA: Harvard University Press 1984.

Stace, Walter, *The Theory of Knowledge and Existence*, Oxford: Clarendon 1932.

Tugendhat, Ernst, *Vorlesungen über Ethik*, Frankfurt: Suhrkamp 1993.

Van Parijs, Philippe, *Real Freedom for All: What (If Anything) Can Justify Capitalism?* Oxford: Clarendon 1995.

Waldron, Jeremy, *Law and Disagreement*, Oxford: Oxford University Press 2001.

———. *Liberal Rights*, Cambridge: Cambridge University Press 1993.

Walzer, Michael, *Just and Unjust Wars*, New York: Basic Books 1977.

———. *Spheres of Justice*, New York: Basic Books 1984.

Williams, Bernard, *Ethics and the Limits of Philosophy*, Cambridge, MA: Harvard University Press 1985.

———. *Moral Luck*, Cambridge, MA: Harvard University Press 1981.

Wolff, Robert Paul, *Understanding Rawls: A Reconstruction and Critique of A Theory of Justice*, Princeton, NJ: Princeton University Press 1977.

A.2.2.3 Essays

Ackerman, Bruce, "Political Liberalisms," *Journal of Philosophy* 91 (1994): 364–86.

Alejandro, Roberto, "What Is Political about Rawls's Political Liberalism?" *Journal of Politics* 58 (1996): 1–24.

Allen, Anita, "Social Contract Theory in American Case Law," *Florida Law Review* 51 (1999): 1–40.

Anderson, Elizabeth, "What Is the Point of Equality?" *Ethics* 109 (1999): 287–337.

Anderson, Perry, "On John Rawls," *Dissent* 140 (1994): 139–44.

Arneson, Richard, "Equality and Equal Opportunity for Welfare," *Philosophical Studies* 541 (1988): 79–95.

Arrow, Kenneth, "Some Ordinalist-Utilitarian Notes on Rawls's Theory of Justice," *Journal of Philosophy* 70 (1973): 245–63.

Audard, Catherine, "The Idea of 'Free Public Reason,'" *Ratio Juris* (1995): 15–29.

Baier, Kurt, "Justice and the Aims of Political Philosophy," *Ethics* 99 (1989): 771–90.

Barry, Brian, "John Rawls and the Search for Stability," *Ethics* 105 (1995): 874–915.

Beggs, Donald, "Rawls's Political Postmodernism," *Continental Philosophy Review* 32 (1999): 123–41.

Beitz, Charles, "Rawls's Law of Peoples," *Ethics* 110 (2000): 669–96.

Benson, Peter, "Rawls, Hegel, and Personhood: A Reply to Sybil Schwarzenbach," *Political Theory* 22 (1994): 491–500.

Binmore, Ken, "Naturalizing Harsanyi and Rawls," in M. Salles and J. Weymark, eds., *Justice, Political Liberalism, and Utilitarianism: Proceedings of the Caen Conference in Honor of John Harsanyi and John Rawls*, Cambridge: Cambridge University Press 1998.

Bohman, James, F., "Public Reason and Cultural Pluralism: Political Liberalism and the Problem of Moral Conflict," *Political Theory* 23 (1995): 253–79.

Brighouse, Harry, "Civic Education and Liberal Legitimacy," *Ethics* 108 (1998): 719–45.

———. "Is There Any Such Thing as Political Liberalism?" *Pacific Philosophical Quarterly* 75 (1994): 318–32.

Brink, David O., "Rawlsian Constructivism in Moral Theory," *Canadian Journal of Philosophy* 17 (1987): 71–90.

Brower, Bruce, "The Limits of Public Reason," *Journal of Philosophy* 91 (1994): 5–26.

Buchanan, Allen, "Justice, Legitimacy, and Human Rights," in Victoria Davion and Clark Wolf, eds., *The Idea of Political Liberalism*, Lanham, MD: Rowman and Littlefield 2000.

———. "Rawls's Law of Peoples: Rules for a Vanished Westphalian World," *Ethics* 110 (2000): 697–721.

Caney, Simon, "Cosmopolitanism and the Law of Peoples," *Journal of Political Philosophy* 10 (2002): 95–123.

Chapman, John W., "Review of *A Theory of Justice*," *American Political Science Review* 69 (1975): 588–93.

Charney, Evan, "Political Liberalism, Deliberative Democracy, and the Public Sphere," *American Political Science Review* 92 (1998): 97–110.

Clark, Barry, and Herbert Gintis, "Rawlsian Justice and Economic Systems," *Philosophy and Public Affairs* 7 (1978): 302–25.

Cohen, G. A., "Incentives, Inequality, and Community," in Grethe Peterson, ed., *The Tanner Lectures on Human Values XIII*, Salt Lake City: University of Utah Press 1992; and in Darwall 1995.

———. "On the Currency of Egalitarian Justice," *Ethics* 99 (1989): 906–44.

———. "The Pareto Argument for Inequality," *Social Philosophy and Policy* 12 (1995): 160–85.

———. "Where the Action Is: On the Site of Distributive Justice," *Philosophy and Public Affairs* 26 (1997): 3–30.

Cohen, Joshua, "Democratic Equality," *Ethics* 99 (1989): 727–51; and in Richardson and Weithman, Vol. I, 1999.

———. "Moral Pluralism and Political Consensus," in David Copp, Jean Hampton, and John E. Roemer, eds., *The Idea of Democracy*, Cambridge: Cambridge University Press 1993, 270–91.

———. "A More Democratic Liberalism," *Michigan Law Review* 92 (1994): 1503–46.

Coleman, James S., "Review of *A Theory of Justice*," *American Journal of Sociology* 80 (1974): 739–63.

Crocker, Lawrence, "Equality, Solidarity, and Rawls' Maximin," *Philosophy and Public Affairs* 6 (1977): 262–66.

Cushing, Simon, "Agreement in Social Contract Theories: Locke vs. Rawls," in Yaeger Hudson, ed., *Technology, Morality and Social Policy*, Lewiston ME: Mellen 1998.

Daniels, Norman, "Equal Liberty and Unequal Worth of Liberty," in Daniels, ed., 1974.

———. "Equality of What: Welfare, Resources, or Capabilities?" *Philosophy and Phenomenological Research* 50 (1990): 273–96.

———. "Wide Reflective Equilibrium and Theory Acceptance in Ethics," *Journal of Philosophy* 76 (1979): 256–82.

Darwall, Stephen, "A Defense of the Kantian Interpretation," *Ethics* 86 (1976): 164–70.

Darwall, Stephen, Allan Gibbard, and Peter Railton, "Toward *Fin de siècle* Ethics: Some Trends," *Philosophical Review* 101 (1992): 115–89.

Davidson, Arnold, "Is Rawls a Kantian?" *Pacific Philosophical Quarterly* 66 (1985): 48–77.

De Marneffe, Peter, "Contractualism, Liberty, and Democracy," *Ethics* 104 (1994): 764–83.

———. "Liberalism, Liberty, and Neutrality," *Philosophy and Public Affairs*, 19 (1990): 253–74.

Dworkin, Gerald, "Contracting Justice," *Philosophical Books* 36 (1995): 19–26.

Dworkin, Ronald, "The Foundations of Liberal Equality," in Grethe Peterson, ed., *The Tanner Lectures on Human Values XI*, Salt Lake City: University of Utah Press 1990.

Estlund, David, "The Insularity of the Reasonable: Why Political Liberalism Must Admit the Truth," *Ethics* 108 (1998): 252–75.

———. "Liberalism, Equality and Fraternity in Cohen's Critique of Rawls," *Journal of Political Philosophy* 6 (1998): 99–112.

———. "The Survival of Egalitarian Justice in John Rawls's *Political Liberalism*," *Journal of Political Philosophy* 4 (1996): 68–78.

Farrelly, Colin, "Public Reason, Neutrality, and Civic Virtues," *Ratio Juris* 12 (1999): 11–25.

Feinberg, Joel, "Duty and Obligation to the Non-Ideal World," *Journal of Philosophy* 70 (1973): 263–75.

———. "Review of *A Theory of Justice*," *Yale Law Journal* 81 (1972): 1004–31.

Fischer, Marilyn, "Associations and the Political Conception of Justice," *Journal of Social Philosophy* 28 (1997): 31–42.

Fleming, James, E., "Securing Deliberative Autonomy," *Stanford Law Review* 48 (1995): 1–71.

Follesdal, Andreas, "The Standing of Illiberal States: Stability and Toleration in John Rawls's *Law of Peoples*," *Acta Analytica* (1997): 149–60.

Freedman, Eric, "Campaign Finance and the First Amendment: A Rawlsian Analysis," *Iowa Law Review* 85 (2000): 1065–105.

Freeman, Samuel, "The Law of Peoples, Social Cooperation, Human Rights, and Distributive Justice," *Social Philosophy and Policy* 23 (2006).

———. "Reason and Agreement in Social Contract Views," *Philosophy and Public Affairs* 19 (1990): 122–57.

———. "Utilitarianism, Deontology, and the Priority of Right," *Philosophy and Public Affairs* 23 (1994): 313–49.

Galston, William A., "Moral Personality and Liberal Theory," *Political Theory* 10 (1982): 492–519.

Gaus, Gerald F., "Reasonable Pluralism and the Domain of the Political: How the Weaknesses of John Rawls's *Political Liberalism* Can Be Overcome by a Justificatory Liberalism," *Inquiry* 42 (1999): 259–84.

Gaut, Berys, "Rawls and the Claims of Liberal Legitimacy," *Philosophical Papers* 24 (1995): 1–22.

Gauthier, David, "Justice and Natural Endowment: Toward a Critique of Rawls's Ideological Framework," *Social Theory and Practice* 3 (1974): 3–26.

George, Robert, "Public Reason and Political Conflict: Abortion and Homosexuality," *Yale Law Journal* 106 (1997): 2475–504.

Gibbard, Allan, "Disparate Goods and Rawls's Difference Principle: A Social Choice Theoretic Treatment," *Theory and Decision* 11 (1979): 267–88.

Giusti, Miguel, "Die liberalistische Suche nach einem 'übergreifenden Konsens,'" *Philosophische Rundschau* 41 (1994): 53–73.

Gutmann, Amy, "Communitarian Critics of Liberalism," *Philosophy and Public Affairs* 14 (1985): 308–22.

Gutmann, Amy, and Dennis Thompson, "Moral Conflict and Political Consensus," in R. Bruce Douglass et al., eds., *Liberalism and the Good*, New York: Routledge 1990.

Guyer, Paul, "Life, Liberty, and Property: Rawls and Kant," in Paul Guyer: *Kant on Freedom, Law, and Happiness*, Cambridge: Cambridge University Press 2000.

Habermas, Jürgen, "Reconciliation through the Public Use of Reason: Remarks on John Rawls's *Political Liberalism*," *Journal of Philosophy* 92 (1995): 109–31.

Haldane, John, "The Individual, the State, and the Common Good," *Social Philosophy and Policy* 13 (1996): 59–79.

Hammond, Peter J., "Equity, Arrow's Conditions, and Rawls's Difference Principle," *Econometrica* 44 (1976): 793–804.

Hampshire, Stuart, "Review of *A Theory of Justice*," *New York Review of Books*, 18: 3 (1972): 34–39.

Hampton, Jean, "The Common Faith of Liberalism," *Pacific Philosophical Quarterly* 75 (1994): 186–216.

———. "Contracts and Choices: Does Rawls Have a Social Contract Theory?" *Journal of Philosophy* 77 (1980): 315–38.

Harrod, R. F., "Utilitarianism Revisited," *Mind* 45 (1936): 281–97.

Harsanyi, John C., "Can the Maximin Principle Serve as a Basis for Morality? A Critique of John Rawls's Theory," *American Political Science Review* 69 (1975): 594–606.

Hart, H. L. A., "Rawls on Liberty and its Priority," in Daniels, ed., 1974.

Hill, Thomas, E., "The Problem of Stability in *Political Liberalism*," *Pacific Philosophical Quarterly* 75 (1994): 332–52; and in Hill 2000.

———. "Review of John Rawls's *Collected Papers*," *Journal of Philosophy* 98 (2001): 269–72.

Hinsch, Wilfried, "Global Distributive Justice," in Thomas Pogge, ed., *Global Justice*, Oxford: Blackwell 2001.

Hittinger, Russell, "John Rawls, Political Liberalism" *Review of Metaphysics* 47 (1994): 585–602.

Hoffman, Stanley, "Dreams of a Just World," *New York Review of Books* 53 (1995): 52–56.

Holmes, Stephen, "John Rawls and the Limits of Tolerance," *New Republic* 39 (1993): 39–47.

Howe, Roger E., and John E. Roemer, "Rawlsian Justice as the Core of a Game," *American Economic Review* 71 (1981): 880–95.

Huemer, Michael, "Rawls's Problem of Stability," *Social Theory and Practice* 22 (1996): 375–95.

Hurd, Heidi M., "The Levitation of Liberalism," *Yale Law Journal* 105 (1995): 795–824.

Ivison, Duncan, "The Secret History of Public Reason: Hobbes to Rawls," *History of Political Thought* 18 (1997): 125–47.

James, Aaron, "Constructing Justice for Existing Practice: Rawls and the Status Quo," *Philosophy and Public Affairs* 33 (2005): 281–316.

Johnson, Oliver, "Autonomy in Kant and Rawls: A Reply," *Ethics* 87 (1977): 251–54.

———. "The Kantian Interpretation," *Ethics* 85 (1974): 53–66.

Jones, Peter, "International Human Rights: Philosophical or Political?" in Simon Caney, David George, and Peter Jones, eds., *National Rights, International Obligations*, Boulder, CO: Westview 1996, 183–204.

Kelly, Erin, "Book Review of John Rawls's *A Theory of Justice*, Revised Edition," *Philosophical Review*, 110 (2001): 421–25.

———. "Justice and Communitarian Identity Politics," *Journal of Value Inquiry* 35 (2001): 71–93.

Kelly, Erin, and Lionel McPherson, "On Tolerating the Unreasonable," *Journal of Political Philosophy* 9 (2001): 38–55.

Kittay, Eva Feder, "Human Dependency and Rawlsian Equality," in Diana Tietjens Meyers, ed., *Feminists Rethink the Self*, Boulder, CO: Westview 1997, 219–66.

Klosko, George, "Political Constructivism in Rawls's Political Liberalism," *American Political Science Review* 91 (1997): 635–46.

———. "Political Obligation and the Natural Duties of Justice," *Philosophy and Public Affairs* 23 (1994): 251–70.

———. "Rawls's Argument from Political Stability," *Columbia Law Review* 94 (1994): 1882–97.

Krasnoff, Larry, "Consensus, Stability, and Normativity in Rawls's *Political Liberalism*," *Journal of Philosophy* 95 (1998): 269–92.

———. "How Kantian Is Constructivism?" *Kant-Studien* 90 (1999): 385–409.

Kraus, Jody S., "Political Liberalism and Truth," *Legal Theory* 5 (1999): 45–73.

Krouse, Richard, and Michael McPerson, "Capitalism, 'Property-Owning Democracy,' and the Welfare State," in Amy Gutman, ed., *Democracy and the Welfare State*, Princeton, NJ: Princeton University Press 1988, 79–106.

Kuper, Andrew, "Rawlsian Global Justice: Beyond the Law of Peoples to a Cosmopolitan Law of Persons," *Political Theory* 28 (2000): 640–74.

Laden, Anthony, "Games, Fairness, and Rawls's *A Theory of Justice*," *Philosophy and Public Affairs* 20 (1991): 189–222.

———. "The House That Jack Built: Thirty Years of Reading Rawls," *Ethics* 113 (2003), 367–90.

———. "Radical Liberals, Reasonable Feminists: Reason, Power and Objectivity in the Work of MacKinnon and Rawls," *Journal of Political Philosophy* 11 (2003): 133–52.

Larmore, Charles, "Lifting the Veil," *New Republic*, 5 February 2001, Issue No. 4490, 32–37 (a review of Rawls's *Lectures of the History of Moral Philosophy*).

———. "The Moral Basis of Political Liberalism," *Journal of Philosophy* 96 (1999): 599–625.

Lavine, Andrew, "Rawls's Kantianism," *Social Theory and Practice* 3 (1974): 47–63.

Lehning, Percy B., "The Coherence of Rawls's Plea for Democratic Equality," *Critical Review of International Social and Political Philosophy* 1 (1998): 1–41.

———. "The Idea of Public Reason: Can It Fulfil Its Task?" *Ratio Juris* 8 (1995): 30–39.

Lloyd, Sharon A., "Family Justice and Social Justice," *Pacific Philosophical Quarterly* 75 (1994): 353–71.

———. "Situating a Feminist Criticism of John Rawls's *Political Liberalism*," *Loyola (Los Angeles) Law Review* 28 (1995): 1319–44.

Lomasky, Loren, "Libertarianism at Twin Harvard," *Social Philosophy and Policy* 22 (2005): 178–99.

Lyons, David, "Rawls versus Utilitarianism," *Journal of Philosophy* 69 (1972): 535–45.

———. "Utility and Rights," in J. Roland Pennock and John W. Chapman, eds., *Ethics, Economics, and the Law*, New York: New York University Press 1982.

MacCallum, Gerald, "Negative and Positive Freedom," *Philosophical Review* 76 (1967): 312–34.

Macedo, Stephen, "Liberal Civic Education and Religious Fundamentalism: The Case of God v. John Rawls?" *Ethics* 105 (1995): 468–96.

Macpherson, C. B., "Class, Classlessness, and the Critique of Rawls: A Reply to Nielsen," *Political Theory* 6 (1978): 208–21.

Mallon, Ron, "Political Liberalism, Cultural Membership, and the Family," *Social Theory and Practice* 25 (1999): 271–97.

Mandle, Jon, "Justice, Desert, and Ideal Theory," *Social Theory and Practice* 23 (1997): 399–425.

———. "The Reasonable in Justice as Fairness," *Canadian Journal of Philosophy* 29 (1999): 75–107.

Marneffe, Peter de, "Liberalism and Perfectionism," *American Journal of Jurisprudence* 43 (1998): 99–116.

———. "Rawls on Public Reason," *Pacific Philosophical Quarterly* 75 (1994): 232–50.

McCabe, David, "Private Lives and Public Virtues: The Idea of a Liberal Community," *Canadian Journal of Philosophy* 28 (1998): 557–86.

McCarthy, Thomas, "Kantian Constructivism and Reconstructivism: Rawls and Habermas in Dialogue," *Ethics* 105 (1994): 44–63.

———. "On the Idea of a Reasonable Law of Peoples," in J. Bohman and M. Lutz-Buhmann, eds., *Perpetual Peace: Essays on Kant's Cosmopolitan Idealism*, Cambridge, MA: MIT Press 1997, 201–18.

————. "Two Conceptions of Cosmopolitan Justice," in I. MacKenzie and S. O'Neill, eds., *Reconstituting Social Criticism*, New York: St. Martins Press 1999.

McClain, Linda C., "Toleration, Autonomy, and Governmental Promotion of Good Lives: Beyond 'Empty' Toleration to Toleration as Respect," *Ohio State Law Journal* 59 (1998): 19–132.

McClennen, Edward, "Justice and the Problem of Stability," *Philosophy and Public Affairs* 18 (1989): 3–30.

Michaelman, Frank I., "Constitutional Welfare Rights and *A Theory of Justice*," in Daniels, ed., 1974.

————. "On Regulating Practices with Theories Drawn from Them," in Ian Shapiro and Judith Wagner DeCew, eds., *Theory and Practice* (Nomos 38), New York: New York University Press 1995.

————. "The Subject of Liberalism," *Stanford Law Review* 46 (1994): 1807–33.

Milo, Ronald, "Contractarian Constructivism," *Journal of Philosophy* 122 (1995): 181–204.

Moellendorf, Darrel, "Constructing a Law of Peoples," *Pacific Philosophical Quarterly* 77 (1996): 132–54.

Moore, Margaret, "On Reasonableness," *Journal of Applied Philosophy* 13 (1996): 167–77.

Mouffe, Chantal, "Political Liberalism: Neutrality and the Political," *Ratio Juris* 7 (1994): 314–24.

Mulhall, Stephen, "Promising, Consent, and Citizenship," *Political Theory* 25 (1997): 171–92.

Munoz-Darde, Veronique, "Rawls, Justice in the Family and Justice of the Family," *Philosophical Quarterly* 48 (1998): 335–52.

Murphy, Liam, "Institutions and the Demands of Justice," *Philosophy and Public Affairs* 27 (1998): 151–91.

Musgrave, R. A., "Maximin, Uncertainty, and the Leisure Trade-Off," *Quarterly Journal of Economics* 88 (1974): 625–32.

Nagel, Thomas, "Moral Conflict and Political Legitimacy," *Philosophy and Public Affairs* 16 (1987): 215–40.

————. "The Problem of Global Justice," *Philosophy and Public Affairs* 33 (2005): 113–47.

————. "The Rigorous Compassion of John Rawls," *New Republic*, 25 October 1999: 36–41 (Review of *Collected Papers, The Law of Peoples*, and *A Theory of Justice, Revised Edition*).

Naticchia, Chris, "Human Rights, Liberalism, and Rawls's *Law of Peoples*," *Social Theory and Practice* 24 (1998): 345–74.

————. "Justice as Fairness: Epistemological Not Political," *Southern Journal of Philosophy* 37 (1999): 597–611.

Neal, Patrick, "Does He Mean What He Says? (Mis)Understanding Rawls's Practical Turn," in Patrick Neal: *Liberalism and Its Discontents*, New York: New York University Press 1997.

Newey, Glen, "Floating on the LILO: John Rawls and the Content of Justice," *Times Literary Supplement*, 10 September 1999: 9–10 (Review of Rawls's *Collected Papers*).

Nussbaum, Martha, "The Enduring Significance of John Rawls," *Chronicle of Higher Education*, 20 July 2001.

———. "The Feminist Critique of Liberalism," in Martha Nussbaum, *Sex and Social Justice*, New York: Oxford University Press 1999, 55–80.

Okin, Susan, "'Forty Acres and a Mule' for Women: Rawls and Feminism," *Politics, Philosophy and Economics* 42 (2005): 233–48.

———. "*Political Liberalism*, Justice and Gender," *Ethics* 105 (1994): 23–43.

———. "Review of *Political Liberalism*," *American Political Science Review* 87 (1993): 1010–11.

O'Neill, Onora, "The Method of *A Theory of Justice*," in Otfried Hoeffe, ed., *John Rawls: Eine Theorie der Gerechtigkeit*, Berlin: Akademic Verlag 1998.

———. "Political Liberalism and Public Reason: A Critical Notice of John Rawls, *Political Liberalism*," *Philosophical Review* 106 (1998): 411–28.

Paden, Roger, "Reciprocity and Intergenerational Justice," *Public Affairs Quarterly* 10 (1996): 249–66.

———. "Reconstructing Rawls's *Law of Peoples*," *Ethics and International Affairs* 11 (1997): 215–32.

Peffer, Rodney G., "Towards a More Adequate Rawlsian Theory of Social Justice," *Pacific Philosophical Quarterly* 75 (1994): 251–71.

Pettit, Philip, "Book Review of John Rawls's *Political Liberalism*," *Journal of Philosophy* 91 (1994): 215–20.

Piper, Adrian, "Personal Continuity and Instrumental Rationality in Rawls' *Theory of Justice*," *Social Theory and Practice* 13 (1987): 49–76.

Pogge, Thomas, "'Assisting' the Global Poor," in Deen K. Chatterjee, ed., *The Ethics of Assistance: Morality and the Distant Needy*, Cambridge: Cambridge University Press 2004, 260–88.

———. "Do Rawls's Two Theories of Justice Fit Together?" in Martin and Reidy, 2006.

———. "An Egalitarian Law of Peoples," *Philosophy and Public Affairs* 23 (1994): 195–224.

———. "Equal Liberty for All?" *Midwest Studies in Philosophy* 28 (2004): 266–81.

———. "Human Flourishing and Universal Justice," *Social Philosophy and Policy* 16 (1999): 333–61.

———. "Is Kant's *Rechtslehre* a 'Comprehensive Liberalism'?" in Mark Timmons, ed., *Kant's* Metaphysics of Morals*: Interpretive Essays,* Oxford: Oxford University Press 2002, 133–58.

———. "The Kantian Interpretation of Justice as Fairness," *Zeitschrift für philosophische Forschung* 35 (1981): 7–65.

———. "On the Site of Distributive Justice: Reflections on Cohen and Murphy," *Philosophy and Public Affairs*, 2000.

———. "Rawls and Global Justice" *Canadian Journal of Philosophy* 18 (1988): 227–56.

————. "Three Problems with Contractarian-Consequentialist Ways of Assessing Social Institutions" *Social Philosophy and Policy* 12 (1995): 241–66.

Proudfoot, Wayne, "Rawls on the Individual and the Social," *Journal of Religious Ethics* 2 (1974): 107–28.

Quinn, Philip, L., "Political Liberalisms and Their Exclusions of the Religious," *Proceedings and Addresses of the American Philosophical Association* 69 (1995): 35–56.

Raz, Joseph, "Disagreement in Politics," *American Journal of Jurisprudence* 43 (1998): 25–52.

————. "Facing Diversity: The Case of Epistemic Abstinence," *Philosophy and Public Affairs* 19 (1990): 3–46.

Rogers, Ben, "Behind the Veil," *Lingua Franca* 9 (1999): 57–65.

Rorty, Richard, "The Priority of Democracy to Philosophy," in Merrill D. Peterson and Robert C. Vaughan, eds., *The Virginia Statute for Religious Freedom*, Cambridge: Cambridge University Press 1988.

Russell, J. S., "Okin's Rawlsian Feminism? Justice in the Family and Another Liberalism," *Social Theory and Practice* 21 (1995): 397–426.

Sandel, Michael, "Political Liberalism," *Harvard Law Review* 107 (1994): 1765–94.

Scanlon, Thomas M., "Contractualism and Utilitarianism," in Amartya Sen and Bernard Williams, eds., *Utilitarianism and Beyond,* Cambridge: Cambridge University Press 1982, 103–28; and in Scanlon, 2003.

————. "The Moral Basis of Interpersonal Comparisons," in John Elster and John Roemer, eds., *Interpersonal Comparisons of Well-Being*, Cambridge: Cambridge University Press 1991, 17–44.

————. "Rawls's *Theory of Justice*," *University of Pennsylvania Law Review* 121 (1973): 1020–69; revised version in Daniels, ed., 1974, 169–205.

Schaller, Walter E., "Rawls, the Difference Principle, and Economic Inequality," *Pacific Philosophy Quarterly* 79 (1998): 368–91.

Scheffler, Samuel, "The Appeal of Political Liberalism," *Ethics* 105 (1994): 4–22.

————. "Justice and Desert in Liberal Theory," *California Law Review* 88 (2000): 965–90.

————. "Moral Independence and the Original Position," *Philosophical Studies* 35 (1979): 288–303.

————. "What Is Egalitarianism?" *Philosophy and Public Affairs* 31 (2003): 5–39.

Schneewind, J. B., "What's Fair Is Fair," *New York Times Book Review*, 24 June 2001: 21 (Review of Rawls's *Justice as Fairness: A Restatement*).

Schwarzenbach, Sibyl A., "Rawls, Hegel and Communitarianism," *Political Theory* 19 (1991): 539–71.

Sen, Amartya K., "Equality of What," in Amartya Sen, *Choice, Welfare and Measurement*, Cambridge, MA: MIT Press 1982.

————. "Justice: Means versus Freedom," *Philosophy and Public Affairs* 19 (1990): 111–21.

————. "Rawls versus Bentham: An Axiomatic Examination of the Pure Distribution Problem," *Theory and Decision* 4 (1974): 301–9.

Simmons, A. John, "Justification and Legitimacy," *Ethics* 109 (1999): 739–71.

Smith, Paul, "Incentives and Justice: G. A. Cohen's Egalitarian Critique of Rawls," *Social Theory and Practice* 24 (1998): 205–35.

Solum, Lawrence, "Inclusive Public Reason," *Pacific Philosophical Quarterly* 75 (1994): 217–31.

Stark, Cynthia, "Hypothetical Consent and Justification," *Journal of Philosophy* 97 (2000): 313–34.

Sterba, James, "Reconciling Public Reason and Religious Values," *Social Theory and Practice* 25 (1999): 1–28.

Strasnick, Steven, "The Problem of Social Choice: Arrow to Rawls," *Philosophy and Public Affairs* 5 (1976): 241–73.

————. "Social Choice Theory and the Derivation of Rawls's Difference Principle," *Journal of Philosophy* 73 (1976): 85–99.

Sunstein, Cass R., et al., "Moral Heuristics," *Behavioral and Brain Sciences* 28 (2005): 531–73.

Tan, Kok-Chor, "Critical Notice: Rawls's *The Law of Peoples*," *Canadian Journal of Philosophy* 31 (2001): 113–32.

————. "Liberal Toleration in Rawls's Law of Peoples," *Ethics* 108 (1998): 276–95.

Tasioulas, John, "From Utopia to Kazanistan: John Rawls and the Law of Peoples," *Oxford Journal of Legal Studies* 22 (2002): 367–96.

Teitelman, Michael, "The Limits of Individualism," *Journal of Philosophy* 69 (1972): 545–56.

Thero, Daniel, "Rawls and Environmental Ethics: A Critical Examination of the Literature," *Environmental Ethics* 17 (1995): 93–105.

————. "The Self in the Original Position," *Dialogos* 33 (1998): 159–74.

Van Parijs, Philippe, "Rawlsians, Christians and Patriots. Maximin Justice and Individual Ethics," *European Journal of Philosophy* 1 (1993): 309–42.

Waldron, Jeremy, "Disagreements about Justice," *Pacific Philosophical Quarterly* 75 (1994): 372–87.

————. "John Rawls and the Social Minimum," *Journal of Applied Philosophy* 3 (1986): 21–33; and in Waldron 1993, 250–70.

————. "The Plight of the Poor in the Midst of Plenty," *London Review of Books* 21: 14 (1999): 3–6 (Review of Rawls's *Collected Papers*).

Weinstock, Daniel, "The Justification of Political Liberalism," *Pacific Philosophical Quarterly* 75 (1994): 165–85

Weithman, Paul, "Contractualist Liberalism and Deliberative Democracy," *Philosophy and Public Affairs* 24 (1995): 314–43.

————. "Liberalism and the Political Character of Political Philosophy," in C. F. Delaney, ed., *The Liberalism-Communitarianism Debate*, Lanham, MD: Rowman and Littlefield 1994.

————. "Rawlsian Liberalism and the Privatization of Religion: Three Theological Objections Considered," *Journal of Religious Ethics* 22 (1994):

3–28, with replies by David Hollenbach, Timothy Jackson, and John Langan, S.J.

———. "Taking Rites Seriously," *Pacific Philosophical Quarterly* 75 (1994): 272–94.

———. "Waldron on Political Legitmacy and the Social Minimum," *Philosophical Quarterly*, 45 (1995): 218–24.

Wenar, Leif, "Contractualism and Global Economic Justice," in Thomas Pogge, ed., *Global Justice*, Oxford: Blackwell 2001, 76–90.

———. "*Political Liberalism*: An Internal Critique," *Ethics* 106 (1995): 32–62.

Westmoreland, Robert, "The Truth about Public Reason," *Law and Philosophy* 18 (1999): 271–96.

Wilkins, Burleigh, "A Third Principle of Justice," *Journal of Ethics* 1 (1997): 355–74.

Williams, Andrew, "Incentives, Inequality, and Publicity," *Philosophy and Public Affairs* 27 (1998): 225–47.

———. "The Revisionist Difference Principle," *Canadian Journal of Philosophy* 25 (1995): 257–82.

Williams, Bernard, "A Fair State," *London Review of Books* 7 (1993): 7–8.

Wolff, Jonathan, "Fairness, Respect, and the Egalitarian Ethos," *Philosophy and Public Affairs* 27 (1998): 97–122.

Wolin, Sheldon S., "The Liberal/Democratic Divide: On Rawls's *Political Liberalism*," *Political Theory* 24 (1996): 97–119.

Wolterstoff, Nicholas, "Why We Should Reject What Liberalism Tells Us about Thinking and Acting in Public for Religious Reasons," in Paul Weithman, ed., *Religion and Contemporary Liberalism*, South Bend, IN: Notre Dame Press 1997.

Young, Iris, M., "Rawls's *Political Liberalism*," *Journal of Political Philosophy* 3 (1995): 181–90.

Yuracko, Kimberly A., "Towards Feminist Perfectionism: A Radical Critique of Rawlsian Liberalism," *UCLA Women's Law Journal* 6 (1995): 1–48.

Zipursky, Benjamin C., "Self Defense, Domination, and Social Contract," *University of Pittsburgh Law Review* 57 (1996): 579–614.

Zuckert, Michael P., "The New Rawls and Constitutional Theory: Does It Really Taste That Much Better?" *Constitutional Commentary* 11 (1994): 227–45.

INDEX

adequacy (of scheme of basic
    liberties), 82–92, 96–99, 102,
    104, 149–52, 154
  three dimensions of, 92,
    149–51, 154
    extent/extensiveness 83, 86,
      88–92, 98, 149–51, 154
    security, 83–84, 90, 92, 98,
      149–51, 154
    (fair) value of basic political
      liberties, 92, 149–51, 154
    See also basic liberties; political
      liberties
affirmative action, 121
age, 122
aggregation (function), 53–54, 67,
    78, 111–12
  maximean, 53, 67
  maximin, 68
Albritton, Rogers, 17–18, 21, 23
Anarchy, State, and Utopia, 178
anonymity condition, 48–53,
    62–67, 107
Aristotelian principle, 54, 188
Aristotle, 185, 188
Arrow, Kenneth, 23

art, 10, 15, 87, 168
Augustine, 11
Austin, John L., 16
autonomy, 56, 145, 173, 189–93, 195

Baltimore, 4–7, 10, 17
Banfield, Edward, 21
Barber, Benjamin, 185
bargaining power, 52, 64–65
basic liberties/rights, 40, 66, 73,
    77–105, 113, 117, 130,
    148–51, 154, 156, 158,
    172–73, 179, 192, 196
  extent/extensiveness of, 83–84,
    86, 89–92, 95–99, 156, 172
    adequate, 83, 98
    constitutional essential, 95, 150
    defined, 83–84
    fully adequate, 86, 88–92,
      149–51, 154
  lexical priority of, 77–80, 84–85,
    96–97, 101–05, 183, 186
  listed, 82–85
  political. *See* political liberties
  reductions of, 97–105, 196
    equal, 98–99

basic reductions of
    liberties/rights (*continued*)
    impermissible, 101–05
    permissible, 96–101
    unequal, 98–99, 105
    restrictions of, 86–88, 97–101
    equal, 97, 99
    impermissible, 96, 101
    permissible, 97
    unequal, 97–98, 105
    scheme of, 82–87, 89, 91–92,
        97, 98, 99, 102, 104, 149,
        151, 154
    adequate, 83–84, 87, 89–92,
        96, 98–99, 102, 104
    fully adequate, 82–92, 97–99,
        102, 149–51, 154
    inadequate, 86, 98, 104
    least adequate, 96, 98–99
    security of, 83–85, 90, 92–93, 95,
        98–100, 102, 148–50, 152,
        154–56, 196
    adequate, 83, 98, 154
    constitutional essential, 95,
        150, 154
    defined, 84
    fully adequate, 84, 90, 92,
        149–51
    threshold, 84–85, 156
    value/worth of, 83, 92, 156, 188
basic needs, 102–04, 117, 173
    constitutional essentials, 104,
        150, 152
    principle of, 117, 133, 148–50, 152
    lexically prior to first principle,
        103–04
basic political liberties. *See* political
    liberties
basic rights. *See* basic liberties
basic structure, 28–44, 54, 58–63,
    70–81, 85–91, 96–99,
    102–04, 106–07, 111–12,
    116–26, 130, 133, 135, 137,
    139–40, 142, 146, 149,
    153–56, 158–9, 162, 173,
    175, 179, 185–87 (*see also*
    institutional order)
    defined, 29
Baumol, William, 16
Bentham, Jeremy, 42, 47, 188
Berkeley, George, 14
Berlin, Isaiah, 16, 23, 187
Black, Max, 14, 17
Bowers, David, 10
Brandt, Richard B., 23
Buckley v. Valeo, 19, 94, 149
burdens of judgment, 139, 173
Butler, Joseph (Bishop), 11, 23

California, 24–25
Cambridge Companion to Rawls, 22
Cambridge, England 10, 24
Cambridge, Massachusetts, 17, 22
campaign finance reform, 19, 93,
    94, 142
capitalism, 115, 133
    laissez-faire, 133, 181, 184–85
    welfare-state, 133, 179
categorical imperative, 189–90, 192
Catholicism, 41, 44, 122, 124, 141,
    143, 168–69, 195
Cavell, Stanley, ix, 21, 23
character, 15, 26, 29, 31, 33, 39, 61,
    171 (*see also* morality)
children, 7, 33, 40, 48, 61, 77, 116,
    122–24, 127, 131, 132, 142,
    147, 181
    Rawls's childhood, 4–9
    Rawls's children, 15, 18
China, 3, 88
Chomsky, Noam, 18
church. *See* religion
citizens, vii–viii, 19, 26, 32, 34–35,
    38–44, 52–56, 58–59, 61–63,
    66–67, 70–93, 95–105,
    116–22, 124–25, 129–32,
    134, 136–43, 145, 147–50,
    152, 154–59, 161–64,

166–70, 172–76, 179–81,
    184, 186–88, 190–96
as free and equal, 66, 172, 173,
    196 (*see also* fundamental
    interests)
citizenship, 93, 104
    equal, 76, 89, 93, 95, 97, 105
civil disobedience, x, 19
civility, duty of, 138–43, 148, 158,
    161, 168–69, 176–77
    defined, 140
class (social), 6–7, 19, 79–80, 92,
    95, 107, 122–34, 136, 152,
    155, 164
Collected Papers (CP), 26
communitarianism, 183, 185–88
comprehensive doctrines, 13–14,
    35, 144–46, 156, 158–59,
    173, 175
    reasonable, 146–47
    unreasonable, 146–47
    See also conceptions of the good;
        ways of life; worldviews
concept of justice, 28, 170–72
conceptions (moral), x, 26, 62, 137,
    165, 170–72, 175–76, 185,
    189, 191 (*see also* concepts;
    ideas)
conceptions of international
    relations, x, 19, 26, 39
conceptions of (social) justice, 15, 26,
    35, 37–41, 43, 45, 55–57,
    59, 62, 72, 135–40, 143–48,
    157–59, 161–63, 165,
    167–76, 178–79, 18–82,
    186, 188, 191–95
    comprehensive, 143
    egalitarian, 137, 148, 152
    liberal, 137, 147–48, 159
    political, 35, 54, 57, 136, 138–40,
        142–44, 146, 153, 158–59,
        169–70, 173, 175
    purely recipient-oriented, 44–45,
        54, 62, 101

stability-achieving, 41, 54, 72,
    104–05, 118
See also theories of justice
conceptions of the good, 34–35,
    55–58, 63, 77, 87–89, 91, 143,
    159, 169, 173, 191–92 (*see also*
    comprehensive doctrines;
    ways of life; worldviews)
concepts, 159, 170–72 (*see also*
    conceptions; ideas)
Condorcet, M. J. A. N. C. de
    (Marquis), 16
Connecticut, 8
consensus, 35–38, 59, 159, 163, 169
    comprehensive, 35, 59
    moral, 35, 37–8
    overlapping, 34–35, 41–42, 59, 63,
        70, 144, 157, 163, 167–69,
        173, 175, 177 (*see also modus
        vivendi*)
consequentialism, 43–45, 47, 73,
    178, 191
considered judgments, 131, 167–69
    (*see also* convictions)
    defined, 162–63
constitution, viii, 4–5, 19, 29, 37, 40,
    70, 83, 85, 94–95, 104, 139,
    142–43, 148–54, 156, 159,
    173, 194
    natural, 73, 77
    of United States, 4–5, 15, 19,
        94–95, 103–04
constitutional essentials, 139,
    148–54, 159, 173
    basic liberties, 104, 149
        extensiveness, 95, 150
        fair value of political liberties,
            149–50, 152, 154, 159
        security, 95, 150, 154
    basic needs, 104, 150, 152
    defined, 148
    formal equality of opportunity, 149
    two kinds of, 149
    See also matters of basic justice

contract (social), 16, 60–61, 119, 165,
    173, 181
  hypothetical, 60, 62, 64–65, 156,
    164–65, 182, 188
contractualism, 42, 60–62, 117,
    131–32, 165
convictions (considered), x, 29,
    99–100, 124, 131, 141,
    162–70, 175–77, 186, 191
  doctrine-dependent, 169–70
  See also considered judgments
Cornell University, 14, 17, 24
crime, 28, 46, 84, 99–101,
    154–55, 193
criteria of (social) justice, 31,
    43–54, 189–90
  middle-tier, 42, 73
  public, vii–viii, 37–44, 46, 49,
    53–55, 60, 62–63, 66–81, 85,
    88, 91–92, 96–99, 102–05,
    114, 116–19, 126, 128–30,
    133, 135, 137–38, 140,
    144, 148–49, 153–57, 161,
    183, 185–86
  purely recipient-oriented, 43–44,
    46–47
  top-tier, 42–43, 47, 51, 53–54, 62,
    67–69, 73
  See also meta-criteria; principles
Critique of Practical Reason, 189
culture, 17, 28, 38, 40, 44, 54, 57, 59,
    78, 84–85, 122, 129, 156,
    158, 161, 166, 172, 174, 175,
    187, 192 (*see also* public
    political culture)
Cuomo, Mario, 141–42

Darwall, Stephen, 190
Davidson, Donald, 24
decent hierarchical societies, 137
democracy, vii, 26, 35, 40, 54, 61, 87,
    90, 95, 118, 133–34, 137,
    143, 148, 152, 154, 168, 171,
    173–75, 187–88, 193

  property-owning, 90, 114,
    133–34, 152, 180
  See also society, democratic
desert, 7, 14, 52, 74, 180, 183–84
difference principle, 94, 106–21,
    123–26, 129–33, 136,
    148–49, 151–53, 159, 162,
    183–84, 188, 194
  relevant to settling constitutional
    essentials, 151–53
disabilities, x, 39, 74–76 (*see also*
    endowments; handicaps)
discrimination, x, 10, 15, 65, 121–25,
    131–32, 147 (*see also* gender;
    race)
disloyalty, 119
distributional profiles, 49–53, 67–68,
    107, 113, 121, 130–31, 135,
    153, 178–81
Dreben, Burton, ix, 18, 21, 23
Dreyfus, Hubert, 17
duties, 14, 18, 31–32, 39, 45, 138–43,
    145, 148, 158, 161, 168–69,
    176, 186–87, 191
  natural, 189
  negative, 31, 33
  positive, 31–32
duty of civility, 138–43, 148, 158,
    161, 168–69, 176–77
  defined, 140
Dworkin, Ronald, 144

economic growth, 114
economic order/regime, 29, 41, 109,
    149, 184 (*see also* institutional
    order)
economics, 3–4, 15–17, 25, 32, 34,
    47–48, 107, 178
education, 7, 14–15, 20, 33,
    39–40, 57, 74–75, 77–78, 83,
    103–04, 120–22, 124, 127–32,
    134, 138, 180, 188, 193
education system, 57, 121, 132, 134,
    138, 180

endowments (natural), 10, 19, 64–66
    73–76, 91–93, 116, 120–25,
    127, 131–32, 150, 152, 155,
    171, 182–84, 193
equality, 5, 15, 19, 84, 92, 94,
    105–06, 117, 121–24,
    126–27, 132, 151–52, 173,
    193 (*see also* inequalities)
equality of opportunity, 15, 106,
    117, 121–24, 126–27, 132,
    151–52, 173
  fair, 106, 109, 121–28, 130–33,
    148–49, 151–52, 159, 162,
    188, 194
    relevant to settling
    constitutional essentials,
    151–53
  formal, 106, 121–22, 126, 147,
    149, 183
    constitutional essential, 149
  See also opportunity principle
ethics, viii, xi, 4, 15–16, 24, 28–29,
    31–35, 46, 142, 144–45,
    175–77, 192
Europe, 3, 34, 133
evil, ix, 11, 13–14, 26, 141
extent/extensiveness. *See* adequacy;
    basic liberties

fact of pluralism, 139
fact of reasonable pluralism, 34–35,
    59, 63, 139, 143, 187
fairness, 173, 194 (*see also justice as
    fairness*)
family, 7, 14, 29, 39, 55, 64, 120,
    123–24, 131–33, 192
  Rawls's, 4–5, 7, 9, 14, 17, 22
Fellner, William, 68
First Amendment, 95
first principle of justice, 79, 82, 84,
    90, 97, 117, 151, 154–55, 183
  lexical priority over second
    principle, 77–80, 84–85,
    96–97, 101–05, 183, 186

  quoted, 82
  See also second principle of justice
Firth, Roderick, 19, 21, 23
Foot, Philippa, 23
foreigners, 32, 44
Frankena, William K., 23
free choice of occupation, 73, 130,
    133, 183 (*see also* equality of
    opportunity, formal)
freedom, 8, 23–24, 52, 73, 76, 82,
    87, 89, 95, 98–99, 105, 130,
    141, 166, 173, 179, 188,
    190, 192–93
  and integrity of the person, 87, 89
  from arbitrary arrest and seizure,
    83, 87
  from physical injury/abuse/
    torture, 83, 87, 154
  from psychological oppression, 83
  from slavery and serfdom, 83, 87
  of assembly, 82
  of association, 82, 87, 89
  of conscience, 82, 87–89, 186, 188
  of expression, 105
  of movement, 73, 83, 87, 130
  of religion, 82
  of speech, 82, 95
  of the press, 82
  of thought, 82, 188
  See also basic liberties
Freeman, Samuel, 24, 26
Fried, Charles, 23
fundamental ideas, 139, 158,
    170–71, 173
  listed, 172–73
fundamental interests, 53, 55–59,
    62–63, 67–68, 70–76, 78–79,
    86–91, 95, 101, 104, 116,
    129–30, 135, 145, 150, 173,
    183, 191 (*see also* moral
    powers)

game theory, 16, 34, 93
Gauthier, David, 52, 64, 182

gender, x, 5–6, 10, 15, 24, 48,
    52–53, 61, 64–65, 85, 89,
    91–92, 121–25, 131–32,
    155, 168, 187
Germany, xi, 9, 13, 188
gifts. *See* endowments
Goodman, Nelson, ix, 21–22
government, 15, 19, 32, 46, 65, 92,
    94, 99–101, 139–40, 145,
    149–53, 155, 179–80, 187
  structure of, 149, 152–53
Great Britain, 9
Grice, H. Paul, 16
Groundwork, 10, 189
guidelines, 38, 88, 137–40, 148,
    153–55, 161 (*see also* criteria
    of justice, public)

Habermas, Jürgen, viii
Hampshire, Stuart, 16, 23
handicaps, 5, 63, 74 (*see also*
    disabilities)
happiness, 30–31, 53–55, 57, 72–73,
    78, 117–19, 138, 143–44,
    157, 191–92
Hare, Richard M., 16
Hart, Herbert L. A., 16, 23, 188
Harvard University, ix, 10, 17–19,
    21–24, 28, 178
health, ix, 4–5, 22, 27
  citizens', 97
health care systems, 40, 78, 97, 155
Hegel, Georg Wilhelm Frierich, viii,
    14, 19, 185
Herzen, Alexander, 16
Hicks, J. R., 16
higher-order interests. *See*
    fundamental interests
Hiroshima, 12
Hitler, Adolf, 14
Hobbes, Thomas, viii, 23, 64,
    185, 188
Höffe, Otfried, 192
Hoffmann, Stanley, 21

Holocaust, 13–14
human rights, 104 (*see also* basic
    liberties)
humanism, 44, 47, 62, 73
Humboldt, Wilhelm von, 58, 188
Hume, David, 23, 188
hypothetical contract. *See* contract,
    hypothetical

Idea of Public Reason Revisited,
    The, 26
ideal theory, 39–41, 80, 88, 92,
    102, 124–26, 157, 190
ideals, x, 27, 34–37, 56, 61, 80,
    89–90, 136, 139, 145,
    155, 157–61, 169, 185–87,
    190, 193
ideas, 15, 34, 60, 62, 65, 139, 142,
    156–57, 163–64, 167, 169,
    175, 181, 187–89
  explained, 170–73
  fundamental. *See* fundamental
    ideas
  listed, 172–73
  See also concepts; conceptions
impartiality, 47, 166, 173, 191
income and wealth. *See* index goods
index goods, 107–08, 110, 116,
    121, 129–30, 132
  income and wealth, 4, 15, 19, 33,
    40, 64, 67–69, 73, 75, 94, 96,
    102, 104, 107–08, 110–12,
    114, 116, 133–34, 152, 155,
    180–81, 184, 193
  leisure time, 107–08
  listed, 107
  powers and prerogatives of offices,
    73, 107
  social bases of self-respect, 73, 107,
    116–17, 132–33
index positions, 109–10, 112–16,
    119–21, 123–29, 131, 153
  absolute, 109–10, 115–16, 120
  relative, 110, 113–16, 120, 152

individualism, 175
  normative, 44, 47–48, 62–63, 73
inequalities, 75, 80, 92–96, 98,
      107, 122–30
  class-based, 6–7, 19, 45, 79–80,
      90–95, 107–09, 112–13,
      116, 119–34, 136, 150,
      152, 155, 193
  economic, 94, 105–06, 113, 121,
      188, 193
  gender-based, 5, 15, 52–53, 61,
      65, 85, 89, 92, 121–25,
      131–32, 155
  natural, 74–75
  political, 65, 81, 92–93, 125
  race-based, 6–7, 51–53, 92, 121,
      123–25, 131–32, 147, 155
  socioeconomic, 79–81, 83,
      94, 107, 109–10, 113–15,
      119, 126
injustices, 7, 28, 31, 33, 40–41, 80,
      101–02, 133, 138, 145, 163,
      171–72, 179
  class-based, 7, 45, 121, 131–32
  gender-based, 15, 65, 121, 131–32
  race-based, 65, 121, 131–32
  Vietnam war, 19–20
  2-S deferments, 20
institutional designs, 32–33, 39, 53,
      55, 72, 84, 97, 101, 108,
      112–15, 120, 124–25, 127,
      137–38, 152, 158, 161–62,
      181, 189
institutional moral analysis, 31, 33–34
institutional order, 4, 32–37, 45, 47,
      78, 83–84, 92, 106, 118, 137,
      159, 180–81, 186, 193–94
      (see also basic structure)
institutions (social), 28–34, 37, 39–41,
      43, 46, 60, 63–64, 70–71, 74,
      76, 77–79, 94, 96, 98, 101, 103,
      106–09, 112–15, 117, 119–21,
      123–25, 128, 134, 136–37,
      144, 166, 171, 179, 186, 188

integrity (physical), 83, 87, 89,
      154–55
interactional moral analysis, 31, 33
interests, fundamental. See
      fundamental interests
interests, higher-order. See
      fundamental interests
international ethics, 19
international relations, x, 4, 26,
      36, 39
intolerance, 98–99 (see also tolerance/
      toleration)
intuitionism, 176
Ithaca, 17–18

Japan, 3, 12–13
John Dewey Lectures, 194
Johnson, Oliver, 190
just savings, 113–14
justice
  concept of, 28, 170–72
  of the world/universe, 28,
      76–77, 160
  See also concept of; conceptions
      of; criteria of; principles of;
      procedural; sense of
justice as fairness, x, 26, 38, 60,
      66–67, 144–46, 148–49, 152,
      154–59, 161, 173, 178–79,
      191, 194
  central elements of, 161
  egalitarian, 137, 148–53, 188,
      193–94
  general conception of, 67, 77–78
  liberal, 137, 139–42, 144–48, 159,
      185–88
  political, 26, 35, 54, 57, 136–48,
      153, 157–59, 169–70, 173,
      175, 194
  six scope restrictions, 39–41
  special conception of, 66–67 (see
      also principles of justice)
Justice as Fairness: A Restatement
      (JFR), 26

justification, ix, 16–17, 28–29, 31,
    35, 37–38, 43, 55–57, 59–64,
    69, 71, 73–77, 95, 97–100,
    103–04, 109, 116, 119, 121,
    124, 127, 129–30, 132, 137,
    139, 142–45, 147, 155–56,
    159, 161–62, 166, 167–77,
    179, 181–83, 185–87, 193, 196
  full, 167,
  public, 72, 142, 168–69, 173
  to oneself, 176 (*see also* reflective
    equilibrium)

Kant, Immanuel, viii, 10, 19,
    23–24, 26, 57, 87, 144–45,
    166, 188–95
  categorical imperative,
    189–90, 192
  Critique of Practical Reason, 189
  Groundwork, 10, 189
  Metaphysics of Morals, 145
  Rechtslehre, 145, 189, 192
Kantian interpretation (of original
    position), 189–92
Kaufmann, Walter, 15
Kent School, 8–9, 12
Keynes, John Maynard, 16
King Jr., Martin Luther, 143
Knight, Frank, 16
Korsgaard, Christine, 23–24

laissez-faire capitalism, 133,
    181, 184–85
law, viii, 4–5, 10, 15–16, 25, 28–29,
    32, 40, 46, 52, 62, 78, 83–88,
    90–95, 99, 101–02, 106,
    121–22, 141–43, 147–50,
    152–55, 157, 168, 177–78,
    193–94
Law of Peoples, The (LP), 19, 26,
    39, 45
*Lectures on the History of Moral
    Philosophy*, 24
legal order, 29, 78, 106

legal rights, 84, 90–93, 102, 121,
    149–50, 152, 154–55
legal system, 19, 94
legitimacy, 153–54, 157, 173–74, 187
  liberal principle of, 153, 177
    quoted, 139–40
leisure time, 107–08
Leon, Philip, 11
Lewis, Clarence I., 10–11
lexical priority
  defined, 79
  of basic needs over first principle,
    103–04
  of first over second principle,
    77–80, 84–85, 96–97,
    101–05, 183, 186
  of opportunity over difference
    principle, 106, 120, 126,
    129, 132
  See also basic liberties, lexical
    priority of
Lexington, Massachusetts, 22, 27
Leyte, Philippines, 12–13
liberal principle of legitimacy,
    153, 177
  quoted, 139–40
liberal socialism, 114–15, 133–34, 152
Liberalism and the Limits of Justice, 185
liberalism, 144–46, 148, 185
  political, 142, 147–48, 173
libertarianism, 45, 170, 178–85
liberties. *See* basic liberties; political
    liberties
  supporting, 87
liberty of conscience, 82, 87–89,
    186, 188
Lincoln, Abraham, 14, 22
Locke, John, viii, 23, 166, 185, 188
loyalty, 120, 185
luck, 7, 21, 75, 123, 127, 130
Lyons, David, 24, 30

MacIntyre, Alasdair, 185
Maine, 8, 22

Malcolm, Norman, 10–11, 14, 16–17
Mansfield, Harvey, 21
Marbury v. Madison, 5
market, 32, 68–69, 180, 184–85
Marshall, Burke, 21
Marx, Karl, viii, 23, 188
Mason, Alpheus, 15
Massachusetts Institute of
        Technology, 17–18, 23–24
matters of basic justice, 148–50, 159
        (*see also* constitutional
        essentials)
maximean
    aggregation, 53, 67
    rule, 69
maximin, 67–72, 80, 102, 117
    aggregation, 68
    rule, 69–72, 75, 77, 86, 94, 98,
        102, 107, 116–18, 126,
        128, 131
        explained, 68–69
McCarthy, Joseph (Senator), 16
Meade, James Edward, 133
meta-criteria of (social) justice,
        42–44, 71, 73
Metaphysics of Morals, 145
method of avoidance, 146, 173,
        175–76, 192
Michigan, University of, 23–24
military, 11–14, 20, 97, 99
Mill, John Stuart, viii, 10, 16, 23, 98,
        144–45, 188
minorities, 19, 85–86, 140
modus vivendi, 35–37, 65 (*see also*
        overlapping consensus)
Moore, George Edward, 16
moral analysis,
    institutional, 31, 33–34
    interactional, 31, 33
moral consensus. *See* consensus
moral justification, 37–38
moral powers, 55–58, 63–64, 73,
        87–90, 173 (*see also*
        fundamental interests)

moral principles, 15–17, 144, 189
        (*see also* principles of justice)
moral universalism, 47
morality, 30, 63, 135–36, 186
Morgenstern, Oskar, 16
motivation/motives, 19, 61, 63–64,
        92–94, 118, 120, 123–24,
        131–32, 134, 140, 155, 157,
        162, 167, 189–92, 193, 196
Musgrave, Richard A., 107

Nagel, Thomas, xi, 24
natural constitutions, 73, 77
natural duties, 189
natural endowments. *See*
        endowments
natural factors, 76, 92, 123–24,
        130–32
natural inequalities, 74–75
natural primary goods, 74–75
natural resources, 64, 67,69, 83,
        181–82
needs. *See* basic needs
Neumann, John von, 16
New Guinea, 11
New York, 10, 17, 141
Niebuhr, Reinhold, 11
normative individualism, 44,
        47–48, 62–63, 73
Nozick, Robert, ix, 45,
        166, 178–84

objectivism, 163, 175, 177
obligations, x, 61, 67
    institutional, 189
opportunities, 7, 15, 40, 52,
        111–12, 121–22, 124,
        126–32, 148, 153
opportunity principle, 106, 120–32
        (*see also* equality of
        opportunity)
    lexical priority over difference
        principle, 106, 120, 126,
        129, 132

original position, vii–viii, 17, 43, 60–67, 71–73, 75, 77, 80, 91, 93, 107, 115, 117, 126, 128, 131, 135, 155–56, 161, 164, 173, 185, 186
  agreement in, 119–20
  constituents of, 62–64
    candidate public criteria, 40–41, 43–44, 63, 69–72, 102, 104, 117, 130
    citizens represented, 54–59, 62–64, 70–79, 86–91, 95, 101, 104, 116, 129–30, 135, 145, 150, 173
    parties contracting. *See* parties
    task description, 63, 70, 102
    veil of ignorance, viii, 64–67, 69, 71, 88, 189, 191
  expository device, 62
  ingredients in, 43
    anonymity, 48–53, 62–67, 107
    consequentialism, 43–45, 47, 73, 178, 191
    humanism, 44, 47, 62, 73
    irrelevance of threat advantage, 62–66, 73
    normative individualism, 44, 47–48, 62–63, 73
  Kantian interpretation of, 189–92
  maximean rule in, 69
  maximin rule in, 68, 75, 77, 102, 107, 117, 128
  meta-criterion, 42–44, 71, 73
  purely recipient-oriented, 43–48, 53–54, 60, 62, 67, 101
  stability considerations in, 72, 90, 118–20
  thought experiment, 42–43, 60–62, 66, 71, 75, 131, 135, 155, 161, 165, 182, 191–92
  top-tier criterion, 42, 67–69, 73
overlapping consensus. *See* consensus
Owen, Gwil E. L., 21
Oxford University, xi, 16–17, 23

Pareto condition, 47–51, 53, 108, 113
Pareto, Vilfredo, 47
parties (in original position), 61, 63–77, 80, 82, 85, 88, 90–91, 94, 96, 98, 100, 102–04, 107, 113, 115–19, 126, 128–32, 137, 140, 156, 161, 164–65, 182, 186
  rationality of, 61–63, 66–70, 76, 102, 118, 128, 131, 164, 189–92
Pearl Harbor, 12
penal system, 157
perfectionism, 75, 166
personal qualities, 123, 130
persons. *See* citizens
Philadelphia, 10, 17
Philippines, 12
philosophy, vii–ix, xi, 3, 10–11, 14–19, 21, 23–24, 27, 34–36, 38, 41, 43, 47, 57, 139–41, 143, 145, 156–57, 159, 163, 168, 174–76, 178, 186, 189, 192–96
  political, vii–x, 3–4, 19, 23–24, 26–27, 172, 174–75, 178, 193, 195–96
Plato, 11
pluralism, 43, 57, 58, 144, 174
  fact of, 139
  limited, 34
  reasonable, 157, 173
    fact of, 34–35, 59, 63, 139, 143, 187
Poland, 9, 13
political constructivism, x, 173, 194
political influence, 19, 92, 94–95, 105, 120, 150, 153
political liberalism, 142, 147–48, 173
Political Liberalism (PL), 26, 141, 194
political liberties, 82, 87, 89–90, 92–95, 97–98, 105, 133, 149–52, 156, 188

(fair) value of, 19, 82, 91–97, 103, 105, 109, 124–25, 133, 148–52, 154–56, 159, 162, 188, 194, 196
  constitutional essential, 149–50, 152, 154, 159
  fully adequate, 92, 149–51, 154
political order, 82, 149
political philosophy, vii–x, 3–4, 19, 23–24, 26–27, 172, 174–75, 178, 193, 195–96
political power, 133, 136, 139–40, 142, 146, 153
  unreasonable use of, 142, 145–46 (*see also* liberal principle of legitimacy)
political virtues, 138, 140, 158, 161, 173, 193 (*see also* civility)
positional goods, 116
poverty, 7, 31–32, 34, 45, 79, 83, 90, 93, 104–05, 114, 116, 120, 122–23, 132, 134, 155, 180–81, 188
power, 20, 36–37, 100, 105, 133, 136, 139–40, 142, 146, 149, 152–53, 193
  bargaining, 52, 64–65
  political, *see* political power
powers and prerogatives of offices, 73, 107
practices, 28, 30, 40, 42, 62, 99
primary goods, 73–79, 85, 104, 118, 128, 130, 132, 173, 179, 190–92
  natural, 74–75
  social, 74–79, 96, 101, 107, 129, 135, 183, 192
Princeton Institute for Advanced Study, 23
Princeton University, xi, 9–11, 14–17
principle of legitimacy, liberal, 153, 177
  quoted, 139–40

principles of justice, 97, 189
  two principles of justice, 31, 42, 117, 185, 190 (*see also* criteria of justice; first principle; lexical priority; priority rules; second principle)
priority. *See* lexical priority
priority rules, 42, 70, 97–98, 161 (*see also* first principle; lexical priority; second principle; two principles)
procedural justice, pure, 164, 173, 179
profiles. *See* distributional profiles
property, 19, 29, 32, 83, 94, 99, 142, 178–79, 183
property rights, 178
property-owning democracy, 90, 114, 133–34, 152, 180
public criteria. *See* criteria of justice
public (political) culture, 19, 57, 136, 139, 147, 156, 158, 168–75, 177
public justification, 72, 142, 168–69, 173
public (use of) reason, 143, 173
  idea of, 139
  ideal of, 139, 155, 157, 161
publicity, 37–44, 54–55, 63, 66–67, 70–81, 83, 85, 88, 91–92, 97, 104, 115–20, 126, 135, 137–43, 154–6, 158, 161, 168–77, 188–89 (*see also* criteria of justice, public)
pure procedural justice, 164, 173, 179
purely recipient-oriented theorizing, 43–48, 53–54, 60, 62, 67, 101
Pusey, Nathan, 21
Putnam, Hilary, ix, 18, 21–22

Quine, Willard V. O., ix, 21–22

race, x, 6–7, 48, 51–53, 64–65, 92, 97, 121, 123–25, 131–32, 147, 155

rationality, 54–56, 58, 68–69, 89,
    116, 139, 173, 189–92
  of the parties, 61–63, 66–70,
    76, 102, 118, 128, 131, 164,
    189–92
Rawls, Alexander Emory (son), 17
Rawls, Anna Abell (mother), 4–5
Rawls, Anne Warfield (daughter), 17
Rawls, Elizabeth Fox (daughter), 17
Rawls, Margaret Warfield (wife), xii,
    15, 18, 22, 26–27
Rawls, Richard Howland (brother),
    5, 9
Rawls, Robert Lee (brother), 5–6
Rawls, Robert Lee (son), 17
Rawls, Thomas Hamilton (brother),
    5–6
Rawls, William Lee (father), 4–5
Rawls, William Stowe (brother),
    5, 9–10, 12
Rawls, William Stowe (paternal
    grandfather), 4
Raz, Joseph, 144
realism, 26–27, 39–40, 67, 71–72,
    80–81, 91, 101, 107–08, 120,
    135–37, 141, 156–60, 167
  moral, 163, 175
realistic utopia, 27, 137
reasonable pluralism. *See* pluralism,
    reasonable
reasonableness, 16, 57, 104, 139,
    141–42, 146–47, 158, 163,
    166, 173–76, 190
  of doctrines, 146–47
  of persons, 145–46, 154
  of ways of life, 146
  of worldviews, 34, 57, 145–47
reasonably favorable conditions, 40,
    63, 66–67, 70–71, 78, 80, 88,
    96, 97, 99, 102–03
Rechtslehre, 145, 189, 192
*Reclaiming the History of Ethics, Essays
    for John Rawls*, 24
redistribution, 178–81, 183

reflective equilibrium, 15, 162,
    165–66, 170, 173,
    175–76, 188
  general, 167
  narrow, 165–66
  wide, 29, 165–70
relativism, 174–75
religion, 8, 11, 13–14, 26–27, 34–35,
    41, 43–44, 51–52, 55, 84, 87,
    92, 97, 99–100, 122, 124–25,
    138–43, 145, 163, 166–68,
    175–76, 187, 192
representative groups, 112
resources, natural, 64, 67, 69, 83,
    181–82
responsibility, 32, 34, 45, 61, 74,
    77, 173, 192
right to a speedy trial, 83, 87
rights, *see* basic liberties
Ritchie, Albert, 5
Roosevelt, Franklin D., 5
Rousseau, Jean-Jacques, viii,
    16, 23, 188
rule of law, 83, 87, 93, 99
Ryle, Gilbert, 16

Sachs, David, 17–18
Samuelson, Paul, 16
Sandel, Michael, 183, 185–87
savings rate, 113–14, 133
Scanlon, Thomas M., 23–24
scheme. *See* basic liberties
Scholastics, the, 185
second principle of justice, 79,
    106, 121
  quoted, 106
  See also difference principle;
    opportunity principle
security, 36–37, 93, 98, 101, 103,
    154, 196 (*see also* adequacy;
    basic liberties)
self-respect, 58, 73, 76, 116, 131, 173
  (residual) social bases of, 73, 107,
    116–17, 132–33

Sen, Amartya K., 23
sense of justice, 6, 55–58, 63, 87,
    131–32, 137, 140, 145, 157,
    164, 166, 173, 193–94
Shklar, Judith, 21, 23
Sidgwick, Henry, viii, 23, 188
Singer, Irving, 17
skin color. *See* race
slaves/slavery, 14, 83, 179, 182
    (*see also* freedom from slavery
    and serfdom)
Smith, Adam, 166
social bases of self-respect, 73, 107,
    116–17, 132–33
social contract. *See* contract
social factors, 123–24, 131–32
social institutions. *See* institutions
social justice, vii, x, 28–29, 31, 35,
    39, 42, 45–46, 102, 166
social order, 35, 37–38, 41–43,
    45–49, 51–56, 58–69, 76,
    105, 118, 120, 133, 136,
    145–47, 157–59, 181–82,
    187–88, 191–94
    stability of, 35, 37–38, 41–42, 55,
        105, 118, 120, 147, 157
    types of, 133
        laissez-faire capitalism, 133,
            181, 184–85
        liberal socialism, 114–15,
            133–34, 152
        property-owning democracy,
            90, 114, 133–34, 152, 180
        state socialism, 133
        welfare-state capitalism, 133, 179
socialism, 34, 114, 133–34
    liberal, 114–15, 133–34, 152
    state, 133
society
    as a fair system of cooperation,
        172–73, 196
    democratic, vii, 26, 35, 54, 61,
        87, 143, 168, 171, 174–75,
        187, 193

ideal, x, 89–90, 139, 161, 186–87,
    190–93
    liberal, 144, 186–87
    well-ordered, 92, 136–40,
        144, 149, 153, 156–59,
        161–62, 173
socioeconomic positions, 89–91,
    93–95, 107–09, 112–13, 116,
    119–21, 131, 150, 183–84, 193
stability, 27, 38, 41, 54, 58–59, 72,
    90, 105, 118, 120, 138, 147,
    160, 173, 187
    achieved by a conception of
        justice, 41, 54, 72,
        104–05, 118
    of a social order, 35, 37–38,
        41–42, 55, 105, 118, 120,
        147, 157
Stace, Walter T., 10, 14
Stanford University, 21, 23
state socialism, 133
strains of commitment, 90, 120, 173
Strawson, (Sir) Peter, 16
students (of Rawls), 24
Stump, Alexander Hamilton
    (maternal grandfather), 4
subjectivism, 175
supporting liberties, 87

talents. *See* endowments
task description (in original position),
    63, 70, 102
taxes, 32, 84, 110, 114, 120, 133,
    151–52, 180–81, 183–84, 194
Taylor, Charles, 185
Theory of Justice, A (TJ), vii–viii, 3,
    18–19, 21–23, 26, 28, 34, 38,
    54, 77, 94, 129, 178, 194
theories of (social) justice, ix–x, 26,
    42, 70, 97, 185, 196
    single-tier(ed), 30
    three-tier(ed), 43, 55, 60, 70
    two-tier(ed), 30, 42–43, 53
    See also conceptions of justice

Thomson, James, 18
threat advantage, 36, 52, 62–66, 73,
        182 (*see also* bargaining power)
Todes, Samuel, 17
tolerance/toleration, 19, 59, 94,
        98–99, 138, 144, 146–47,
        173, 188
Tower, Anna, 21
truth, 141, 145, 163, 174–77
two principles of justice. *See*
        principles of justice

U.S. *See* United States
unemployment, 31–32, 34, 46
Unger, Roberto, 185
United Nations, 104
United States, viii, ix, 4–5, 9, 11,
        15, 19, 22, 24, 33–34, 45, 67,
        94–96, 99, 112, 133, 136,
        141–42, 150, 155, 170,
        179, 185
    Buckley v. Valeo, 19, 94, 149
    constitution, 4–5, 15, 19, 94–95,
        103–04
        First Amendment, 95
    Marbury v. Madison, 5
universalism, 47
Urmson, James O., 16
utilitarianism, 10, 30–31, 42, 45–47,
        51, 53, 55–56, 63, 68, 71, 75,
        117–18, 137–38, 143–44,
        157, 170
utopia, 27
    realistic, 27, 137

value/worth. *See* adequacy; basic
        liberties; political liberties
veil of ignorance, viii, 64–67, 69, 71,
        88, 189, 191

Vietnam, ix, 19, 21
Viner, Jacob, 15
virtues, 4, 28, 138, 146, 192
    political, 138, 140, 158, 161, 173,
        193 (*see also* civility)

Walras, Leon, 16
Walzer, Michael, 21, 185
war, 19, 28, 36, 64, 97, 103, 196
    Civil, 14
    civil, 72, 97
    First World, 9
    on terror, 196
    Second World, 7, 9–14, 99
    unjust, 19–20, 28
    Vietnam, ix, 19–21
ways of life, 54, 58, 144
    reasonable, 146
wealth. *See* income and wealth
Webster, John, 7
welfare-state capitalism, 133, 179
well-ordered society. *See* society,
        well-ordered
White, Morton, 21
Williams, Bernard, 185, 187
Willkie, Wendell, 5
Wilson, Woodrow, 5
Wittgenstein, Ludwig, 10–11, 14
world
    goodness of, 26–27, 136
    justice of, 28, 76–77, 160
worldviews, 34–36, 38, 41, 43,
        53, 57, 65, 138–48,
        157–58, 163, 168–69,
        175, 195
    reasonable, 34, 57, 145–47
    See also comprehensive doctrines;
        conceptions of the good;
        ways of life